Dornier Do 335

Dornier Do 335
An Illustrated History

Karl-Heinz Regnat

Schiffer Military History
Atglen, PA

Translated from the German by David Johnston
Book Design by Ian Robertson.

Printed in China.
ISBN: 0-7643-1872-1

This book was originally printed under the title,
Dornier Do 335: Mehrzweck-Jagdflugzeug by Aviatic Verlag

We are interested in hearing from authors with book ideas on related topics.

Published by Schiffer Publishing Ltd.
4880 Lower Valley Road
Atglen, PA 19310
Phone: (610) 593-1777
FAX: (610) 593-2002
E-mail: Schifferbk@aol.com.
Visit our web site at: www.schifferbooks.com
Please write for a free catalog.
This book may be purchased from the publisher.
Please include $3.95 postage.
Try your bookstore first.

In Europe, Schiffer books are distributed by:
Bushwood Books
6 Marksbury Avenue
Kew Gardens
Surrey TW9 4JF
England
Phone: 44 (0) 20 8392-8585
FAX: 44 (0) 20 8392-9876
E-mail: Bushwd@aol.com.
Free postage in the UK. Europe: air mail at cost.
Try your bookstore first.

Contents

1. Origins

The Use of the Tandem Engine Configuration in Dornier Designs

Claude Dornier

This book begins with a brief biography of Claude Dornier, whose career was both successful and fraught with difficulties. Together with men such as Junkers, Messerschmitt and Heinkel, he left his mark on German aviation. Born on 14 May 1884 in Kempten, Dornier received his professional training at the Munich Technical College. In 1907 he graduated as an engineer trained in bridge building and in 1910 moved into another field with Zeppelin. His work there included calculations for an all-metal airship. The first patents soon followed, for example for a rotating airship hangar. In 1913 Dornier began calculations for a steel airship capable of crossing the Atlantic.

Because of his obvious gift for solving technical problems, Zeppelin gave him his own development section. Initially it consisted of two offices, a modest workshop and an area for experiments and prototype construction. This opportunity formed the basis of his ground-breaking activities. Meanwhile Dornier had obtained German citizenship, a wise decision in view of the approaching war with France, his father's homeland. Dornier's career would probably have been much different had he decided otherwise. Meanwhile the designer had earned an outstanding reputation as an engineer, and Zeppelin gave him the task of designing all-metal aircraft. This came at a time when wooden fabric-covered aircraft were the norm. In autumn 1914 Dornier moved to a facility in Seemoos, near Manzell on Lake Constance, to begin work. It was there that the long line of Dornier aircraft had its beginning.

First Flying Boat Designs

The R.S.I, a three-engined flying boat with pusher propellers, was completed in October 1915. The next year saw the advent of the R.S.II, the first Dornier design with engines in a tandem arrangement. This flying boat, equipped with four engines, two pusher and two tractor, was the initial spark for dozens of future designs.

Claude Dornier (14 August 1884 – 5 December 1969).

Dornier adopted the tandem engine arrangement long before the appearance of the Wal family. Illustrated here is the Rs III giant flying boat.

Top left: The ultimate development of the Wal, the four-engined Superwal. Top right: Regrettably the Seastar has no future. Center, left: The catapult Wal "Passat". Center right: The Do X flying boat powered by Siemens Jupiter engines. Bottom left: A racing seaplane project from 1928. Bottom right: A Wal on land – the Do N.

Next came the R.S.III. Also powered by four engines, this giant made its first flight on 4 November 1917. Following the Dornier philosophy, the engines were installed in tandem arrangement. This arrangement was to be a feature of future flying boats up to the Do 18 and Do 26. The R.S.IV was completed in the last year of the war. Spanning 37 meters, the R.S.IV was a giant by the standards of the day. The R.S.IV made its first flight on 12 October 1918. Development of this flying boat was hindered by the German surrender and the resulting consequences.

Dornier Tandem Designs Between the Wars

Space limitations prevent a detailed description of Dornier's activities between the two wars. Readers in search of more information on the consequences of the Versailles Treaty may refer to Aviatic Verlag's publication on the Dornier Do X. This huge aircraft represented the apex of German aviation technology at the end of the 1920s. Twelve engines in tandem-mounted pairs powered this giant.

The following is a brief summary of the aircraft with tandem engines produced by Dornier from the end of the First World War to the 1930s:

Dornier *Wal* — built in numerous versions, including some with four engines, from 1922.

Dornier N – land version of the Wal intended for the civil transport role. First flown on 19 February 1926.

Dornier K2 – Developed from the K1, powered by four engines. First flown in December 1929.

Dornier Do X – final product of numerous preliminary studies, powered by twelve engines. First flown on 21 October 1929.

Dornier Do P – land-based military aircraft based on the design of the four-engined *"Superwal"*.

Dornier Do S – four-engined flying boat capable of carrying up to 30 passengers. First flown on 23 September 1930.

Dornier Do K3 – four-engined land-based aircraft, tested by DLH. First flown on 17 August 1931.

Dornier Do 18 – twin-engined long-range flying boat used in civilian and military guises. Used on the South Atlantic mail route by DLH. First flown on 15 March 1935.

Dornier Do 26 – four-engined trans-Atlantic flying boat operated by DLH. Military versions were also built for the *Luftwaffe*. First flown on 21 May 1938.

The legendary "Seeadler", prototype of the Do 26 series, completed its first flight on 21 May 1938.

The Do 18 V1 LR flying boat first flew on 15 March 1935.

Table 1: Technical Data

Model	Wal 1922	K2	Do X	Do P	Do S	Do K3	Do 18	Do 26
Wingspan	22.5 m	20.6 m	48.0 m	30.0 m	31.0 m	25.0 m	23.7 m	30.0 m
Length	17.3 m	15.0 m	40.1 m	23.4 m	25.8 m	16.7 m	19.3 m	24.6 m
Height	5.2 m	4.1 m	10.1 m	7.3 m	7.9 m	4.6 m	5.4 m	6.9 m
Tare weight	3560 kg	3400 kg	28250 kg	8000 kg	10620 kg	4265 kg	6260 kg	11240 kg
Takeoff weight	5700 kg	5000 kg	48000 kg	12000 kg	16000kg	6200 kg	8500 kg	15000 kg
Power plants	z.B. BMW	Gnome-Rhone	Siemens	Siemens	Hispano-Suiza	Walter	Junkers	Junkers

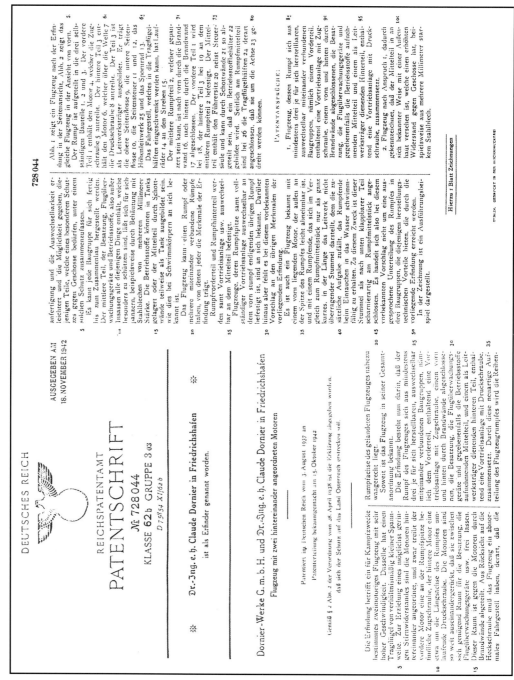

Pages 1 and 2 of patent specification No. 728044 from the year 1937.

Detailed information on these aircraft may be found in Volume 9 of the Bernard & Graefe series *Die Deutsche Luftfahrt*. These aircraft with tandem engines proved the correctness of the Dornier design philosophy.

In addition to this drag-minimizing method of construction, Dornier was also working on a completely different engine arrangement with the same operating principle. Instead of placing the engines directly behind one another, they were installed in the nose and tail of the aircraft (see patent drawing).

Yet another configuration was represented by the Dornier Do 14 flying boat.

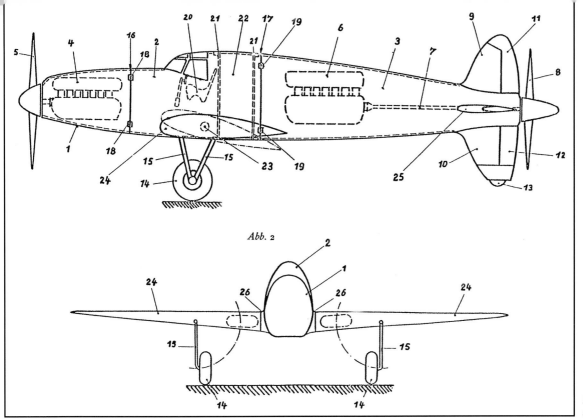

Abb. 2

Page 3 of patent specification No. 728044.

Dornier Do 14

The energy produced by two BMW VI in-line engines in the aircraft's fuselage drove a huge four-blade propeller by way of a hollow shaft and ***angle drive***. This method of operation is confirmed by two technical drawings. The shaft led vertically to a "*head*" mounted on the wing containing the gearing and the huge propeller. Another interesting feature of this aircraft was the surface radiator mounted on the underside of the wing. In spite of all its technical innovations, the Do 14, a product of the early 1930s, was not proceeded with. Designed for *Luft Hansa* as a long-range mail plane, the aircraft made its maiden flight, which lasted one minute, on 10 August 1936. In the course of more than 50 hours of flight testing by Dornier (until January 1937) the aircraft displayed various serious shortcomings. The aircraft's lack of power was addressed by a two-speed transmission. This made it possible for Dornier to increase the original gross weight of 8 000 kg to 11 400 kg. In spite of this the Do 14 did not progress beyond the prototype stage. By the late 1930s wing-mounted engines and variable-pitch propellers had become standard design features, making the Do 14's technology appear outdated.

Considerable difficulties with the drive system, which was prone to failure, also contributed to the Do 14's failure. In 1939, overtaken by technical advances, this interesting flying boat was scrapped.

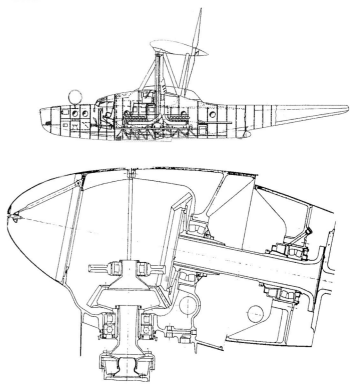

Above Right: The Do 14, an experimental trans-Atlantic flying boat. Center: Location of the propulsion system within the fuselage of the flying boat. Right: The angle drive in detail.

Two BMW VI in-line engines provided the required power.

figuration, however in each case their designs failed to progress beyond the prototype stage.

Foreign Designs

Fokker D. XXIII

This type of engine arrangement was not the sole domain of the Dornier company. On 30 May 1939, several years before the first flight of the "Anteater", the first prototype of a fighter aircraft with a similar engine arrangement took to the air in the Netherlands. The Dutch aircraft, the Fokker D. XXIII, had a much inferior performance.

The aircraft consisted of an all-metal fuselage gondola combined with a boom-mounted tail and trapezoid-shaped wing of wooden construction. Two Walter Sagitta I-SR engines were installed in the nose and tail of the fuselage gondola. Each twelve-cylinder engine produced 530 H.P. and drove a three-blade metal propeller. It was hoped that more powerful Rolls-Royce or Daimler-Benz engines would produce the desired performance. It was also

Let us now turn to aircraft whose engines were installed in the nose and rear fuselage. As the following photographs and drawings show, designers outside Germany were also interested in this con-

The short-lived Fokker D.XXIII.

hoped to install an ejector seat to enable the pilot to clear the rear propeller in the event of a bail-out. Neither of these plans was realized.

Testing revealed cooling problems with the rear engine. Unlike the Do 335, D. XXIII did not have an extension shaft linking the rear engine to its propeller. The tandem fighter's intended armament consisted of two 7.9-mm and two 13.2-mm machine-guns. Designed by Marius Beeling, this interesting Dutch design failed to reach production. In May 1940 the German invasion brought development of the D. XXIII to an abrupt halt. The aircraft's calculated maximum speed with two Rolls-Royce or Daimler-Benz engines was 615 km/h.

Tachikawa Ki-94 (Model I)

In 1943 a very unusual fighter aircraft took shape on a drawing board in distant Japan. Similar in layout to the D. XXIII, the Ki 94-I was a much larger and more powerful aircraft and was intended as

Table 2: Technical Data Fokker D.XXIII

Wingspan	11,50 m
Length	10,20 m
Height	3,80 m
Wing area	18,50 m^2
Tare weight	2180 kg
Takeoff weight	2950 kg
Maximum speed	525 km/h
Service ceiling	9000 m
Range	840 km
Power plants (2)	Walter Sagitta I-SR
Output	530 PS
Armament	2 x 7,9 mm MG
(planned)	2 x 13,2 mm MG
Crew	1

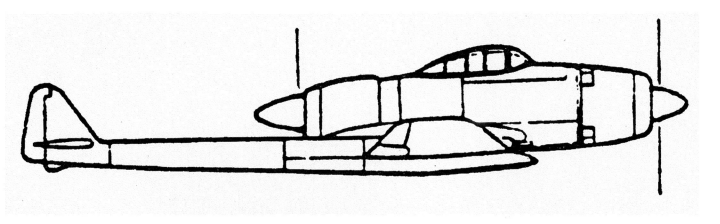

The Tachikawa Ki-94 (Version I) progressed no further than the mockup stage.

a high-altitude interceptor to counter the American B-29s, against which existing Japanese fighters had little chance of success. In spite of the adverse military situation and severe fuel shortage, work on the project proceeded apace. From a Japanese point of view, this configuration was extremely innovative. Two Ha 211 Ru engines were situated fore and aft in a central fuselage gondola. These 18-cylinder radial engines were capable of producing 2,200 H.P. and drove large four-blade propellers. The pilot sat in a central position between the two engines.

Twin booms extending back from the wing supported the tail surfaces. The aircraft was designed with a tricycle undercarriage. Armament was supposed to consist of two 30-mm Ho 105 and 37-mm Ho 203 cannon. Calculations suggested a maximum speed of 780 km/h at a height of 10 000 meters, however the Ki-94 never got the chance to prove this. A mock-up was completed in 1943.

Further development was halted by order of the military command. Tachikawa was subsequently ordered to conceive a high-altitude fighter of conventional design with a pressurized cockpit.

Testing of the new design, the Ki-94-II, began in August 1945 shortly before the end of the war.

Table 3: Technical Data Tachikawa Ki-94-I

Wingspan	15,00 m
Length	13,05 m
Wing area	37,00 m²
Wing loading	238 kg/m²
Takeoff weight	8800 kg
Maximum speed	780 km/h in 10000 m
Power plants (2)	Mitsubishi Ha-211 Ru
Output	2200 PS
Armament	2 x Ho 105 (30 mm)
(planned)	(37 mm)
Crew	1

JONA 10

Regrettably, little is known about this Italian design which is believed to have been patented in 1935. It was a single-seat fighter-bomber with wings mounted in the mid-fuselage position. The tail consisted of a central vertical fin combined with horizontal tail surfaces on the underside of the aft fuselage.

The aircraft was powered by two engines, a two-row radial in the fuselage nose and an inline liquid-cooled engine in the fuselage driving a pusher propeller by means of an extension shaft. It is especially interesting that the design included a tailwheel undercarriage, resulting in unusually little ground clearance.

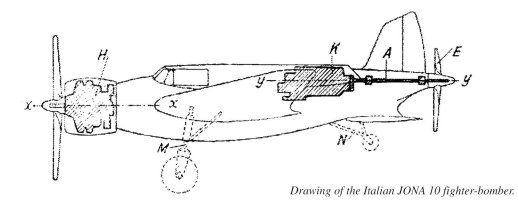

Drawing of the Italian JONA 10 fighter-bomber.

2. Background to the Do 335

The Dornier P.59 Project

The Do 18 of 1936 may well have provided the inspiration for the P.59 project. This flying boat was unique in one respect: it was powered by two engines in tandem, with the rear engine driving a propeller by way of an extended drive shaft. This configuration probably gave birth to the idea of placing the pilot between two engines powering separate propellers, one a conventional tractor, the other a pusher propeller. This was a brilliant idea that made it possible to design a twin-engined aircraft which, because of its engine arrangement, produced no more drag than a single-engined machine. According to *Major* Schreiweis, later *Kommandeur* of EK 355, it was Claude Dornier's son Peter who was responsible for the concept. *Major* Schreiweis remarked: "As you know, I was the *Geschwader* technical officer in 1942. For more than six months during that period the younger of the two Dornier sons was with me. From statements made by Peter during fireside chats in the May house (where the *Geschwaderstab* was located) I know that the Do 335 can be traced back to his initiative and that he had more or less formulated the idea." The concept resulted in patent number 728044, dated 3 August 1937. This now protected design concept led in a direct line to the P-59-04 high-speed bomber project. This design, which proceeded no further than the drawing board, possessed all the basic features of the later Do 335. The P-59-04 subsequently served as the basis for Project P.231, the predecessor of the Do 335, however many hurdles had to be overcome before the realization of the final product. These will be described in detail, but first let us turn to the P-59.04.

Project P.59.04

The aircraft's long slender fuselage included a single-seat cockpit. Proposed power plants were two Daimler-Benz DB 605s mounted fore and aft. The latter powered the pusher propeller by means of an extension shaft. The fuselage ended in a cruciform-shaped tail. The wing had a swept leading edge. In contrast to the Do 335, the P.59.04 did not have a tricycle undercarriage. To those in the *Reichsluftfahrtministerium* (RLM) the project seemed too ambitious, and, given the military situation in 1940, it was felt that there was no need to develop such an unconventional aircraft. Instead they turned to conventional concepts, which could be turned into a front-line aircraft quickly. On 3 February 1940 Göring, who was responsible for the four-year plan, wrote to the Reich Economic Minister:

"Therefore, all efforts must be concentrated on those plans which can yield results in 1940 or the spring of 1941. All programs which will come to fruition at a later date will have to be set back in favor of the above plans in order to avoid overtaxing the economy."

This decision was to have far-reaching consequences which would affect the subsequent development of this category of weapon. No one expected the war to last until 1945, and so at that time of the "Blitzkrieg" all efforts were devoted to follow-on types which would be needed in the immediate future. Dornier's P-59-04 project was one of those affected by the decision and the design was consigned to the desk drawer. Approximately two years were to pass before a specification was issued for a high-speed bomber. Dornier, deeply convinced of the correctness of its concept, continued developing it privately. The result was the Göppingen Gö 9, a flying test-bed for the pusher principle, which was used to solve significant technical problems and to convince the skeptics in the RLM.

Preliminary Experiments – The Göppingen Gö 9

The RLM was extremely skeptical about the principle of a rear-mounted engine driving a pusher propeller. This, together with other factors, had led to the rejection of the Dornier P.59. In order to demonstrate the trouble-free operation of this concept to its doubters, Dornier issued a development contract to Schempp-Hirth. The

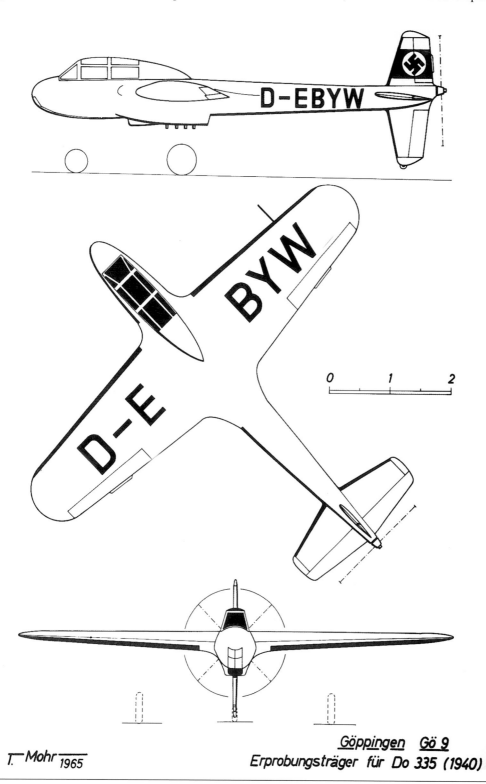

T. Mohr 1965

Göppingen Gö 9
Erprobungsträger für Do 335 (1940)

Three-view drawing of the Göppingen Gö 9.

The aircraft's relationship to the Do 17 is unmistakable.

result was the Gö 9 designed by Wolfgang Hütter. Hütter's design was based on that of the Do 17, reduced to a scale of 1 to 2.5. This method reduced costs and the time required to construct the prototype. The Gö 9, which was built in Nabern, was ready for its maiden flight in June of 1941. That same month it took to the air for the first time, towed by a Bf 110 or Do 17. The Hirth engine, which did not have an electric starter, was started prior to takeoff as it could not be started in the air. Dornier company pilot Ivan Quenzler, formerly of the Rechlin Test Station, piloted the unusual miniature. At a height of 1 000 meters the tug released the Gö 9. Quenzler ended the debut of the Gö 9 with several aerobatic maneuvers. At a very early stage of testing the aircraft proved the reliability of a pusher propeller powered by way of a drive shaft.

This photo of the Göppingen Gö 9 was taken in Wüsterberg in 1940.

Lacking a starter, the aircraft's engine had to be started the old-fashioned way.

Technical Features of the Göppingen Gö 9

In contrast to the Do 17, on which it was based, the Gö 9's airframe was made of wood with plywood skinning. The slender club-shaped fuselage was 6.8 meters long. The pilot's cockpit was in the nose with a sliding canopy. Beneath the cockpit was the nosewheel, which retracted rearwards. The engine, a HM 60 developed by the company of Hellmuth Hirth, Wolf Hirth's brother, was installed behind the pilot. The energy produced by the HM 60 was transmitted to the pusher propeller by a drive shaft four meters in length. The engine was installed roughly at the aircraft's center of gravity. Numerous preliminary experiments were necessary to come up with an ideal configuration for this unusual method of propulsion. Unlike the Do 17, the Gö 9 was fitted with a so-called cruciform tail consisting of two vertical and two horizontal elements. In addition to the usual two elevators, it therefore also had two rudders. The ventral fin was fitted with a skid to prevent damage in the event of ground contact. This configuration also protected the rear-mounted propeller. It was originally planned to equip the Gö 9 with a variable-pitch propeller, however a propeller of the required size could not be jettisoned in an emergency. Had Quenzler been forced to abandon the aircraft in flight, the propeller would have posed an unacceptable danger. It

The Göppingen Gö 9 completed its first flight in 1941.

was therefore decided to use a four-blade wooden propeller which met requirements. The aircraft's horizontal stabilizer was equipped with a Flettner tab and the angle of incidence could be adjusted by means of a spindle. The elevators were fitted with external mass balances. The wing was patterned on that of the Do 17 and was constructed of wood. The Gö 9's wingspan was just 7.2 meters with a wing area of 8.8 m2. The wing was a two-spar structure with wooden ribs and plywood skinning. The ailerons, which had external mass balances, were also made of wood. The wing also included two split landing flaps and housed the fuel tanks and main undercarriage. Fuel was contained in two tubular tanks in the leading edge of the wing of 180-mm diameter. The tanks had plexiglass bottoms to allow the pilot to visually monitor their contents. This obviated the need for a fuel gauge in the cockpit. The wing tanks were mounted in a higher position than the engine, and thus no fuel pump was necessary. Gravity forced the fuel into a collector tank behind the pilot's seat, from where it was fed to the Hirth engine.

The following specification applies to the Göppingen Gö 9:

Table 4: Technical Data Göppingen Gö 9

Wingspan:	7.2 m
Length:	6.8 m
Wing area:	8.8 m^2
Wing loading:	82 kg/m^2
Takeoff weight:	720 kg
Maximum speed:	220 km/h
Engine:	Hirth HM 60 R
Engine output:	80 H.P. for takeoff, 66 H.P. for cruise
Capacity:	3.596 l
Length of drive shaft:	400 cm
Propeller:	four-blade propeller
Crew:	1

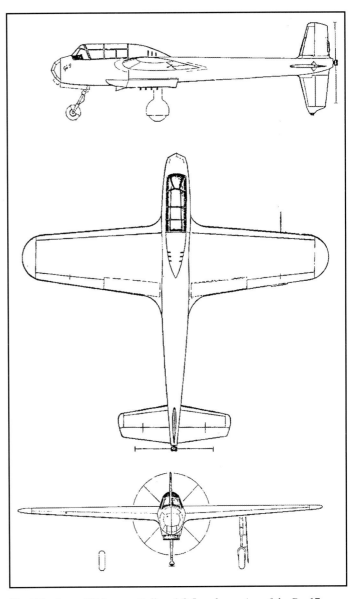

The Göppingen Gö 9, essentially a 1:2.5 scale version of the Do 17.

Hirth HM 60

The story of the Hirth Motorenwerke, which was founded by Hellmuth Hirth, brother of Wolf Hirth, began in 1927. Hirth subsequently developed the HM 60, which was to prove an outstanding success in the *Deutschlandflug* competition flight of 1931. The HM 60 was first installed in a Klemm L25. Hirth soon became one of the most important manufacturers of engines for sporting aircraft. The HM 60 R was developed from the HM 60 and it also proved to be a major success. The new HM 60 R was first installed in a Heinkel He 71 in 1933. The engine performed well in the *Deutschlandflug* competition flights in 1934-35. The one-thousandth engine was completed in October 1936.

The HM 60 R and the earlier HM 60 were four-cylinder inline engines with the cylinders in a suspended arrangement. The displacement of the HM 60 R was 3.6 liters, up from the 3.46 liters of the earlier engine, and compression ratio was increased from 5.3 to 5.6 to 1. These measures resulted in an increase in available takeoff power from 65 H.P. (HM 60) to 80 H.P. Both versions of the engine were equipped with roller bearings and a multipart crankshaft. Division of the crankshaft into several segments made possible the system of "face-serration", which was developed and patented by Hirth's father, Albert Hirth. The joining ends of the shaft segments consisted of intermeshing fixed serrated faces which were also self-centering. Hirth's invention became widely used in machine design and remains in use in the present day.

The Hirth HM 60 from various angles.

Crankshaft

The crankshaft is manufactured in sections following the patents of Dipl.Ing. Albert Hirth.

The linkage and precise centering of the components is accomplished using the Hirth "face serration" method, which guarantees a problem-free connection of such high stress components. (Hirth's invention is still used today in general machinery design: author's note.) All crankshaft throws are on a single plane.

The shaft is statically and dynamically balanced.

Both the main and connecting rod bearings are rolling contact bearings, which is possible without difficulty given the design of the Hirth crankshaft. The segmented nature of the shaft makes possible the use of bearings whose dimensions are determined by the load to be borne, not assembly considerations.

The known advantages of the rolling contact bearing, such as reduced frictional drag and minimal use of lubricants, do not come with the cost of a heavy and expensive design.

Building the shaft in segments also makes it possible to select the most suitable materials for each segment.

This makes it possible to dispense with the use of inner racers for the rolling contact bearings, making the design simpler, lighter and more reliable.

The main crankshaft bearing and the connecting rod bearing are double row roller bearings.

It is planned to install a deep-groove-type radial ball bearing on the front end of the crankshaft for mounting the propeller.

The front of the shaft has a Hirth face serration which engages the matching serration on the Hirth propeller hub, while the end has gearing for installation of a starter dog.

Connecting Rods

The connecting rods are drop-forged from chrome-nickel steel. The shaft is of H cross-section. Because of the segmented crankshaft, no division of the connecting rod bearing is necessary. The bearing is a sealed unit, with the bearing rollers running directly in the connecting rod, whose hardened bearing face is ground and machine-lapped. Two rows of rollers are used.

The piston pin bearing is a double-row needle bearing, whose bearing face in the connecting rod head is also ground and machine- lapped.

Pistons

The light metal piston is cast from aluminum alloy. It is fitted with three piston rings and beneath these a stripper ring, which effectively prevents oil from entering the combustion chamber. The piston pin is hardened, ground and machine-lapped. It is float-mounted in the piston pin socket and held in place by spring washers. Note: In Series 2 engines (HM 60 R/2) the safety plate on the bearing block was replaced by a one-piece safety rod, which prevents the piston pins from being pushed to the side.

Cylinder

The cylinder is made of a special iron alloy and has very closely-spaced ribs. Approximately one-fourth of its length is inserted into the crankcase, where it rests on a narrow flange.

Inserted in the flange is a small ring nut, into which opens the oil line from the Bosch lubricator. The oil separates into the ring nut and flows through four small holes directly onto the races.

Cylinder Head

The cylinder head is made of a special aluminum alloy. It is cast and liberally provided with cooling ribs. Intake and outlet valves are arranged suspended at 40° to the cylinder axis. The valve guides and valve seats are made of forged special bronze and are shrink-mounted in the cylinder head.

The valve shafts with springs, spring collars and toggler levers are completely enclosed and are thus protected against external influences (dust, oil). The toggler levers are seated in needle bearings. Each cylinder head has two sparkplugs, which are connected to independent ignition systems.

The mating of cylinder and cylinder head is achieved by means of four trough bolts, which are seated in the crankcase. Two of these trough bolts are made hollow to accept the pushrods.

Care has been taken to enclose the pushrods to where they enter the cylinder head in order to seal them against dust and oil.

Valves

The valves are made of a high-grade special steel. The intake and exhaust valves are identical and interchangeable. The valve timings are: intake open: 6° before dead center position, intake closed: 50° after bottom dead center position, exhaust open: 65° before top dead center position, exhaust closed: 5° after top dead center position. Cold, intake and exhaust valve play is 0.2 mm.

Camshaft

The valves are controlled by two short camshafts, which are seated in special guide bearers between Cylinders 1 and 2 and Cylinders 3 and 4.

These guide bearers also house the main crankshaft bearings. The camshafts are driven by hardened, ground gear wheels with a reduction ratio of 1 : 2.

The gear wheels which sit on the crankshaft and the corresponding crankshaft section are manufactured from a single piece.

The correct position of the two gear wheels in relation to one another is precisely indicated by markings on the gear wheels. This simplifies reassembly should the parts have to be removed. The camshafts are seated in ball bearings. The cams, which convey control movements to the pushrods, are seated in needle bearings.

These control elements are lubricated from the associated crankshaft main bearings.

Note: In Series 2 engines (HM 60 R/2) the safety plate for the toggler levers on the mounting bearer has been replaced by a one-piece safety rod.

This ends the handbook description of the principal areas of the HM 60 R and HM 60 R 2 engines. The design of this engine formed the basis for various other Hirth engines which much higher power ratings.

The rapid realization of these engines was aided in part by the advent of the standard one-liter cylinder. On this basis, from 1934 Hirth produced engines with four, eight and twelve cylinders.

Hellmuth Hirth died a few years after the first of these successful engines began running.

Three years after Hirth's death, in 1941, Ernst Heinkel purchased the Hirth production facilities. These later performed valuable service in the development of jet engines.

The following table provides a general description of the HM 60 engine.

Table 5: Technical Data Hirth HM 60 R

Number of cylinders	4
Bore	102 mm
Stroke	110 mm
Displacement per cylinder	0.899 l
Displacement (total)	3.596 l
Compression ratio	5.8 to 1
Dimensions	
Length (without hub)	840 mm
Width	390 mm
Height	722 mm
Weights	
Dry weight	91 kg
Installed weight	97 kg
Performance	
Takeoff power	80 H.P. (2,400 rpm)
Continuous power	72 H.P. (2,320 rpm)
Cruising power	66 H.P. (2,240 rpm)
Cylinder output	20 H.P. (maximum)
Output per unit of displacement	1.12 H.P./kg
Fuel consumption (74 octane)	
Takeoff power	235 g/H.P.
Continuous power	230 g/H.P.
Cruise	230 g/H.P.

Table 6: General Information Hirth HM 60 R

Engine Type	Air-cooled carburetor four-stroke engine with four cylinders in inverted-vee configuration
Intake and Exhaust Valves	One intake and one exhaust valve per cylinder
Crankshaft	Direction of turn clockwise
Reduction Gearing	None
Idle Speed	320-350 rpm
Limiting Speed	2,430 rpm
Components and Systems	
Crankcase	Two-piece, cast Elektron. Crankcase cover also serves as accessory mount.
Crankshaft	Composite Hirth crankshaft with hardened crank and tempered flanges.
Connecting Rods	I cross-section, undivided heads, roller-mounted.
Pistons	Die-cast ECY alloy, three compression rings, one oil control ring.
Cylinders	Cylinders of special gray cast iron, cylinder heads of heat-proof cast light metal alloy.
Carburetor	SUM carburetor, Type JHF 36
Ignition	Two separate Bosch ignition systems consisting of battery and magneto ignition.

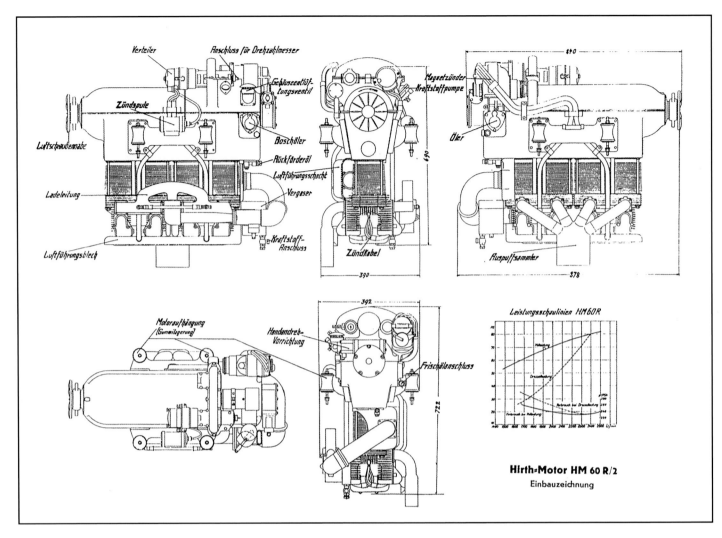

The labels in the diagram read:

Verteiler — Anschluss für Drehzahlmesser — Gehäuseentlüftungsventil — Zündspule — Boschöler — Luftschraubennabe — Rückförderöl — Luftführungsschacht — Ladeleitung — Vergaser — Luftführungsblech — Kraftstoff-Anschluss — Magnetzünder — Kraftstoffpumpe — Öler — Auspuffsammler — Zündkabel

Motoraufhängung (Gummilagerung) — Handandreh-Vorrichtung — Frischölanschluss — Leistungsschaulinien HM 60 R

Hirth-Motor HM 60 R/2
Einbauzeichnung

The Hirth HM 60 R/2 from various angles (handbook 1936).

Project P.231 – Predecessor to the Do 335

In spite of the success of the Gö 9 in flight tests, the RLM remained unconvinced of the potential of drive shaft technology. All subsequent work on the system was done independently by Dornier, which conceived Project P.231. Developments in the military situation in 1942 clearly demonstrated that the types currently available to the *Luftwaffe* would be inadequate to meet future requirements. The air force's standard types, which had earlier earned such high praise, were not well suited to the increased demands in the period which followed the time of the Blitzkrieg. Some types had reached the limit of their development potential and enemy types were gaining the upper hand in performance. The glaring errors of 1940 were now beginning to show their effects. As in other areas, the RLM continued to react hesitantly in developing a new generation of com-

bat aircraft. Not until the latter months of 1942 did it find itself compelled to revise its shortsighted method of planning and issue a specification for a new aircraft within the framework of the high-speed bomber competition.

Numerous points had to be clarified before a firm specification could be issued to the aviation industry. In November 1942 Professor Hertel of Junkers met with Milch to work out with the RLM the necessary guidelines and key features of the future high-speed bomber. Maximum speed was to be 760 km/h and the aircraft was to be able to carry a 1 000-kg bomb load. At a subsequent conference in December 1942 these requirements were lowered. Maximum speed was to be 750 km/h with a bomb load of 500 kg and a range of 2 000 kilometers. The specification was subsequently issued to five manufacturers: Arado, Dornier, Heinkel, Junkers and Messerschmitt. The five companies were invited to a conference scheduled for 11 January 1943. Dornier's submission was the P.231, based on the P.59 project and offered in three different versions.

The cantilever low-wing monoplane, which included a cruciform tail, front and rear motors and a tricycle undercarriage, was certainly an unconventional design. Nevertheless, the performance demonstrated by the Do 335 V1 later silenced most skeptics. As stated earlier, the predecessor to the Do 335 was developed in three versions:

P.231/1 A design with two Daimler-Benz DB 605 E inline engines. Other sources give the DB 605 A as the intended power plant. (wingspan 15 m, length 12.9 m).

P.231/2 Powered by the DB 603 G. The aircraft also had a modified wing planform (increased chord, wing area 36 m2).

P.231/3 This design had a hybrid propulsion system, meaning a combination of piston and turbojet power plants. The P.231/3 formed the basis (until May 1943) for the follow-on Project P. 232/2 (DB 603/Jumo 004)

On that January day Dornier himself traveled to Berlin to attend the meeting, in order to present his unconventional project. The following summary of his statements is taken from the minutes of the meeting:

"We began work on this project at a somewhat later date, however we have been able to take advantage of earlier work. From this we reached the conclusion that the conventional bomber configuration of wing-mounted engines has become obsolescent. Our solution is the tandem motor arrangement: one engine with a tractor propeller, installed conventionally as in a fighter aircraft, and one engine behind the pilot driving a propeller located in the tail by means of an extended drive shaft. The preliminary work was done five years ago. We presented such a project to the department, which was probably premature at that time. But we have quietly continued our work and have built a model aircraft (the Gö 9, author's note), a smaller version of the Do 17 with a pusher propeller, and we have carried out tests with this aircraft. The results have confirmed our wind tunnel measurements in all respects. The tail surfaces are not affected."

Claude Dornier's design principle so to speak overcame its previous hurdles in its second attempt. Dornier was issued a contract.

3. The High-Speed Bomber Competition

The Dornier P.231's Competitors in the High-Speed Bomber Design Competition

With the long-desired construction contract in his pocket, in his mind's eye Dornier probably saw an armada of production aircraft leaving his factories' final assembly lines. At first, however, it was decided to construct ten prototypes. In reality, quantity production never progressed beyond the planning stage. This will be addressed later. We will now turn to some of the designs which competed against the P.231. In some cases detailed information has survived to the present day. Unfortunately such is not the case for the P.231 and the P.1063.

The clear losers in this competition were Arado, Heinkel, Junkers and Messerschmitt. The competing projects will now be described in alphabetical order.

Arado Project E 561

The Arado E 561, which bore an outward resemblance to the Bf 110, was distinguished by a very interesting propulsion system. The concept for a heavy long-range fighter (Zerstörer) was developed in 1937-38. It was a low-wing cantilever monoplane with trapezoid-shape wings and twin fins and rudders. The wide forward fuselage was designed for a crew of three. The pilot and radio operator sat side by side. Located behind them was the gunner's station. Another gunner was positioned prone in the lower aft fuselage. The E 561's proposed armament consisted of four MG 81 Z machine-guns (*B*- and *C-Stand*) and four cannon of unspecified caliber in the fuselage nose. The aircraft had a conventional tailwheel undercarriage with single mainwheels. The airframe was unquestionably of conventional design, What was unconventional was the power plant arrangement. Instead of being housed in conventional nacelles in the wings, the engines were placed in the wing root area. A system of shafts and drives transmitted their energy to the four-blade variable-pitch propellers. The propellers were situated in conventional fashion in front of streamlined nacelles, which housed drives, shafts

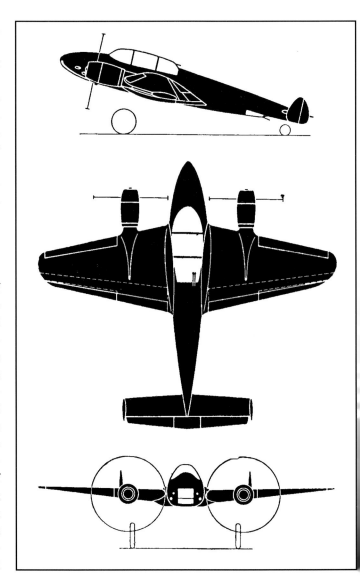

The Arado E 561, whose engine power was transmitted to the propellers by a system of shafts and drives, did not proceed beyond the drawing board.

and annular radiators. The power transmission system, the so-called "remote drive system", was combined with a free-wheel clutch. This arrangement made it possible to continue to provide power to both propellers in the event of the loss on an engine. This was an interesting design, however it was rejected by the RLM, and the Arado E 561 proceeded no farther than the project stage.

Heinkel Project P.1063

Regrettably, almost no information about this project has survived. This mid-wing monoplane was designed in 1942.

Junkers Projects EF 115.0 / EF 130.0 / EF 135.0

The Junkers submission was the EF 115.0. The following is a summary of the project's design features:

The Junkers EF 115.0 was a low-wing monoplane powered by two Jumo 211 J engines in a tandem arrangement in front of and behind the pilot. The engines were not coupled, and they powered counter-rotating propellers in the nose (2 x 3 blades). The use of counter-rotating propellers eliminated the usual torque effect.

Also worthy of mention are the Projekt EF 130.0 and the EF 135.0 design, both contemporaries of the Do 335. These were the

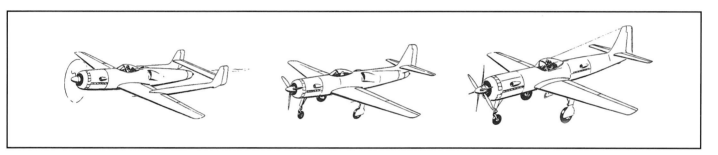

Three high-speed bomber proposals by Junkers (from left to right: EF 135.0, EF 130.0, EF 115.0).

first examples of Junkers' mixed propulsion method. The airframe of the EF 130.0 was largely similar to the EF 115.0, however the propulsion system was much different. The piston engine behind the pilot was replaced by a Jumo 004 turbojet engine. In the case of the EF 135.0, a twin-boom structure replaced the aft fuselage. It, too, was of mixed propulsion, with a single piston engine and a Junkers Jumo 004 turbojet. The air intakes for the jet engine were located on the sides of the fuselage aft of the cockpit. The accompanying drawings illustrate the three configurations. All three versions were rejected. The reasons given for this were:

EF 115.0 – The counter-rotating propellers represented new technology which was as yet unproven.

EF 130.0 – Delays in the Jumo 004 program eliminated this design.

EF 135.0 – As this model was also based on the 004 turbojet, there was no chance of realization.

Junkers and Heinkel were thus out of the running. In the end the only serious competitor for Dornier's P.231 was the Messerschmitt Me 109 Z. The main reason for the rejection of the Messerschmitt design was a lack of production capacity rather than any aspect of its design. Dornier, on the other hand, had adequate production capacity. As previously mentioned, Messerschmitt countered with a design similar to the Dornier one. While the decisive conference which resulted in confirmation of the Do 335 took place in January 1943, in July of that year the notion of a turbojet-powered bomber was raised. Associated planning extended into 1949!

The following are selected statements by Pasewaldt and Milch from the conference held on 19 July 1943 concerning high-speed bomber planning until 1949:

Pasewaldt: *"We are in a critical situation here, for in terms of range at the required speed we are at a technical end in the medium bomber field."*

Milch: *"In the area of propeller-driven machines. However I believe that turbojet engines will mark the beginning of a new, healthy period."*

Pasewaldt: *"But we are beginning with a relatively disappointing range."*

Milch: *"Yes, so far the jet engines have not progressed beyond the testing stage. We have pushed ahead bravely on the fighter side, because something absolutely has to be done in that area. But we have so many other fighters that we can endure a possible setback. We would like to run a similar risk on the bomber side, but with a somewhat later timetable. The Chief of Aircraft Procurement and Supply has no intention whatever of delivering inferior materiel. He is determined to deliver the best available. We must, however, be clear as to what can be done and what cannot. I am therefore convinced that we are directed to the Ju 188 in this class, even in 1945 and 1946. We will get no relief from larger machines, as there are too few of them, nor from the faster aircraft, which we urgently need, as they are lacking in range and payload. I am disregarding the area of navigation, although there may yet be difficulties in this area. I am also of the opinion that we will need the best available medium bomber for the next three years. We will not see an improvement until the new system, Dornier with his counter-rotating propellers fore and aft, arrives. There will be an increase in speed, although it will not be as great as he promised. We will have to be satisfied with less. I believe that the next advance in this area will only be possible through the jet engine, and even if the first Dornier machines really enter front-line service at the end of 1945, I will say: perhaps we will have a future jet bomber by the end of 1948, perhaps even earlier in the year. I cannot say for sure, but I don't believe that it can go into production much earlier. I am thinking of a range of 2 300, 2 400 kilometers with a single 1 000 kg bomb or an equivalent weight of smaller bombs. Obviously we will be working to complete the project sooner, but even if we shave off half a year we will still be into 1946-47. I believe that we should not be under any illusions in this regard."*

This extract reveals that by that stage they were already prepared for a war whose outcome was uncertain and whose end might not come until the end of the 1940s. The next part of this documentation will deal with the events surrounding the rival Do 335 and the Me 262. The latter type, originally conceived as a fighter aircraft, was supposed to see action as a high-speed bomber by order of the *Führer*. To complete this survey of the P.231 a brief description of its last competitors, which were ultimately rejected:

Messerschmitt Me 109 Z-1 and Z-2

In December 1942 Messerschmitt responded to the high-speed specification with the Me 109 Z-2. The corresponding heavy fighter version was designated the Z-1. The aircraft was a quick solution based on two Me 109 fuselages.

Drawings of the aircraft reveal that relatively few new components would have to be produced. Messerschmitt's initial design consisted of two Me 109 G fuselages joined by a wing center-section. This version (Z-1 *Zerstörer*) was to be armed as follows:

3 x MK 108 cannon in the wings
2 x MK 108 cannon (firing through the propeller hubs)
alternative armament of 4 x MK 108 and 1 x MK 103 cannon
2 x 250-kg bombs
alternative armament of 1 x 500 bomb

The Z-2 also made extensive use of Me 109 G components, nevertheless this variant included many new components in the port and starboard wings. The center-section also consisted largely of new components and there was redesigned horizontal stabilizer between the twin tails. The undercarriage was equipped with larger wheels and the wheel wells were revised. The aircraft's fuel capacity was increased and the ailerons and leading edge slats were lengthened. Proposed power plants were the DB 605 and Jumo 213. Beneath each fuselage was a bomb rack with a capacity of 500 kg.

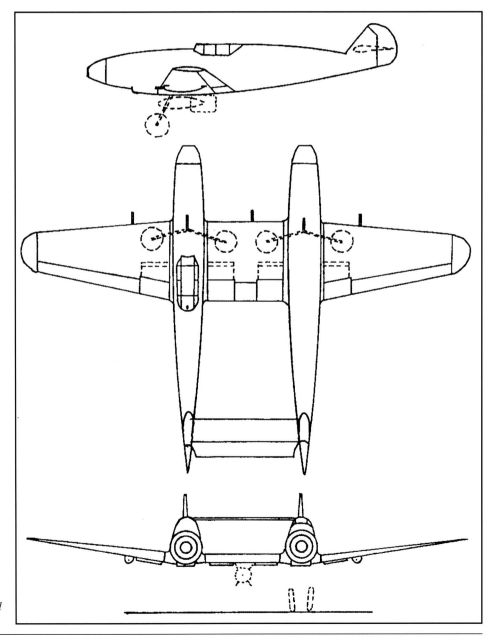

The Messerschmitt Me 109 Z-2 high-speed bomber.

Table 7: Technical Data for the Me 109 Z High-Speed Bomber Variants

	Me 109 Z (DB 605)	Me 109 Z (Jumo 213)
Wingspan	13.27 m	13.27 m
Length	8.92 m	8.92 m
Power plants	DB 605	Jumo 213
Equipped weight	4 900 kg	5 300 kg
Takeoff weight	6 200 kg	6 600 kg
Maximum speed	690 kph	750 kph
Armament	2 x MK 108	2 x MK 108
	2 000 kg of bombs*	2 000 kg of bombs*

*Calculated speed loss with external bombs was approximately 75 km/h.

The "Counter Project"

Messerschmitt subsequently offered the Me 609, another "twin" project based on the Me 309. At a later stage Messerschmitt even decided on a configuration similar to that preferred by Dornier (see drawing). Messerschmitt's so-called "Counter-Project" was to be equipped with two DB 605 or DB 603 engines in a push-pull arrangement. It was calculated that the aircraft would have a maximum speed of 757 km/h powered by the DB 605, however the DB 603 version exceeded this, with a projected maximum speed of 800 km/h. These were purely theoretical values, however, and the project proceeded no further than the drawing board.

Table 8: Technical Data Messerschmitt "Counter Project"

Wingspan	15.75 m
Length	13.53 m
Height	4.94 m
Wing area	36 m²
Equipped weight	6 620 kg
Takeoff weight	9 040 kg
Power plants	2 x DB 605 or
2 x DB 603 G	
Armament	2 x MK 108
Bomb load	1 x 500 kg
Crew	1

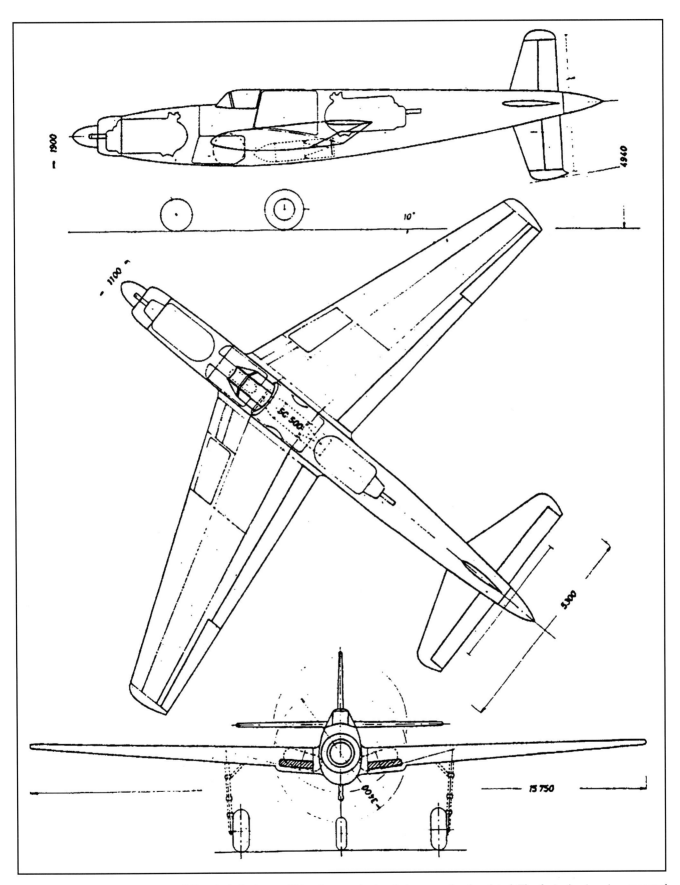

Messerschmitt's counter-project and Dornier's design could be characterized as being very closely related. The design's wings incorporated significantly more sweep than the Do 335.

4. Propeller versus Jet Propulsion

Do 335 and Me 262

With the start of construction of the Do 335 V1 Dornier's project finally left the years-long planning phase. Construction of the first prototype's fuselage began in a barracks in Manzell in spring 1943, while the wings were built in a facility southwest of Ravensburg. After completion both components were shipped to Mengen for final assembly of the V1. These processes were unnecessarily hindered, first by a lack of interest on the part of the RLM, and later by constant changes in the priorities of the building program which reduced the urgency attached to the high-speed bomber. The situation is reflected in several hundred pages of conference minutes.

Opinions concerning the Do 335 also varied wildly. Pasewaldt, head of the Technical Department, viewed the Do 335 rather skeptically, while Milch was a firm advocate of the unconventional aircraft. After Pasewaldt delayed the issuing of a contract, Dornier went directly to Milch, who subsequently ordered ten prototypes. Initially, however, only eight of these were built. In his book *Tragedy of the Luftwaffe*, David Irving wrote that Milch issued a contract for twenty prototypes in January 1943. Milch's other favorite was the Me 262, which Hitler was demanding be built in large numbers as a high-speed bomber. In June 1943 Hitler ordered that both the

The Me 262 A-2a high-speed bomber. Aircraft of this type were supposed to help defeat the Allied invasion of Europe.

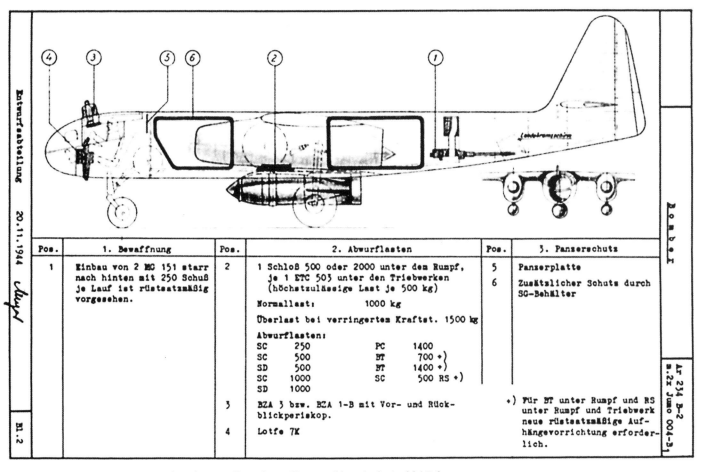

The following table appears within the illustration:

Pos.	1. Bewaffnung	Pos.	2. Abwurflasten	Pos.	3. Panzerschutz
1	Einbau von 2 MG 151 starr nach hinten mit 250 Schuß je Lauf ist rüstsatzmäßig vorgesehen.	2	1 Schloß 500 oder 2000 unter dem Rumpf, je 1 ETC 503 unter den Triebwerken (höchstzulässige Last je 500 kg)	5	Panzerplatte
			Normallast: 1000 kg	6	Zusätzlicher Schutz durch SG-Behälter
			Überlast bei verringertem Kraftst. 1500 kg		
			Abwurflasten:		
			SC 250 PC 1400		
			SC 500 BT 700 *)		
			SD 500 BT 1400 *)		
			SC 1000 SC 500 RS *)		
			SD 1000		
		3	BZA 3 bzw. BZA 1-B mit Vor- und Rück-blickperiskop.		*) Für BT unter Rumpf und RS unter Rumpf und Triebwerk neue rüstsatzmäßige Auf-hängevorrichtung erforder-lich.
		4	Lotfe 7K		

The Arado 234 also saw service, though in small numbers. Illustrated here is the Ar 234 B-2.

Do 335 and the Me 262 should retain a high priority within the high-speed bomber program. In September 1943, one month before the Do 335 V1's maiden flight, Hitler issued a directive which stated that priority would now only be given to the Me 262. The directive also gave instructions for the Do 335 to be kept in reserve for the possibility that jet technology might prove a failure. As a result, large-scale production of the Do 335, which was supposed to begin in February 1945, was pushed back. This also applied to the Ar 234. On that 7 September Hitler also spoke with Messerschmitt, who confirmed that the Me 262 was capable of carrying bombs. It should be noted that, contrary to often-made claims, several bomb-carrying versions of the Me 262 had already taken form on Messerschmitt's drawing boards prior to his discussion with Hitler. This is confirmed by a Messerschmitt technical description dated 25 March 1943, which depicted several variants armed with one 1 000-kg or two 500-kg bombs. Also proposed was a version with provision for bombs carried within an enlarged fuselage. More information on this theme was provided by Hitler's *Luftwaffe* adjutant, Nicolaus von Below. The purpose of examining the topic

of the Me 262, the Do 335's true competitor, is to give the reader an understanding of the prevailing situation at that time and the thinking of those responsible for the development of the two types. Von Below described the events as follows:

"More and more Germany was becoming a helpless target of British air attacks. On 7 September Hitler summoned Professor Messerschmitt and asked him about the state of development of the jet aircraft. To everyone's surprise, he asked if this aircraft was also suitable for use as a bomber, to which Messerschmitt responded in the affirmative. He also added that Feldmarschall Milch had been giving him nothing but trouble and was not providing him with sufficient labor. This was the result of a struggle between Milch and Messerschmitt which had been smoldering for years. I was able to explain this to Hitler and told him that Messerschmitt always demanded too much without actually achieving the general standard which would have justified his demands. He liked to present isolated achievements in such a way as to give the impression of being ready for production. I asked Hitler to discuss the matter with Milch again."

Von Below had the following to say about Hitler's visit to Insterburg, where he witnessed a demonstration by the Me 262 V6:

"Assembled there were all those responsible for the production of aircraft: Göring, Milch, Speer. Saur, Messerschmitt, Galland, Vorwald, etc. In my opinion the Luftwaffe had once again made the mistake of presenting almost exclusively weapons and equipment which were not yet sufficiently developed for service use. Hitler very quietly inspected the long row of aircraft, among them the latest Me 109 and Me 410, the Ar 234, the Do 335 and the Me 262. Milch accompanied him and was able to answer all his questions. Hitler saw the Me 262 for the first time and was very impressed by its appearance. He called Messerschmitt over and asked him if the aircraft could also be built as a bomber. Messerschmitt responded in the affirmative and said that the machine was capable of carrying two 250-kg bombs. Hitler responded, "This is the high-speed bomber", and demanded that the Me 262 be outfitted exclusively as such. Milch tried to convince Hitler to release only some of the Me 262s for bomber production, however Hitler was insistent. Göring, who returned to this theme several days later, was also harshly rebuffed.

On the drive back to the Wolfsschanze I once again had the opportunity to speak to him about the problem and tried to rescue the Me 262 as a fighter aircraft. He agreed with me in principle, and admitted that he wanted more fighter aircraft for the defense of the Reich, however he justified his demand with pressing political problems.

In his view the greatest threat in the near future was an Allied landing in France. We had to do everything possible to prevent this landing."

As reported by von Below, the Me 262 V6 was demonstrated to Hitler at Insterburg. It is obvious that Hitler was deeply convinced that the Me 262 was the weapon which could turn back an Allied invasion of "Fortress Europe". This happened in November, one month after the maiden flight of the Do 335 V1. In spite of Hitler's directive, however, work on the Messerschmitt high-speed bomber remained on the back burner. This situation changed radically, however, when in May 1944 Hitler inquired about the state of affairs and learned that not a single Me 262 high-speed bomber was as yet available. At a hastily convened conference at the Obersalzberg attended by Messerschmitt and Galland, the problem of the Me 262 was discussed intensively, with the result that the Me 262 program was placed in the hands of the commander of bombers, *Oberst* Marienfeld. It was a decision which spared numerous Allied heavy bombers, for in the fighter role the Me 262 would have undoubtedly resulted in a drastic increase in Allied bomber losses. Nevertheless, even this "wonder weapon" could not have turned the tide of the air war in Germany's favor. By the time the Me 262 went into action Germany no longer had an intact infrastructure. Qualified pilots, a reliable supply of fuel and intact bases were absolutely vital for successful operations. Without them, even an advanced weapons system such as the Me 262 must fail. The situation was further exacerbated by the Allies' overwhelming air superiority, which made it necessary for piston-engined fighters to protect the jets during takeoffs and landings, when the Me 262 was particularly vulnerable. The unproven jet engines were reacted to throttle inputs much more slowly than piston engines and as well were very unreliable. As a result, many jet pilots died without ever firing a shot.

The Do 335 program undoubtedly suffered as a result of the events surrounding the jets. Like so many other promising projects, it was allowed to continue as a back-up project with low priority. But even if the Do 335 had proceeded into production, it would have had little effect on the final outcome. The same was even true of the Ar 234 jet bomber. Claims that this or that "miracle weapon" could have turned the tide of the war must be seen as nonsense. Herr Schliebner, who participated in the Do 335 program, wrote of the aircraft:

"The Do 335 was not any aircraft. It was a special aircraft. But it had been overtaken by the Me 262 and Ar 234. The Arado and Messerschmitt were available in small numbers, however, largely because our leaders could not decide who would get them and for what role. It should be noted that in no air force is an aircraft developed, built and flown by the men who are to take it into action. General Galland had clear ideas in this regard, however the military situation frustrated them all. The Do 335 was not an aircraft which any pilot could climb into and fly. The Do 335 required the touch of an experienced pilot, a great deal of caution and flying skill. This is why the aircraft was only flown by the Gruppe's experienced officers. The aircraft were simply too valuable to be placed at risk. My commanding officer ordered no aerial combat. If enemy aircraft were encountered, pilots were to escape at high speed."

Major Schreiweis on the same theme:

"The bomb bay with doors showed that it had been designed as a high-speed bomber. That everyone wanted the "Bee" (reconnaissance, fighters, night fighters) is another story. The fighters only wanted it because Hitler would not give them the Me 262. The demands of various operational roles meant that we never got the machine for the high-speed bomber role. As a result of the various changes for different roles, it was never built in large numbers. And that was the reason why I then resigned (subsequently on operations with the Ju 88 G-6)."

Major Schreiweis, *Kommandeur* of EK 335, was not personally convinced that the Do 335 was the answer, as he saw jet aircraft as the way of the future. The table below lists the most important dimensions and performance figures for the contenders, including the Ar 234 B.

Table 9: Comparison of the Do 335 with the Me 262 and Arado Ar 234

Technical Data	Dornier Do 335 A-0 *	Messerschmitt Me 262 A-2a **	Arado Ar 234 B ***
Wingspan	13.80 m	12.50 m	14.20 m
Length	13.85 m	10.60 m	12.60 m
Height	5.00 m	3.83 m	4.42 m
Wing area	38.50 m²	21.70 m²	26.4 m²
Equipped weight	7320 kg	NA	4650 kg
Takeoff weight	9580 kg	7100 kg	9410 kg
Maximum speed	775 km/h	750 km/h	745 km/h
Landing speed	190 km/h	175 km/h	NA
Service ceiling	11400 m	11300 m	9500 m
Power plants	2 x DB 603 A 12-cyl. inline engines	2 x Jumo 004 turbojets	2 x Jumo 004 turbojets
Output	1750 PS	2 x 860 kp	2 x 860 kp
Armament	2 x MG 151/15 später -20 1 x MK 103	2 x MK 108	2 x MG 151/20
Crew	1	1	1

* The Do 335 A-0 was a pre-production variant.

** The V10 served as prototype for the high-speed bomber version (first flight 15 April 1944).

*** The V9 was the first prototype of the B-version (first flight 10 March 1944).

5. The Test Phase Begins

The Maiden Flight of the Do 335 V1

The previously-described events had an influence on the Do 335 project even before the prototype was able to demonstrate its performance. The big moment for all those involved in the project came on 26 October 1943. On that day Dornier's curiosity took to its natural element for the first time. No less a personality than Hans Dieterle, who had piloted the He 100 on its record-breaking flights, was at the controls when the Do 335 made its first flight at Mengen near Sigmarinen. Dieterle got some idea of the performance potential of Dornier's tandem design after just a few minutes in the air.

His flight test report, dated 26 October 1943, was largely positive. The following is an extract from that report:

"One immediately felt at home in this aircraft, a sign that no unpleasant characteristics or peculiarities appeared. The unusual power plant arrangement revealed no unpleasant characteristics—as far as could be determined. In point of fact, in single-engined flight it is far superior to conventional twin-engined aircraft. As far as could be determined, the rear propeller has no negative effects

The fuselage of the first Do 335 prototype.

on the control surfaces. Takeoff and landing are simple, which is due in part to the special undercarriage arrangement. There are no significant trim changes. Controllability is generally good, however the ailerons will probably need some modification as control forces are too heavy. Stability about the longitudinal axis is too weak, but very strong about the vertical axis."

Dieterle was unfortunately forced to break off the flight prematurely after the main undercarriage refused to lock in the retracted position. The reason for this was a failure in the system which retracted the circular mainwheel covers into the closed position. As a result, the wheel covers were removed and three days later Dieterle took the aircraft into the air again for a repetition of the first flight. In spite of some minor complaints, it was obvious from Dieterle's test report that the Do 335 was a "hit". This did not mean, however, that the aircraft would not have "teething troubles" to overcome, like every other new aircraft design. Milch, a strong advocate of the Do 335, was encouraged. He expressed his positive impression in a letter to the Reich Chancellery. So far he had only been able to offer theoretical calculations, but now, after the V1's

maiden flight, there was positive proof that the Do 335 was an outstanding aircraft. Furthermore, its 1 000-kg payload was twice that of the Me 262. Its speed at low level was an impressive 640 km/h. The RLM subsequently ordered fourteen prototypes, ten A-0 pre-production aircraft and eleven examples of the A-1 production version. The contract also included a requirement for three examples of a two-seat training aircraft. Slowly, after much valuable time had been lost, things began moving. Work began on a heavy fighter (*Zerstörer*) version, which required major design changes. Galland foresaw the addition of two wing-mounted MK 103 cannon for the *Zerstörer*. The Do 335 was no longer seen strictly as a high-speed bomber to compete with the Me 262. The following is an extract from a meeting held on 9 June 1944, three days after the invasion of Normandy:

Knemeyer: *"We know that. You are speaking about the Me 262, but not the Do 335. The program calls for 300 aircraft. I would like to inform you of the following. The V1, which is equipped for the special mission, has now flown. It made the flight from southern Germany to Rechlin at its maximum permissible cruising speed of*

The aircraft's relatively bulky appearance gave little clue to the high speeds of which it was capable.

580. We have the fastest fighter. We also have a fighter with a range superior to all enemy types (this was undoubtedly false in June 1944—the author). We are allowing 2,000 single-engined fighters to be produced and this one only 300. That is no ratio. Another advantage to producing the 335 in larger numbers is that production shortfalls will not hurt us because the aircraft can be used in both roles. It should also be mentioned that much effort is being expended to convert the Do 335 to a wooden wing, which will result in some relief.

Vorwald: *"If we reduce the number of He 177s, which is now set at 120 or 130, to 100, the number that was planned earlier, this should immediately result in at least double or even triple the number of Do 335s."*

Knemeyer: *"That is correct. As well, the General der Jagdflieger will now have to decide whether a certain percentage of fighter production should not be converted to the Do 335, for it is a far superior fighter aircraft. We have once again reviewed its range compared to the jet fighter. At altitude the jet fighter has a greater range. However it has been shown that low-level range can only be met by the 335."*

Factory Testing

The first flight on 26 October 1943 was soon followed by an extensive factory test program, which was organized into six different series of tests. This was done with the objective of revealing the unconventional design's strengths as well as its weaknesses. In the absence of further test reports, the testing of the V1 can only be described in rough outlines. Too many files went up in flames shortly before the end of the war, while others were destroyed or fell into enemy hands. The aircraft could not be tested over its entire speed range. One of the reasons for this was a defect in the machine's cooling system. Because of this, the aircraft often had to be flown with the radiator gills full open, which reduced the speed of the V1 by as much as twenty kilometers per hour. As well the skinning was damaged in many places as a result of modification work. This affected the aerodynamic qualities of the airframe, resulting in a further loss of airspeed. In addition, test flights were often carried out with aileron seals or wing root fairings. The aircraft also did not reach its calculated maximum boost altitude, which was blamed on incorrectly sized air intakes. While these problems gave cause for complaint, they were corrected in a relatively short time. All in all, the tests showed that Dornier was capable of providing the air force with an exceptionally capable aircraft. Following the completion of factory trials the V1 was transferred to the *Luftwaffe* test station in Rechlin.

The Do 335 V1 was assigned the factory code CP+UA.

The "Anteater" demonstrated an impressive performance on its very first flight on 26 October 1943.

The usual procedure before a test flight, here involving the Do 335 V1.

Testing at Rechlin

Testing of the aircraft with its DB 603 E power plants began in September 1944 and included high-speed flights in which speeds approaching 650 km/h were reached at low level. In tests simulating the failure of one engine, the Do 335 V1 achieved a maximum speed of 560 km/h. The aircraft's maneuverability was assessed as extremely good considering its size. The pilots of the *Luftwaffe* and the *Technische Amt* who flew the machine came to the same conclusion. Once again the V1 was unable to demonstrate its full performance potential. The aircraft's aerodynamic finish was negatively affected by the previously mentioned unevenness of the skinning and the loss of putty on the leading edge of the wing. Once again maximum speeds were not achieved. An accident on 20 November 1944 brought testing of the V1 to an abrupt end.

A fractured hydraulic line was responsible for the accident. The loss of hydraulic pressure made it impossible to lower the nose-wheel, forcing the pilot to attempt a landing on the mainwheels only. The V1 was damaged in the landing, however none of the surviving documents confirm that it was repaired. It is very likely that the aircraft sustained serious damage in the area of the forward engine and airframe and as a result no repairs were attempted.

Identifying Features of the Do 335 V1

Two prominent external features of the V1 were the chin intake beneath the forward engine and the large round wheel covers associated with the main undercarriage. Like the V2 and V3, the aircraft was unarmed. The design armament was two MG 151 cannon. Another difference was the camouflage scheme. The Do 335 V1 was the only aircraft without a splinter scheme. It was finished in a scheme of Dunkelgrün 71 on all upper surfaces and Hellblau 65 on all under surfaces. Both spinners and the V1's code CP+UA were in black.

The V1 and V2 were finished in a camouflage scheme of RLM 71 dark green on the upper surfaces and RLM 65 pale blue on the under surfaces.

Table 10: Technical Data Dornier Do 335 V1

Wingspan	13.8 m
Length	13.85 m
Height	5 m
Wing area	38.5 m²
Equipped weight	7105 kg
Takeoff weight	8700 kg
Maximum speed	770 km/h
Landing speed	180 km/h
Service ceiling	11500 m
Power plants	2 x DB 603A
	44.5 l/V-12
Output	1750 H.P.
Armament	2 x MG 151 (planned)
Crew	1

Above Right: The air intake beneath the forward engine and the circular mainwheel covers were features of the first prototype.

Center Right: Front view of the Do 335 V1.

Right: The aircraft's controls could be optimized for high-speed flight by use of the so-called "variable input system".

Note the different shapes of the nose and tail spinners.

6. Continued Testing

The Do 335 V2-V8

Dornier Do 335 V2 (*Werknummer* 230 002, CP+UB)

The second prototype (CP + UB) completed its maiden flight on 31 December 1943 with Hans Dieterle at the controls. The flight trials that followed were carried out in southern Germany and basic flight tests and performance measurements were planned, however the aircraft's life was a short one. The V2 was lost in an accident in April 1944. The original plans called for the V2 to be sent to Rechlin for additional testing. On 14 April pilot Altrogge was assigned to take the aircraft up on a test flight. Shortly after takeoff, the pilot reported severe vibration from the area of the aft engine. Radio contact was subsequently lost and all further information came from eye witnesses. The pilot was seen to jettison the canopy, however the pilot was still on board when the aircraft crashed near a kindergarten in Buxheim. An investigation revealed that Altrogge had sustained severe head injuries when he jettisoned the canopy, making it impossible for him to use his ejection seat. Tests were carried out in a so-called "water tow bath" to determine precisely the canopy's behavior when jettisoned. The information gained resulted in modifications to the jettisoning mechanism on all subsequent Do 335s.

The most significant difference between the Do 335 V2 and the first prototype was the former's use of a modified cooling system. Designed by Dornier, the new system produced less drag than the original Daimler-Benz system. The V1 was equipped with a chin-mounted oil cooler, which increased frontal drag, whereas the V2's oil cooler was integrated into the annular radiator. This resulted in a more streamlined nose section with less drag. To improve cooling of the rear-mounted engine, vents were added to the engine cover panels. These were used only on the V2 and V3. In addition, the V2 used modified radiator gills. The V2 was powered by two DB 603 A-1 engines. The canopy folded upwards, a feature only seen on the V2 and V3, and teardrop-shaped fairings were added to the sides of the canopy to improve vision for the pilot.

Dornier Do 335 V3 (*Werknummer* 230 003, CP+UC)

On 20 January 1944, three weeks after Altrogge's fatal crash, the next prototype took to the air on its maiden flight. CP+UC was subsequently used for endurance trials, which were carried out at Mengen and Oberpfaffenhofen airfields. During testing, in May 1944 the V3 was fitted with a mock-up wing-mounted weapons

Table 11:

Prototype	Code	*Werknummer*	First Flight
Do 335 V2	CP+UB	230 002	31 December 1943
Do 335 V3	CP+UC*	230 003	20 January 1944
Do 335 V4	CP+UD	230 004	9 July 1944
Do 335 V5	CP+UE	230 005	2 August 1944
Do 335 V6	CP+UF	230 006	25 March 1944
Do 335 V7	CP+UG	230 007	19 May 1944
Do 335 V8	CP+UH	230 008	30 or 31 May 1944

*The V3 wore the code CP+UC in the period July to November 1944, after which it wore T9+ZH.

The Do 335 V3 was later assigned the tactical code T9+ZH.

The face of the Do 335 V3.

The identifying feature of the V3 was its ventral fin, which was painted in RLM 65. Note the dented access panels.

The cockpit of the third prototype.

installation. The weapons were most likely 30-mm cannon. Approximately two months later, on 26 July, work began to convert the V3 into an interim reconnaissance machine. Reconnaissance equipment (Rb 50/30 camera) was installed in the bomb bay. Thus equipped, the aircraft was transferred to the *Versuchsverband des Oberkommandos der Luftwaffe* (Test Unit of the *Luftwaffe* High Command). The V3 was given a new tactical code, T9+XH. The aircraft was supposed to conduct operational missions to determine its suitability for the reconnaissance role. The V3 was attached to the unit from August to October 1944. Plans called for it to be flown over Corsica and Sardinia in that time. Lt. Ziese may also have made several flights over the British Isles, however, this remains

The Do 335 V3 was assigned to the OKL's experimental unit for use as a photo-reconnaissance aircraft. It was then that it received the tactical code T9+ZH.

The fuselage of the V3 was damaged in several places (for example next to the fuselage cross).

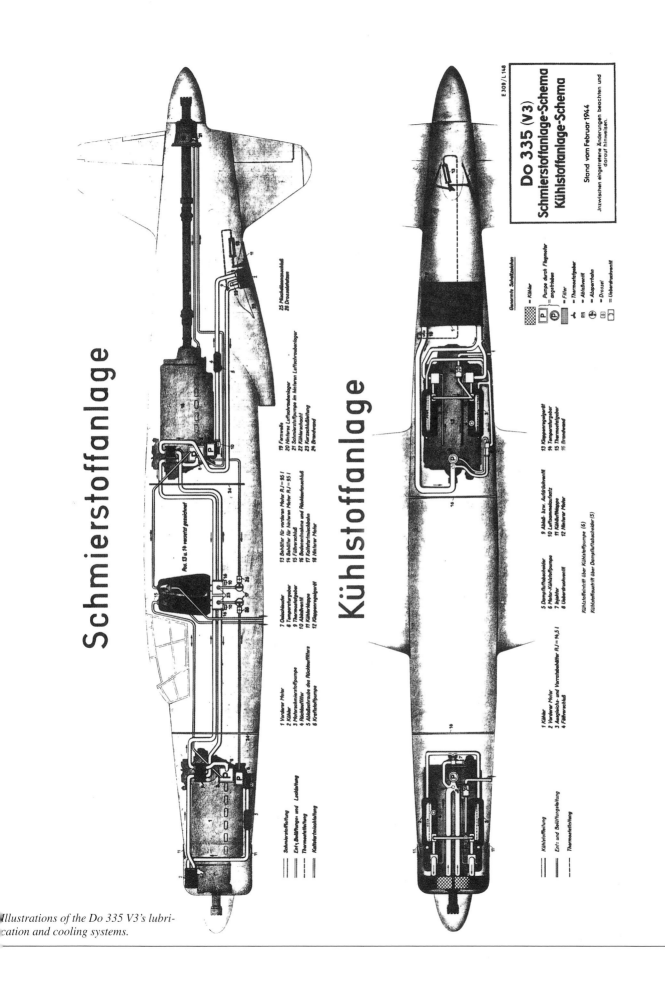

Schmierstoffanlage

Kühlstoffanlage

Do 335 (V3)
Schmierstoffanlage-Schema
Kühlstoffanlage-Schema

Stand vom Februar 1944

Inzwischen eingetretene Änderungen beachten und
darauf hinweisen.

E 309 / L 148

Gesamte Schaltzeichen

= Kühler
= Pumpe durch Flugmotor angetrieben
= Filter
= Thermostatgeber
= Ablaßventil
= Absperrhahn
= Drossel
= Ueberdruckventil

Schmierstoffanlage:

Schmierstoffleitung
Ent-, Belüftungs- und Leckleitung
Thermostatleitung
Kühlwasserbeimischleitung

1 Vorderer Motor
2 Kühler
3 Motorschmierstoffpumpe
4 Rücksaugfilter
5 Ablaßschraube des Rücksaugfilters
6 Kraftstoffpumpe

7 Ölabscheider
8 Temperaturgeber
9 Thermostatgeber
10 Ablaßventil
11 Kühlerklappe
12 Klappenregelgerät

Pos. 13 u. 14 vierseitig gezeichnet

13 Behälter für vorderen Motor RJ = 95 l
14 Behälter für hinteren Motor RJ = 95 l
15 Füllverschluß
16 Bodenentnahme und Rückbeförderschluß
17 Kraftstoffzuleitung
18 Hinterer Motor

19 Fernwelle
20 Hinteres Luftschraubenlager
21 Schmierstoffpumpe im hinteren Luftschraubenlager
22 Kühlverschluß
23 Kurzschlußleitung
24 Brandwand

25 Mischdüsenanschluß
26 Drosselabhahn

Kühlstoffanlage:

Kühlstoffleitung
Ent- und Belüftungsleitung
Thermostatleitung

1 Kühler
2 Vorderer Motor
3 Ausgleichs- und Vorratsbehälter RJ = 14,5 l
4 Füllverschluß

5 Dampfluftabscheider
6 Motor-Kühlstoffpumpe
7 Injektor
8 Ueberdruckventil

Kühlstoffeintritt über Kühlstoffpumpe (6)
Kühlstoffaustritt über Dampfluftabscheider (5)

9 Absd.- bzw. Aufströmventil
10 Luftsammelanschritz
11 Kühlstoffklappe
12 Hinterer Motor

13 Klappenregelgerät
14 Temperaturgeber
15 Thermostatgeber
16 Brandwand

*Illustrations of the Do 335 V3's lubri-
cation and cooling systems.*

Unlike the V1 and V2 prototypes, the third prototype was finished in a splinter scheme of RLM 70/71/65.

speculation as no supporting documents have been found. Following two months of service with the unit the V3 was supposed to be flown to Rechlin for more tests, however a landing accident in November initially made this impossible. Not until 30 November, after the damage had been repaired, was testing of the prototype resumed. Trials at Rechlin were limited to testing of the FuG 218 night fighter antenna system and were completed by mid-December. The aircraft's subsequent use and ultimate fate are not known.

The annular radiator, power plants and cockpit canopy of the V3 were similar to those of the V2, which was also unarmed. One area that was different, however, was the wing-fuselage fairing. Externally, the V2 and V3 were otherwise indistinguishable. One fact of significance to the modeler is that the ventral fin of the V3 was painted *Hellblau 65*. Only the V3 was painted in this way.

Dornier Do 335 V4 (*Werknummer* 230 004, CP+UD)

The fourth prototype made its first flight on 9 July 1944 with test pilot Quenzler at the controls. Problems developed after about thirty minutes in the air, when the rear engine caught fire. Fortunately Quenzler was able to activate the fire-extinguishing system, which put out the fire. He then landed the aircraft without incident. Following repairs, the V4 was flight-tested from Mengen until October 1944. The V4 was later fitted with a revised wing. It was the extended wing of the planned B-series with a span of 18.40 meters. The V4 became the prototype of the B-4 reconnaissance version. The aircraft was with Dornier in 1945.

Dornier Do 335 V5 (*Werknummer* 230 005, CP+UE)

This prototype first flew on 2 August 1944. Its subsequent use was limited to the armament test-bed role. In the course of these tests CP+UE was initially used by Dornier for static firing trials. On 30 September the aircraft was flown to Rechlin. Modifications to the weapons system, which initially consisted of one MK 103 and two MG 151 cannon, began the next day. The new configuration consisted of two MK 103 cannon in the fuselage and two MG 151 cannon in the wings. It has been suggested, but not confirmed, that an engine-mounted MK 103 was also installed. The series of tests at Lärz ended on 23 December 1944, after which the machine was attached to *Erprobungskommando 335* (Test Detachment 335) in Mengen. The subsequent use and ultimate fate of the V5 are not known.

Dornier Do 335 V6 (*Werknummer* 230 006, CP+UF)

On 25 March 1944, several weeks before his death, Werner Altrogge took the V6 (CP+UF) up on its maiden flight. The sixth prototype was subsequently to be used exclusively in factory trials (electrics). These plans were frustrated when the V6 was disabled at the Löwenthal airfield (Friedrichshafen) as a result of undercarriage damage. On 24 April 1944, barely one month after its maiden flight, the V6 was destroyed in an American air raid on Löwenthal. Technically, the V6 was largely similar to the V5. The aircraft was powered by two DB 603 A-2 engines. Armament equipment consisted of one MK 103 and two MG 151 cannon.

One of the few photographs of the seventh prototype.

It is known for certain that the Jumo 213 was tested in the nose position of the Do 335.

Dornier Do 335 V7 (*Werknummer* 230 007, CP+UG)

Assembled at Löwenthal, the V7 (CP+UG) first took to the air on 19 May 1944 with Hans Dieterle at the controls. The seventh prototype was subsequently used mainly for factory trials. Various sources state that the V7 was later sent to Junkers, where the machine was used in static tests. In the course of these tests two Junkers Jumo engines, of the A and E versions, were installed. During these tests the V7 was destroyed in an Allied air raid.

Dornier Do 335 V8 (*Werknummer* 230 008, CP+UH)

This AC began taxiing trials on 22 May 1944. The exact date of the aircraft's first flight is not known, but it may have been 30 or 31 May 1944. Test pilot Quenzler ran into problems on the maiden flight of the V8 (CP+UH). The undercarriage refused to retract and the flight had to be ended prematurely. The V8, which was built in Löwenthal, was subsequently handed over to Daimler-Benz for tests relating to the installation of improved engines. In the process it became the first Do 335 to be fitted with the DB 603 E-1, resulting in modifications to the engine cowlings. Test flights were carried out at Stuttgart-Echterdingen. On 1 July the aircraft was moved to Mengen for another series of tests, once again related to the engines. There the eighth prototype was fitted with flame dampers to determine their suitability for a planned night fighter version. Experimental night flights were conducted from Neuburg airfield in the second half of August. In October 1944 the V8 was used for high-altitude test flights from Mengen. On the last day of February 1945 the V8 left Mengen for Rechlin. The *Luftwaffe* test station was most likely the prototype's last stop.

7. The Pre-Production Series

Do 335 A-0

The Do 335 V9 Prototype
(*Werknummer* 230 009, CP+UI)

The realization of the Do 335 A-0 marked the beginning of a new phase in the type's development. It was the final stage leading up to production. The first example was completed in June 1944. The Do 335 V9 (CP+UI) was built to A-0 standard and as such was the forerunner of the Do 335 production aircraft.

The prototype of the A-0 series (*Werknummer* 230 009) completed its first flight on 29 June 1944. Test pilot "Ivan" Quenzler took the aircraft into the air for the first time. The next month found the V9 at the Tarnewitz weapons test station, where tests were carried out with the engine-mounted MK 103. The prototype's next, and probably last, station was the *E-Stelle Rechlin*.

In the course of testing at Rechlin the aircraft was flown by a *Staffelkapitän* from JG 26. His task was to evaluate the Do 335's performance and assess the type's suitability for the day fighter role. *Leutnant* Schild came to the conclusion that the Do 335 was too demanding to fly, given the level of training of new fighter pilots at that late and critical stage of the war. In the hands of an experienced pilot, however, he felt that the aircraft would be an effective weapon.

On 18 August 1944 the Do 335 V9 was damaged in a crash-landing. It is very likely that the aircraft was repaired, however no information on its subsequent fate has survived. It may be assumed that the V9 was still at Rechlin when the war ended.

Side view of the Do 335 V9. The V9 was essentially the prototype of the A-0 pre-production version.

Pre-Production Aircraft
(*Werknummer* 240 101 – 240 110)

In late summer 1944 the Do 335 cleared the hurdle from purely experimental flying to level of the A-0 pre-production series. The first pre-production aircraft was *Werknummer* 240 101, which was immediately delivered to the *Erprobungskommando 335* in Mengen. Four more aircraft followed in October 1944.

As mentioned earlier, some elements of III./KG 2's ground personnel were assigned to the aviation industry to assist in production of the Do 335. Production was decentralized, which meant that in 1944 the wings were built in an aircraft hangar in Konstanz, whereas in the final weeks of the war fuselages were built in a sawmill on Ummendorf, near Biberach. These components were subsequently assembled in Oberpfaffenhofen.

The following information concerning the construction and subsequent fates of the ten Do 335 A-0s should not be considered definitive on account of gaps in the surviving documents.

Werknummer 240 101 (VG+PG)
Werknummer 240 102 (VG+PH)
Werknummer 240 103 (VG+PI)
Werknummer 240 104 (VG+PK)
Werknummer 240 105 (VG+PL)
Werknummer 240 106 (VG+PM)
Werknummer 240 107 (VG+PN)
Werknummer 240 108 (VG+PO)
Werknummer 240 109 (VG+PP)
Werknummer 240 110 (VG+PQ)

The huge cruciform tail of the Do 335 V9. The two vertical fins could be jettisoned explosively.

Do 335 A-0
(*Werknummer* 240 101)

The first example of the A-0 series was assigned the tactical code VG+PG. After company acceptance flights the machine was transferred to Mengen for type testing. It is believed that the aircraft later served as a replacement for the Do 335 V2, which was lost in a crash. One identifying feature was the numerical code 2/1 on the vertical stabilizer instead of the usual last three digits of the *Werknummer*. In his book *War Prize*, Phil Butler states that 240 101 arrived in America with an American registration. This topic will be examined further in the chapter *War Booty*.

Dornier Do 335 A-0
(*Werknummer* 240 102)

The events surrounding this machine are very well known. The now famous VG+PH, the sole surviving Do 335, has had a long and eventful life. Transported to the USA aboard an auxiliary carrier after the war, decades later it returned to its birthplace. Following restoration in Oberpfaffenhofen, it spent several years in the

In this photograph VP+GH is still in standard Luftwaffe *markings. Oberpfaffenhofen was already in American hands when this photo was taken.*

The second pre-production aircraft in American markings.

Deutsches Museum in Munich before returning to the United States once more. A separate chapter is dedicated to this last survivor of the Do 335 family. Several flights by "102" can be confirmed from logbook entries. The three examples given here were made from Rechlin:

13/1/1945   From 1313 to 1330 hours.

14/1/1945   Ferry flight from Rechlin to Lärz (0920 to 0934 hours).

14/1/1945   Return flight from Lärz to Rechlin (1631 to 1641 hours).

Dornier Do 335 A-0
(*Werknummer* 240 103)

This third pre-production aircraft (VG+PI) was first flown on 30 September 1944 by Hans Dieterle. The aircraft almost came to grief in the process, when the aircraft's troublesome undercarriage again caused an in-flight emergency. When a hydraulic failure made it impossible to lower the undercarriage, Dieterle resorted to the emergency compressed air system, preventing a forced landing. The aircraft was supposed to be flown to Rechlin, however an accident during a night landing en route prevented this. The incident is believed to have occurred sometime between 18 and 25 November 1944. The weekly report for the period 26 November to 2 December 1944 had this to say:

"Aircraft is to be repaired. Date of completion uncertain."

The machine was repaired, however it was not used for engine trials at Rechlin as was originally planned. After repairs had been completed, Lt. Lerche was ordered to ferry the machine to Oberpfaffenhofen. A flat tire caused by bomb splinters prevented Lerche from carrying out the order, and so VG+PI stayed at Rechlin. For reasons which are not known, repairs proved impossible. Instead, Lerche ferried 240 102 (VG+PH), the sole surviving example of the type. It was originally thought that "103" was still at Rechlin when the Russians arrived, however recently uncovered information indicates that the aircraft was flown to Oberpfaffenhofen. This is confirmed by a photograph (with an American soldier) in which the numbers "0" and "3" are clearly visible. The aircraft displays splinter damage.

Dornier Do 335 A-0
(*Werknummer* 240 104)

The date of this aircraft's maiden flight is not known. The weekly report for the period 5 to 12 November 1944 reveals that VG+PK was also used for a time by Junkers at Dessau. The report states:

The same aircraft following restoration.

The fifth pre-production aircraft, displaying considerable splinter damage. Note that the cockpit canopy has been removed.

"During the ferry flight from Oberpfaffenhofen to Dessau (and Rechlin) the aircraft had to make a stop at Merseburg for fuel. The aircraft suffered hydraulic failure during the subsequent takeoff."

The weekly report for the period 18 to 25 November 1944 confirmed its arrival in Dessau and Rechlin.

"Ferried from Dessau to Rechlin on 22/11/1944. Start of acceptance checks. Elimination of complaints received to date."

Two other reports, dated 8 to 15 December and 17 to 23 December of the same year, confirm the installation of the engine-mounted cannon and other modifications. Armament then consisted of one MK 103 engine-mounted cannon and two MG 151/15 cannon mounted above the forward engine. The last-mentioned report

documented the completion of the radio system and contained information on a series of hydraulic tests. Rechlin is the last known station for this aircraft.

Dornier Do 335 A-0
(*Werknummer* 240 105)

The date of the fifth pre-production aircraft's maiden flight is also unknown. The aircraft was intended mainly for tests with the aircraft's deicing system, which were to take place in Rechlin. Several weekly reports confirm that the aircraft was flown to the *E-Stelle*. The first noted that "105" had made an en route stop in Illesheim after developing a problem with the cooling system. The second report (26 November to 2 December 1944) reported the aircraft in flyable condition once again. The next report, dated 2 to 15 December, confirmed that the aircraft had been flown to Rechlin by *Hauptmann* Maier. Other sources state that 240 105 was flown to Munich in January 1945 for deicing tests. At a later date the type sustained considerable damage from bomb splinters. When Germany surrendered the aircraft was most likely at Oberpfaffenhofen, but possibly Mengen.

Dornier Do 335 A-0
(*Werknummer* 240 106)

No proof exists, in word or photo, that this pre-production aircraft was ever completed, or if it was, how it was used. The only reference in the available literature is by Smith, Creek and Hitchcock, who believe that the aircraft was destroyed in a bombing raid. If the previous sequence of manufacturer's codes was followed, the aircraft would have been VG+PM.

Parked on the airfield perimeter, the fate of 105 was sealed.

Above Left: Werknummer 240 107, a Do 335 A-0 pre-production aircraft.
Above Right: 240 107 bore no factory code when this photo was taken.
Center Left: The seventh pre-production machine was undoubtedly one of the most-photographed "Anteaters".
Center Right: The seventh pre-production aircraft was used to obtain performance data for the Do 335 A-1 series.
Right: This previously unpublished photograph reached the author shortly before the book went to press. Taken in Mengen and dated September 1944, the photo depicts Do 335 pilots of III./KG 2 (front row). (A. Schliebner)

Dornier Do 335 A-0
(*Werknummer* 240 107)

Whereas the very existence of *Werknummer* 240 106 remains questionable, there are numerous photographs to confirm that the seventh pre-production machine (VG+PN) was completed. Its ultimate fate remains a mystery, however. Documents confirm its existence from September 1944. It is also known that "107" was used to provide data for the Do 335 A-1 fighter-bomber. In that configuration the aircraft was armed with an engine-mounted MK 103 cannon and two MG 151 cannon above the forward engine. The aircraft was powered by two DB 603 A-2 engines.

Dornier Do 335 A-0
(*Werknummer* 240 108)

This aircraft was used as a prototype for the A-1 series. From December 1944 until at least February of the following year VG+PO was involved in a test program at the *E-Stelle Rechlin*. "108" was also used for engine trials with the DB 603 E-1. In April 1945 it was flown back to Oberpfaffenhofen, where it was captured by American troops.

Dornier Do 335 A-0
(*Werknummer* 240 109)

Here again, gaps in the record make it impossible to describe this aircraft's complete history. A flight report dated 15 January 1945 describes an accident during flight trials at Oberpfaffenhofen which led to the loss of the aircraft. The pilot of VG+PP set the aircraft down on an icy runway with a very high sink rate. The impact broke the aircraft's back resulting in a total write-off.

Dornier Do 335 A-0
(*Werknummer* 240 110)

This aircraft (VG+PQ) was the last A-0 and the ultimate prototype for the Do 335 A-1 fighter-bomber series. It was powered by two DB 603 E-1 engines. The aircraft was probably destroyed in a bombing raid.

A total of ten pre-production aircraft was built. They were followed by the A-1 version, the first variant of the Do 335 intended for operational service. It should also be mentioned that A-0 air-

frames were used to construct the V11 and V12 prototypes, which may be seen as predecessors of the A-10 training aircraft.

Erprobungskommando 335

The following history of *Erprobungskommando 335* is based on information provided by Major Schreiweis:

"It should be noted that this was the only time in the history of the Luftwaffe that a unit was its own test detachment, meaning it was responsible for developing the very aircraft it was supposed to take into action."

The order for the formation of this detachment was issued on 4 September 1944. The unit's existence was initially frozen for six months, as a result of which all of III./KG 2's personnel were assigned to Dornier to work in the Do 335 program. Their tasks included production, development of servicing procedures and the writing of technical manuals.

"At the beginning of November 1944 I was summoned by General Galland. I gave to him a set of detailed, illustrated pilot's notes for the Do 335. He thumbed through the manual and said that he wanted to read it in detail. He then declared:
"This is terrific. We have and have had many test detachments, but this is the first time I have been given anything like this.""

Major Schreiweis described the events of those days:

"I was made Kommandeur of III./KG 2 in July 1943 and for nearly four weeks we flew mission against the invasion forces. On one of the last of these missions my crew and I were forced to bail out. Much later, in May 1944, I was ordered to report to the commander of XI. Fliegerkorps, Gen. Peltz. He said something to the effect of: "Technically and as a pilot, you have been judged the best commander in my area. You and your entire Gruppe (augmented strength about 800 men) are being sent to Lake Constance. There you will assist Dornier in developing a completely new high-speed bomber, after which you and your Gruppe will return to action." Apparently no one in our command, whether in the army or air force, had any idea of the industry's production potential. Moreover, everyone was telling everyone else lies, in any case General Peltz said we would be going back into action in about three months. In my opinion he really believed this, but the lying went from the top to bottom. In this case he was the bottom.".

I considered the propeller age to be ended, especially since I knew that some bomber units were being retrained on the Me 262 after Hitler's refusal to release the aircraft for use in the fighter role. I naturally assumed that the new Dornier aircraft was a jet bomber. Had I known otherwise, I would have asked General Peltz for another assignment.

Our aircraft, all Dornier Do 217 M bombers powered by two DB 603 engines, were transferred to other Geschwader. Everything else, especially our technical equipment and vehicle, we kept and took with us to Lake Constance. Despite what we had been told, we found that absolutely no preparations had been made there. The Friedrichshafen base commander had merely received a letter telling him that we were arriving and that he was to provide quarters. It was not mentioned that we were a bomber unit. They assumed that we were a bunch of cast-offs.

The Gruppe carried out the move. I still had my Do 217 and flew to see Oberstleutnant Meister, who was with his unit at Lager Lechfeld converting to the Me 262.

I had him brief me on what he was doing in preparation for my anticipated task. Two days later when I rejoined the bulk of my unit, I found them squeezed into the flak barracks in Friedrichshafen. The place was in bad shape and its location, right next to the Dornier works, exposed it to the threat of air attack. The Friedrichshafen gear factory was also not far away. One can imaging what the morale of my people was like!

My disappointment was great when the Dornier people told me that the aircraft was a propeller-driven fighter-bomber, even if it was the fastest in the world. It would have been even faster if Dornier had been given the Jumo 213 instead of the DB 603.

The first thing I did was try to find out from those in charge at Dornier what was actually going on. They tried to put me off with a lot of big talk, but I wasn't taken in by the exaggerations then customary from the aviation industry. I took the necessary brutal approach and in two days learned that it would be at least six months before we could take the new aircraft into action…"

One of the basic requirements was suitable accommodations for the unit's personnel, however in the case of III./KG 2 there were problems. Once again *Major* Schreiweis:

"The first thing to be done was find proper accommodations for the men. I soon wore out my feet but received only rejections. It should be borne in mind that I could not state the unit's real purpose for security reasons. Langenargen was a big army barracks camp. The army had also occupied a large hotel with approximately 30 men present there. The barracks camp alone would have accommodated our entire company. At first there was nothing they could do, as the camp was supposed to be occupied in the next fourteen days, but by January 1945 it was still empty. We later learned that it was the supply and recreation base for the Brandenburg Division. Farther out of town, by the lake, there was an old barracks camp housing an Abwehr listening station manned by six layabouts. We were also prevented from moving there. Afterward we simply took what we needed by force and the Stab and I remained there until we left the Lake Constance area. After I realized that nothing was going to happen in the next six months, I began debating what to do with my men. Together with the Dornier managers, I came up with the idea of using them on the production line, which would also solve the accommodations problem. Because of air raids production had been dispersed to numerous towns in the Vorarlberg and Upper Swabia south of Wurttemberg. Flight operations were conducted from Mengen. And so my people were assigned to various positions. Believing that the aircraft would soon be available, the generals began fighting to get it for their units. There were new RLM orders daily. One day the aircraft was to be a bomber, then a fighter, then a reconnaissance machine, then a night fighter, then a bomber again. There was even talk of using it as a close-support aircraft. The Dornier people constantly made changes, there was no talk of production anymore…"

In September 1944 *Major* Schreiweis was ordered to Rechlin. There he saw the Ar 234, which he would gladly have exchanged for the "old" Do 335.

"In September 1944 I was sent to Rechlin for three weeks. There I was introduced to the Ar 234, the world's first jet bomber. It was even faster than the Me 262. Designed as a fighter, it had no bomb-aiming mechanism. Neither did the Do 335. Both machines were thought of as nothing more than "terror bombers", which meant that they were to be used in random revenge attacks. In contrast the

Ar 234 had been conceived as a bomber, with a Lotfe 7K in the clear nose for accurate bombing. The aircraft was equipped with a Patin three-axis autopilot. As a result, while on the bomb run the pilot could release the controls and devote his full concentration to dropping the bombs. At Rechlin I also learned of developments with four and six jet engines and the Ju 287 jet bomber. Not only was the Do 335 out of date compared to these machines, Arado also had a lead on Dornier of almost a year. Why the same nonsense again now? Why fool around with the Do 335?

Why did Dornier not release the Do 335 for license production? Some said that there were not enough jet engines available, but I didn't accept that. Why hadn't they switched engine production in time?"

In the meantime the use of military personnel in industry had had drastic consequences for some of Dornier's employees. *Major Schreiweis:*

"It was November 1944. A "press gang" turned up at Dornier. The most pitiful of Dornier's personnel, the lame, the sick, the grandfathers, were drafted. They were replaced by our professional soldiers. Out went grandpa, replaced by a tough career soldier. I couldn't take any more of it."

The events that followed ended the sojourn at Dornier and the soldiers returned to their intended roles. *Major* Schreiweis' final account does not relate to the book's actual theme, however it does describe the general chaos which prevailed in Germany at that time:

"I took my idea to General Galland. Less than two weeks later we were transferred to Munich-Neubiberg. There we were redesignated V./NJG 2. I never saw anything of that Geschwader or its Kommodore. We were attached directly to the 7. Jagddivision. We received forty Ju 88 G-6s. By the end of December 1944 we were ready for night fighter operations, but in fact we never flew any. It is little known that as of January 1945 no more night fighter missions were flown, at least not conventional missions by twin-engine machines. The night fighter units were retrained for night ground attack, for which we were better trained than our night fighter comrades. We did a lot of practice air-ground firing on the range, and we were given two unserviceable locomotives with which to practice on. As time went on it became increasingly difficult to obtain fuel, bombs and ammunition.

We flew out last attacks on the night of 27-28 April 1945.

I received the mission order early on the morning of the 28th. That afternoon I tried to call division to confirm, but received no answer.

I didn't think anything of it, assuming that the line was down. I should have been suspicious, because we also could not make radio contact. We flew the mission, and afterwards there was still telephone and radio silence. On 29 April we were forced to realize that the 7. Jagddivision had disbanded itself or had fled. At first I assumed that we would we transferred south, but on 30 April there was still no radio contact. It finally dawned on us that there was no longer a 7. Jagddivision.

Our thoughts now turned to avoiding capture if possible. The Amis took Munich on 30 April.

What happened next is a story of its own. On the morning of 1 May three aircraft took off, almost over the heads of the Americans.

Hauptmann Deuring and Lt. Maier belly-landed on a football field in Tailfingen, Wurttemberg.

Oberleutnant Felder made a normal landing near Lindau. Oberfähnrich Zobernig landed at his home field in Klagenfurt. I had given him papers indicating that he was the advance party for our transfer. He later told me that this was a good thing, for after he landed he was checked by military police. They told him that things would have gone badly for him if he hadn't had those papers."

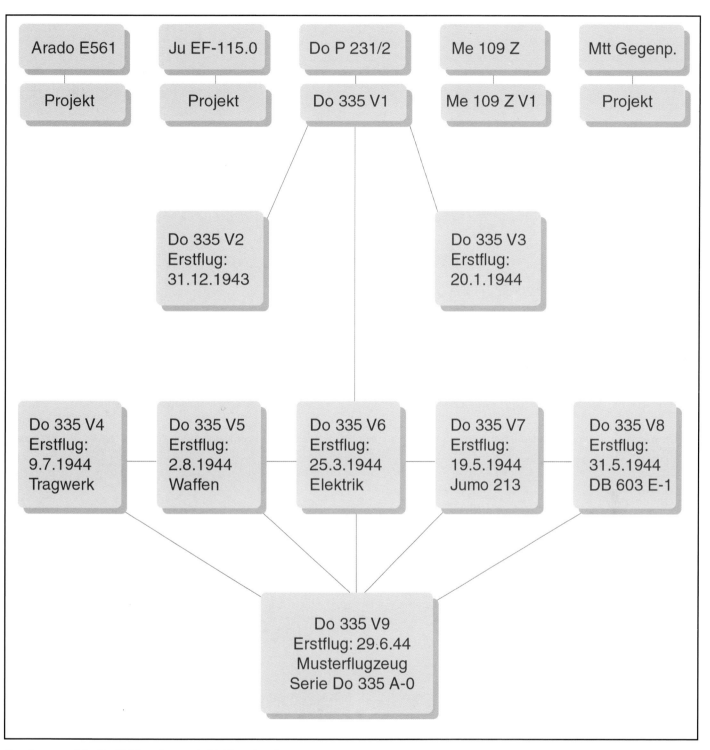

Arado E561	Ju EF-115.0	Do P 231/2	Me 109 Z	Mtt Gegenp.
Projekt	Projekt	Do 335 V1	Me 109 Z V1	Projekt

Do 335 V2
Erstflug:
31.12.1943

Do 335 V3
Erstflug:
20.1.1944

Do 335 V4
Erstflug:
9.7.1944
Tragwerk

Do 335 V5
Erstflug:
2.8.1944
Waffen

Do 335 V6
Erstflug:
25.3.1944
Elektrik

Do 335 V7
Erstflug:
19.5.1944
Jumo 213

Do 335 V8
Erstflug:
31.5.1944
DB 603 E-1

Do 335 V9
Erstflug: 29.6.44
Musterflugzeug
Serie Do 335 A-0

Development of the Do 335 from Project P. 231/2 to the V9 prototype.

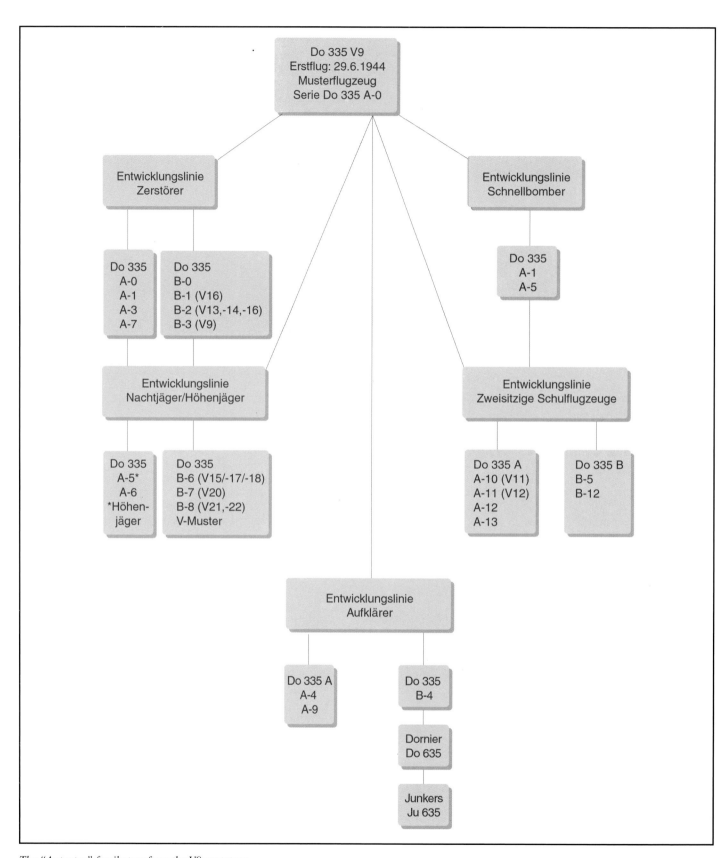

Do 335 V9
Erstflug: 29.6.1944
Musterflugzeug
Serie Do 335 A-0

Entwicklungslinie
Zerstörer

Entwicklungslinie
Schnellbomber

Do 335
A-0
A-1
A-3
A-7

Do 335
B-0
B-1 (V16)
B-2 (V13,-14,-16)
B-3 (V9)

Do 335
A-1
A-5

Entwicklungslinie
Nachtjäger/Höhenjäger

Entwicklungslinie
Zweisitzige Schulflugzeuge

Do 335
A-5*
A-6
*Höhen-
jäger

Do 335
B-6 (V15/-17/-18)
B-7 (V20)
B-8 (V21,-22)
V-Muster

Do 335 A
A-10 (V11)
A-11 (V12)
A-12
A-13

Do 335 B
B-5
B-12

Entwicklungslinie
Aufklärer

Do 335 A
A-4
A-9

Do 335
B-4

Dornier
Do 635

Junkers
Ju 635

The "Anteater" family tree from the V9 prototype.

8. Production Status

The Do 335 A-1 - First Production Version

In November 1944 the A-0 pre-production series was followed by the first example of the Do 335 A-1. The aircraft, *Werknummer* 240 111, was assembled in Oberpfaffenhofen. In keeping with the original plans, twelve machines were supposed to be completed in the A-1 configuration. The aircraft were assigned the *Werknummer* 240 111 to 240 122. The following summary is based on documents held by the Deutsches Museum.

Do 335 A-1 (*Werknummer* 240 111, RP+UA, A-11 configuration)

The aircraft was rolled out in Oberpfaffenhofen in 1945. It was not a "pure" A-1, rather it was an unarmed two-seat trainer. In this configuration it was designated the A-11. By way of comparison, the A-10 trainer was derived from the A-0 airframe.

At some point 240 111 was damaged as a result of undercarriage trouble, however it was repaired.

Do 335 A-1 (*Werknummer* 240 112, RP+UB, A-11 configuration)

240 112 was also assembled in Oberpfaffenhofen. Like the first aircraft, it was also completed in the two-seat configuration (A-11). The aircraft was captured by American forces at

112 in the colors of its original owners.

This Do 335 A-11 was allocated to the British. It was lost in England while under test.

Oberpfaffenhofen at the end of the war. It was repaired and flown to England, where it was lost in a crash. More details are contained in the chapter *War Booty*. A logbook entry dated 20 January 1945 confirms a 22-minute test flight (1410 to 1432 hours) in which "112" developed engine trouble.

Do 335 A-1 (*Werknummer* 240 113, RP+UC)

This aircraft (RP+UC) was most likely the only one which remained in the original A-1 configuration. The fighter-bomber was severely damaged in a crash. "113" was repaired and flown again. The aircraft was captured by American forces in Bindlach.

Do 335 A-1 (*Werknummer* 240 114, RP+UD, completed as A-11)

Like "111" and "112", his aircraft was also built with dual cockpits. In April 1945 "114" (RP+UD) was captured by the Allies at Oberpfaffenhofen in flyable condition.

Do 335 A-1 (*Werknummer* 240 115)

At war's end, this aircraft (RP+UE) was captured by the Americans at Oberpfaffenhofen before production was complete. The state of the aircraft and its subsequent fate are not known (also see the B-Series).

Do 335 A-1 (*Werknummer* 240 116, for B-Series)

The aircraft was intended as a prototype for the Do 335 B. The airframe was still under construction when the war ended. Further information is contained in the chapter dealing with the B-version.

Do 335 A-1 (*Werknummer* 240 117)

This aircraft served as a prototype for the Do 335 B. The aircraft was tested at Rechlin in October 1944. Whether this was done in the B-series configuration is not known.

Do 335 A-1 (*Werknummer* 240 118, for B-Series)

This aircraft was planned as a test-bed for the B-2 variant.

Do 335 A-1 (*Werknummer* 240 119, for B-Series)

Various sources claim that this machine was a prototype for the B-6 variant and was designated the V15. Not completed.

Do 335 A-1 (*Werknummer* 240 120)

This modified version was equivalent to the A-12 variant. It is not certain if the aircraft was later used for the B-series.

240 113 was repaired in spite of serious damage.

The wreck of 240 122 at Oberpfaffenhofen. The aircraft's back was broken in a heavy landing.

Do 335 (*Werknummer* 240 121, completed as A-11)

Aircraft "121" (RP+UL) was assembled in Oberpfaffenhofen and was built in the two-seat configuration of the A-11. Work on this machine was at an advanced stage.

Do 335 (*Werknummer* 240 122, completed as A-11)

Like the other late machines in this series, it is impossible to say when it made its first flight. The machine was completed as a two-seater. In the course of its brief career the aircraft was involved in accident at Oberpfaffenhofen in which the rear fuselage was damaged. A decision was made not to repair "122". The aircraft was subsequently captured by the Americans at Oberpfaffenhofen and was scrapped after the war.

From the surviving records it may be concluded that eleven examples were completed in a variety of configurations or were in an advanced state of assembly when the war ended. These included five A-11 trainers, just one A-1 and five prototypes of various B-series aircraft. Plans called for these to be followed by numerous sub-variants of the A-1 series, covering a wide spectrum of operational roles.

Table 12

Version	Remarks
Do 335 A-2	*Zerstörer* version. Based on the A-1, but with modified bombing system.
Do 335 A-3	*Zerstörer* version. Also based on the A-1 with revised armament.
Do 335 A-4	Based on the A-0. Reconnaissance aircraft with cameras in the bomb bay. Two lens openings roughly at the mid point of the bomb bay doors, one at the rear.
Do 335 A-5	Projected high-altitude fighter.
Do 335 A-6	Two-seat night fighter equipped with FuG 217 radar. The V10 served as prototype. A drawing by Arthur L. Bentley documents another version of the A-6 with a blown hood for the radar operator plus FuG 220 and FuG 350 radar equipment. Armament consisted of one MK 103 and two MG 151/20 cannon. Two drop tanks were carried for increased range.
Do 335 A-7	High-speed bomber version powered by the Jumo 213 (single-seat).
Do 335 A-8	*Zerstörer* version powered by the Jumo 213 (single-seat).
Do 335 A-9	Single-seat reconnaissance aircraft powered by the Jumo 213.
Do 335 A-10	First two-seat trainer variant. Two prototypes of this unarmed version were tested.
Do 335 A-11	Two-seat trainer based on the A-1 airframe.
Do 335 A-12	Projected two-seat version for flight and weapons training.
Do 335 A-13	Another projected two-seat trainer.

The following section deals with the V10/V11 and V12 prototypes, which were associated with the development of the A-version.

Do 335 V10 (*Werknummer* 230 010, CP+UK)

This aircraft was the prototype for a two-seat night fighter variant (A-6). It was based on an A-1 airframe, which was modified for the night fighter role by Heinkel in Vienna. The prototype (CP+UK) was mentioned in a letter dated April 1944 and its completion and readiness to fly were confirmed in mid-November. Flight testing did not begin until 24 January 1945, however. The aircraft was subsequently assigned to the *E-Stelle Werneuchen* for type testing for the proposed A-6 series. According to Nowarra in *Die Deutsche Luftrüstung*, the V10 saw action with the *Stab* of *I./NJG 3*. The aircraft fell into French hands at the end of the war and was later heavily damaged in a landing accident.

The development of a Do 335 night fighter called for numerous design changes. The most significant of these were provision of a second work area for the radar operator and installation of the extensive radar equipment. The second cockpit was placed behind and above the pilot's position. This move drastically reduced the aircraft's fuel capacity. In order to create the necessary room for the second cockpit, the single-seater's main tank fuel volume of 1 830 liters was halved. Aerodynamically, the raised second cockpit and the tube-type flame dampers on the sides of the fuselage increased drag significantly. External radar antennas were another source of drag. The airframe's dimensions were identical to the previously-produced aircraft. Power was provided by two DB 603 A-2 engines, each producing 1,750 H.P. for takeoff. The armament of the A-6 consisted of one MK 103 and two MG 151/20 cannon. Performance was inferior to that of the single-seat versions. The increases in weight and drag resulted in a maximum speed of 688 km/h. By comparison, the A-1 single-seater was capable of 763 km/h. Nevertheless, the A-6 had an excellent performance for a night fighter. Cruising speed was 606 km/h. Service ceiling was reduced from 11 000 to 10 200 meters. One of the reasons for this was the increase

in weight beyond the ten ton range (10 090 kg). Overall the type impressed the officials at the *Technische Amt* and the night fighter was assigned high priority. The type was supposed to be produced in quantity by Heinkel in Vienna, however these plans, like so many others, were never realized.

Major Schreiweis expressed the following opinion:

"Had the military situation been different the Do 335 night fighter would have been ready for service in May-June 1945.

We would have had sufficient night fighter experience and could easily have converted to the Do 335. That is probably why we were transferred to the night fighters."

Do 335 V11 (*Werknummer* 230 011, CP+UL)

The Do 335 V11 served as prototype for the A-10, an unarmed trainer variant. Its design was based on the A-0 airframe, to which a second cockpit was added. As in the case of the V10, this resulted in a reduction in fuel capacity and thus range. The forward cockpit was occupied by the student, while the instructor was placed in the raised second cockpit. The large main fuel tank of the single-seater was deleted. It was replaced by significantly smaller L-shaped tank located behind and beneath the instructor's seat. The aircraft was powered by two DB 603 A-2 engines. At the present time the fate of the V11 is unknown.

The topic of the V11 concludes with a flight report (167/335) dated from 11 to 16 October 1944, concerning the explosive jettisoning of the rear propeller, written by pilot Appel:

"After extensive static tests, the Do 335 V11 was used f to jettison the rear propeller in flight for the first time. The climb and combat power setting was selected for the moment of jettisoning. At a speed of 500 km/h, with 1.3 atm of boost and 2,500 rpm, the engine ignition was switched off, and one to two seconds later the jettison switch was activated. Engine speed at that point was 2,000 rpm. The propeller separated smoothly. Prior to jettisoning the pro-

The V11 two-seat prototype formed the basis of the A-10 trainer variant.

peller I trimmed the machine slightly tail-heavy to counter the sudden c.g. shift of 6.7 percent and resulting change in trim. In fact, however, the actual moment about the lateral axis which resulted from the sudden c.g. shift was so minor that I could have dispensed with this measure. Stansingenieur Baist of the E-Stelle Rechlin observed the test from the cockpit of the Do 335 V8. He reported that the propeller separated smoothly, trailed the aircraft briefly, very quickly ceased to rotate and then tumbled to the earth.

Contrary to the original plan, to jettison the propeller onto the Heuberg troop training grounds, following the introduction of necessary safety measures it was jettisoned over Mangold airfield in order to save time and fuel."

The V11 subsequently suffered undercarriage damage in a landing accident.

The Do 335 V11 was also used to test the rear propeller jettisoning system in flight.

Do 335 V12 (*Werknummer 230 012, RP+UO*)

Like the V11, the V12 was a two-seat trainer, in this case the prototype for the A-11 version. The aircraft was completed in the last quarter of 1944. After factory tests, in November 1944 the V12 was flown to Rechlin. After general testing the machine was used to test the P8 propeller developed by Messerschmitt and for elevator control measurements. In April the aircraft was at Friedrichshafen, where its remains were found by American troops.

Technical Details

The V12, coded RP+UO, differed from the V11 in many respects. The most significant change concerned the nosewheel leg, which rotated 45 degrees during retraction into the nosewheel bay. The same system was incorporated in the B-series. As mentioned, the V12 was used to test the Messerschmitt P8 propeller, a three-blade variable-pitch propeller with a diameter of 3.5 meters and electric pitch control. The P8 was designed for power plants in the 2,000 H.P. range and was being developed for use with the DB 603 and Jumo 213 engines. By order of the RLM, in 1942 Messerschmitt

had transferred its work on propellers to VDM. Testing of the P8 began the following year. In spite of the design's simplicity, which was praised by the RLM, and its ease of servicing, no production was undertaken. Another change compared to the V11 was the use of DB 603 E-1 engines rated at 1,800 H.P. armament similar to that of the A-1 could be installed. Speed and ceiling figures were similar to the A-10 series. The V12 was the last prototype in the A-series development program. The V13 was associated with the Do 335 B, the next stage in development.

The story of the Do 335 so far has concerned company and service testing using prototypes and pre-production machines. According to the original plans, the Do 335 was to be assigned to the units and see action quickly. Some initial steps were taken in this direction. III./KG 2 was withdrawn from action and on 22 June 1944 it was transferred to Achmer. The necessary technical personnel and pilots were sent to Friedrichshafen for retraining at the beginning of July 1944. In September 1944 the *Geschwader* was disbanded except for III./KG 2, however the unit subsequently abandoned its retraining activities.

From 1 December 1944 until its final actions (27-28 April 1945) the unit served as V./NJG 2. After conversion training the unit flew the Ju 88 G-6 on night fighter missions from Neubiberg and Riem.

Table 13

Technical Data	A-0	A-1	A-4	A-6	A-10	A-11
Wingspan	13.8 m	13.8 m	13.8 m	13.8 m	13.8 m	13.8 m
Length	13.85 m	13.85 m	13.85 m	13.85 m	13.85 m	13.85 m
Height	5.0 m	5.0 m	5.0 m	5.25 m	5.25 m	5.25 m
Wing Area	38.5 m^2	38.5 m^2	38.5 m^2	38.5 m^2	38.5 m^2	38.5 m^2
Empty Weight (kg)	7 320	7 400	—	7 730	7 700	7 700
Takeoff Weight (kg)	9 580	9 600	—	10 090	10 090	10 090
Maximum Speed (km/h)		775	763	780	688	690 690
Cruising Speed (km/h)	693	685	700	606	650	650
Service Ceiling (m)	11 400	11 400	11 400	10 190	10 190	10 190
Range (km)	1 400	1 400	—	2 065*	1 480*	—
Power Plants (2)	DB 603 A	DB 603 E	DB 603 E	DB 603 A	DB 603 A	DB 603 E
Output (H.P.)	1,750	1,800	1,800	1,750	1,750	1,800
Crew	1	1	1	2	2	2

*According to Nowarra: *Die Deutsche Luftrüstung*

9. Technical Description of the Do 335A

This objective of this part of the book is to provide the most detailed technical description of the Do 335 possible. Descriptions of the various components of the aircraft are based for the most part on original documents. Only where such documents are not available has the author resorted to secondary literature.

The unusual Do 335, jokingly called the "*Ameisenbär*" (Ant-Eater), was certainly not the beauty queen of German aircraft designs. Equally unconventional in design and appearance, Dornier's superlative deserves a closer look from the technical standpoint. The Do 335 undoubtedly pushed the limits of piston-engine technology and as such it was flying toward a future which would belong to the jet. The following description of the type's advanced technology is based on the A-version.

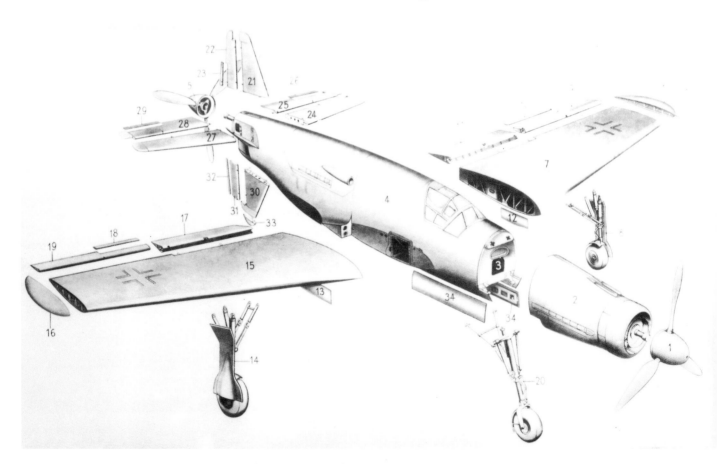

The main components of the Do 335 using the Do 335 A as an example.

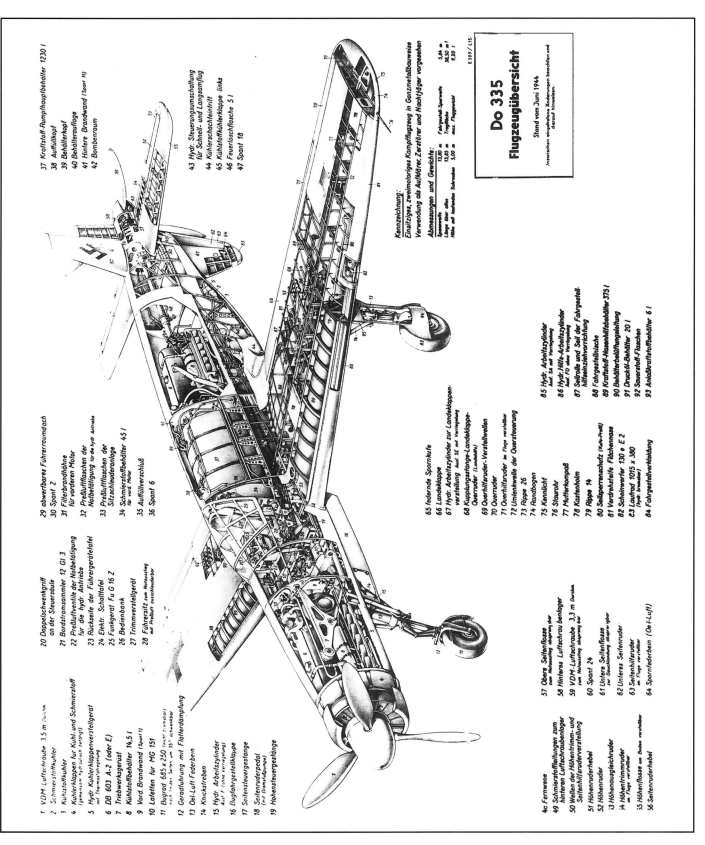

1 VDM Luftschraube 3,5 m Durchm.
2 Schmierstoffkühler
3 Kühlstoffkühler
4 Kühlerklappen für Kühl- und Schmierstoff (gemeinsam hydraulisch betätigt)
5 Hydr. Kühlerklappenverstellgerät mit Thermostatregelung
6 DB 603 A-2 (oder E)
7 Triebwerksgerüst
8 Kühlstoffbehälter 14,5 l
9 Vord. Brandwand (Spant 11)
10 Lafetten für MG 151
11 Bugrad 685 x 250 (nicht bremsbar) nach beiden Seiten um 35° schwenkbar
12 Geradführung mit Flatterdämpfung
13 Oel-Luft-Federbein
14 Knickstreben
15 Hydr. Arbeitszylinder Ausf. F (ohne Verriegelung)
16 Bugfahrgestellklappe
17 Seitensteuergestänge
18 Seitenruderpedal (mit Bremszylinder)
19 Höhensteuergestänge

20 Doppelschwenkgriff an der Steuersäule
21 Bordstromsammler 12 Gl 3
22 Preßluftventile der Notbetätigung für die hydr. Antriebe
23 Preßluftflaschen der Notbetätigung für die hydr. Antriebe
24 Elektr. Schalttafel
25 Funkgerät Fu G 16 Z
26 Bedienbank
27 Trimmverstellgerät
28 Führersitz zum Notausstieg mit Preßluft ausschleuderbar
29 abwerfbares Führerraumdach
30 Spant 2
31 Filterbrandhöhe für vorderen Motor
32 Preßluftflaschen der Notbetätigung für den hydr. Antrieb
33 Preßluftflaschen der Sitzschleuderanlage
34 Schmierstoffbehälter 45 l für vord. Motor
35 Auffüllverschluß
36 Spant 6

37 Kraftstoff-Rumpfhauptbehälter 1230 l
38 Auffüllkopf
39 Behälterkopf
40 Behälterauflage
41 Hintere Brandwand (Spant 11)
42 Bombenraum

43 Hydr. Steuerungsumschaltung für Schnell- und Langsamflug
44 Kühlerschachteintritt
45 Kühlstoffkühlerklappe links
46 Feuerlöschflasche 5 l
47 Spant 18

4c Fernweae
49 Schmierstoffleitungen zum hinteren Luftschraubenlager
50 Wellen der Höhentrimm- und Seitenhilfsruderverstellung
51 Höhenruderhebel
52 Höhenruder
53 Höhenausgleichruder zur Beschleunigung abgeschrägt
54 Höhentrimmruder im Fluge verstellbar
55 Höhenflosse am Boden verstellbar
56 Seitenruderhebel

57 Obere Seitenflosse zum Notausstieg abgespreagt über
58 Hintere Luftschraube benlager
59 VDM-Luftschraube 3,3 m Durchm.
60 Spant 24
61 Untere Seitenflosse zum Notausstieg abgespreagt über
62 Unteres Seitenruder
63 Seitenhilfsruder im Fluge verstellbar
64 Spornlederbein (Oel-Luft)

65 federnde Spornkufe
66 Landeklappe
67 Hydr. Arbeitszylinder zur Landeklappen-verstellung Ausf. SE mit Verriegelung
68 Kupplungsstange-Landeklappe-Querruder (Landestellg.)
69 Querruder
70 Querruder
71 Querhilfsruder im Fluge verstellbar
72 Umlenkwelle der Quersteuerung
73 Rippe 26
74 Randbogen
75 Kennlicht
76 Staurohr
77 Mutterkompaß
78 Kastenholm
79 Rippe 14
80 Seitspannschutz (Rohr-Draht)
81 Verdrehsteife Flächennase
82 Scheinwerfer 130 e E 2
83 Laufrad 1015 x 380 (hydr. bremsbar)
84 Fahrgestellverkleidung

85 Hydr. Arbeitszylinder Ausf. SA mit Verriegelung
86 Hydr. Hilfs-Arbeitszylinder Ausf. FO ohne Verriegelung
87 Seilrolle und Seil der Fahrgestell-hilfseinziehvorrichtung
88 Fahrgestellinie be
89 Kraftstoff-Nasenhilfsbehälter 375 l
90 Behälterbefüllungsleitung
91 Drucköl-Behälter 20 l
92 Sauerstoff-Flaschen
93 Anlaßkraftstoffbehälter 6 l

E 309 / L15/

Do 335
Flugzeugübersicht

Stand vom Juni 1944

Inzwischen eingetretene Änderungen beachten und darauf hinweisen.

Kennzeichung:
Einsitziges, zweimotoriges Kampfflugzeug in Ganzmetallbauweise
Verwendung als Aufklärer, Zerstörer und Nachtjäger vorgesehen

Abmessungen und Gewichte:

Spannweite	13,80 m	Fahrgestell-Spurweite	5,04 m
Länge über alles	13,85 m	Tragfläche	38,50 m²
Höhe mit laufender Schraube	5,00 m	max. Fluggewicht	9,30 t

Cutaway drawing of the Do 335 A, dated June 1944.

69

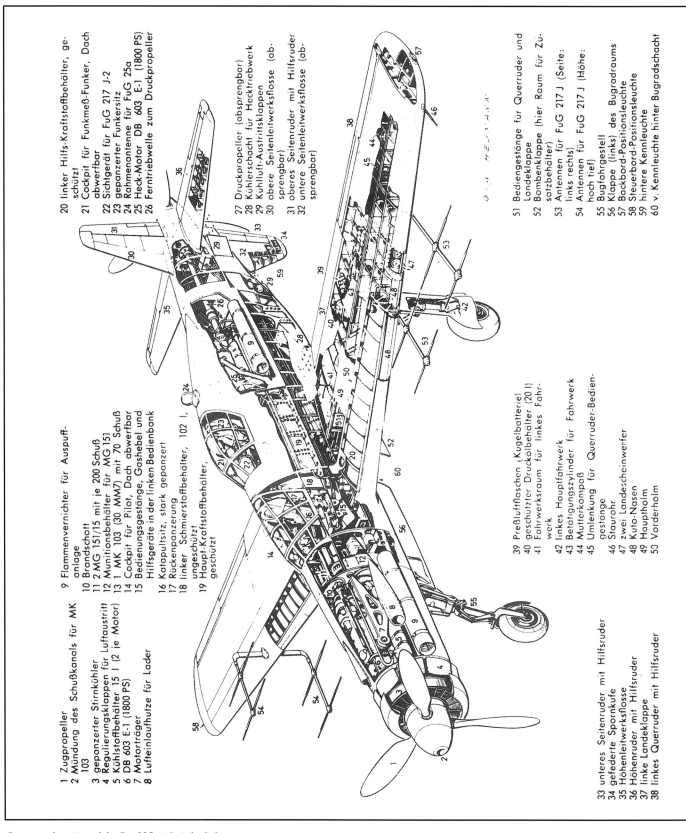

1 Zugpropeller
2 Mündung des Schußkanals für MK 103
3 gepanzerter Stirnkühler
4 Regulierungsklappen für Luftaustritt
5 Kühlstoffbehälter 15 l (2 je Motor)
6 DB 603 E-1 (1800 PS)
7 Motorträger
8 Lufteinlaufhutze für Lader
9 Flammenvernichter für Auspuff-anlage
10 Brandschott
11 2 MG 151/15 mit je 200 Schuß
12 Munitionsbehälter für MG 151
13 1 MK 103 (30 MM7) mit 70 Schuß
14 Cockpit für Pilot, Dach abwerfbar
15 Bedienungsgestänge, Gashebel und Hilfsgeräte in der linken Bedienbank
16 Katapultsitz, stark gepanzert
17 Rückenpanzerung
18 linker Schmierstoffbehälter, 102 l, ungeschützt
19 Haupt-Kraftstoffbehälter, geschützt

20 linker Hilfs-Kraftstoffbehälter, ge-schützt
21 Cockpit für Funkmeß-Funker, Dach abwerfbar
22 Sichtgerät für FuG 217 J-2
23 gepanzerter Funkersitz
24 Rahmenantenne für FuG 25a
25 Heck-Motor DB 603 E-1 (1800 PS)
26 Ferntriebwelle zum Druckpropeller

27 Druckpropeller (absprengbar)
28 Kühlerschacht für Hecktriebwerk
29 Kühlluft-Austrittsklappen
30 obere Seitenleitwerksflosse (ab-sprengbar)
31 oberes Seitenruder mit Hilfsruder
32 untere Seitenleitwerksflosse (ab-sprengbar)

33 unteres Seitenruder mit Hilfsruder
34 gefederte Spornkufe
35 Höhenleitwerksflosse
36 Höhenruder mit Hilfsruder
37 linke Landeklappe
38 linkes Querruder mit Hilfsruder

39 Preßluftflaschen (Kugelbatterie)
40 geschützter Druckölbehälter (20 l)
41 Fahrwerksraum für linkes Fahr-werk
42 linkes Hauptfahrwerk
43 Betätigungszylinder für Fahrwerk
44 Mutterkompaß
45 Umlenkung für Querruder-Bedien-gestänge
46 Staurohr
47 zwei Landescheinwerfer
48 Kuto-Nasen
49 Hauptholm
50 Vorderholm

51 Bediengestänge für Querruder und Landeklappe
52 Bombenklappe (hier Raum für Zu-satzbehälter)
53 Antennen für FuG 217 J (Seite: links rechts)
54 Antennen für FuG 217 J (Höhe: hoch tief)
55 Bugfahrgestell
56 Klappe (links) des Bugradraums
57 Backbord-Positionsleuchte
58 Steuerbord-Positionsleuchte
59 hintere Kennleuchte
60 v. Kennleuchte hinter Bugradschacht

Cutaway drawing of the Do 335 A-6 night fighter.

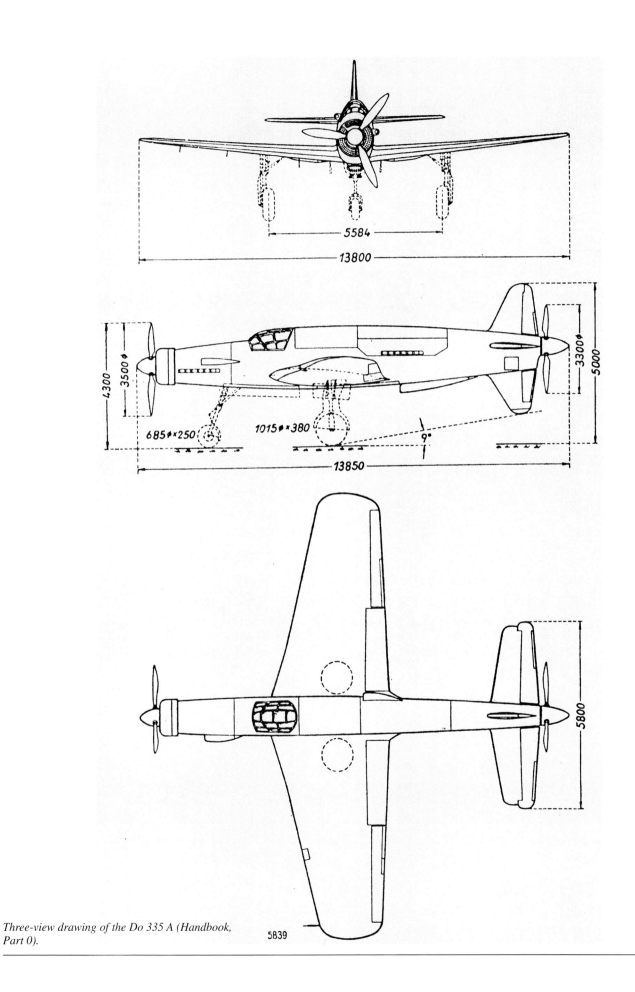

Three-view drawing of the Do 335 A (Handbook, Part 0).

The Fuselage

The stressed-skin all metal fuselage was 13.85 meters long. Twenty-four bulkheads gave shape to the fuselage, while numerous stringers and the stressed skin resulted in a structurally strong unit. So-called L, U and Z stringers were used in the basic fuselage structure. The fuselage nose was circular in section and concealed the annular radiator and oil cooler. Directly behind the nose ring were the hydraulically-activated cooling gills. Behind the cooling unit was the twelve-cylinder DB 603 in-line engine, which in the case of the Do 335 A-1 was the DB 603 E model. The engine was attached to two V-shaped engine mounts, each of which was joined to Bulkhead 1 at two attachment points. Beneath the engine, between Bulkheads 1 and 6, was the nosewheel bay. The fixed armament, consisting of one MK 103 and two MG 151/20 cannon, was installed between Bulkheads 1 and 2. The barrels of the two MG

A fuselage ready for installation of equipment. The machine in the background has already been painted.

The radiator air intake with external fairing removed.

72

The three main elements of the fuselage (from left to right the rear engine compartment, area for the fuselage fuel tank, the cockpit with rails for ejection seat).

The rear engine compartment extended from Frame 11 to Frame 17.

151/20s passed over the engine with their muzzles in the area of the cooling gills. The MK 103, on the other hand, was engine mounted, firing through the propeller hub. Behind this area was the cockpit (Bulkheads 2 to 6), which minor variations in the different versions of the aircraft. Details of these variations may be found in the relevant sections of this documentation. Pilot protection consisted of armor-glass sections in the windscreen and an armor plate behind the pilot seat. An additional safety feature was the ejector seat, an innovation at that time. Ejector seat technology was in its infancy in those days and the seat used in the Do 335 was relatively simple in design. Immediately aft of the single-seat cockpit, separated by the armored bulkhead, were two oil tanks, followed by a self-seal-ing fuel tank. These tanks were installed between Bulkheads 6 and 11. Tank volume varied between the different versions. Located beneath this area, between Bulkheads 7 and 14, was the bomb bay, which could accommodate free-fall bombs or additional fuel tanks. The rudder and elevator control cables also ran through the interior of the bomb bay. Separated by another firewall was the aft engine, which was fed by a large air intake on the starboard side of the fuselage. A large ventral air intake fed cooling air to the oil cooler, whose hydraulically-activated flaps were positioned in front of the ventral fin. The rear engine transmitted power to the jettisonable rear propeller by means of an extension shaft. The installation area extended from Bulkhead 11 to Bulkhead 18.

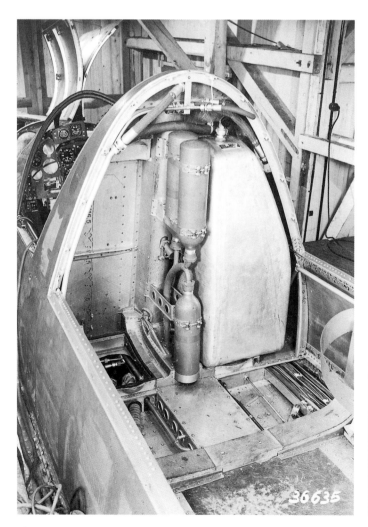

This area accommodated two oil tanks plus three compressed air bottles, the latter for operation of the ejection seat.

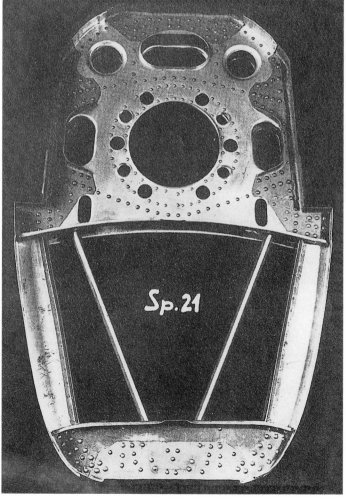

Fuselage Frame 21.

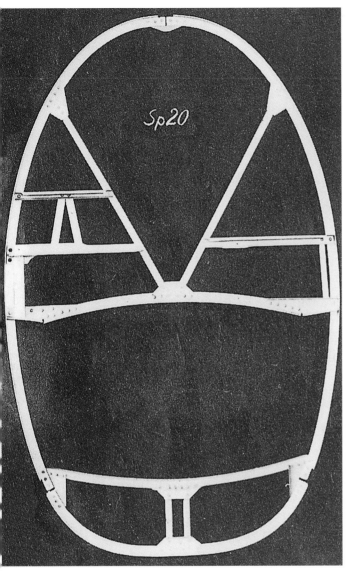

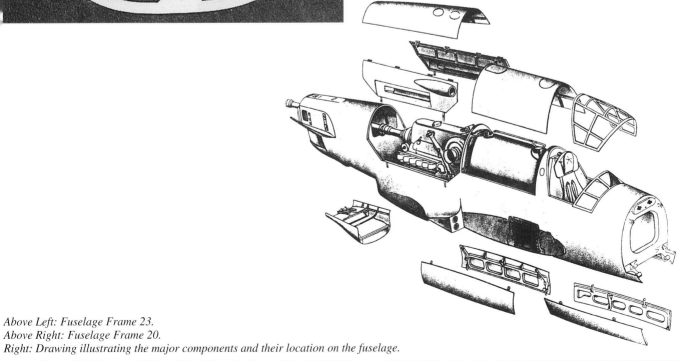

Above Left: Fuselage Frame 23.
Above Right: Fuselage Frame 20.
Right: Drawing illustrating the major components and their location on the fuselage.

The cruciform tail of the V3.

The Empennage

The fuselage terminated in a cruciform tail. The ventral fin was equipped with a sprung tail skid, so as to prevent damage to the tail in the event of ground contact. The cruciform tail was an unconventional solution which Dornier had only used in predecessor designs to the Do 335. This design was made possible by the use of a tricycle undercarriage, allowing the usual tailwheel to be dispensed with. The empennage consisted of four fins attached to the rear fuselage. All components were of metal construction.

The Vertical Stabilizer

This consisted of two components (both NACA Profile 23012.5) which were attached to the top and bottom of the rear fuselage by massive bolts. These were not bolts in the conventional sense, instead they were so-called explosive bolts. These bolts, which were ignited electrically, made it possible to quickly separate the two vertical stabilizers from the fuselage in the event of emergency. The stabilizers could be blown off singly or together. The dorsal stabilizer structure consisted of two spars and seven ribs which gave

The dorsal fin and rudder.

The ventral fin and rudder with tail skid.

ribs. It had two attachment points (Ribs 1 and 7) and was fitted with a trim tab. The rudder ended in a rounded cap.

The following description appears in Part 3 of the aircraft handbook:

"Dorsal stabilizer: the internal structure consists of 2 spars and 7 ribs. It is covered with Dural skinning and has recently been strengthened. The leading edge is made of wood and includes a recess for installation of an antenna and antenna adjuster. It is screwed to the forward spar and is removable. The curved stabilizer cap is also made of wood and is attached to Rib 7 by screws. Both components may thus be easily replaced.

Two mounts are provided for the control surface, on Ribs 1 (rigid) and 7 (flexible). The upper mount is an integral part of the control surface, while the lower one is attached by screws. The stabilizer is attached to the upper side of the fuselage using four special fittings between Frames 21 and 22.

To achieve the desired ability to jettison the stabilizer, the design includes explosive attachment bolts. If the pilot is forced to abandon the aircraft, the stabilizer (together with the aft propeller) can be jettisoned by electrical activation of the explosive bolts. The

it its aerodynamic shape. The entire unit was covered with Dural skinning with the exception of the leading edge, which was made of wood. A recess in the leading edge housed the antenna attachment point and tensioner. For ease of servicing the leading edge could be removed quickly. The stabilizer ended in a rounded cap. The rudder was also a metal structure, consisting of a spar and ten

1. Flossennase
2. Flossenvorderholm
3. Flosse
4. Flossenhinterkante
5. Ruder
6. Trimmruder
7. Spornkufe
8. Schmiegungsblech
9. Rumpfanschluß
10. Ruderholm
11. Trimmgestänge
12. Federbein zu „7"
13. Kufenlenker
14. Kufenvekleidung
15. Oberes Ruderlager
16. Unteres Ruderlager
17. Ruderhebel

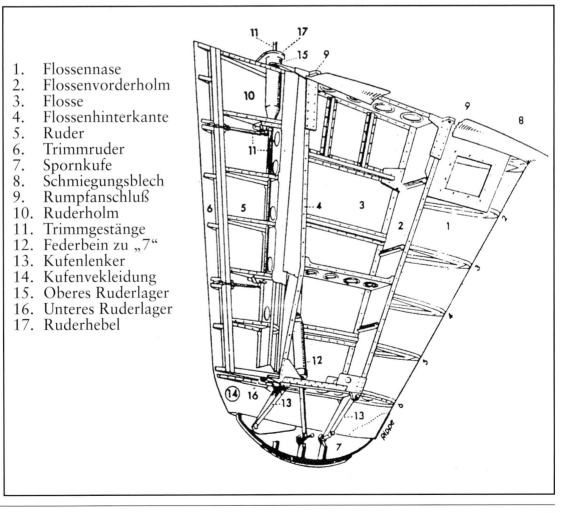

Construction of the ventral fin and rudder.

stabilizer is faired into the fuselage by means of recessed fairings attached by recessed screws."

Dorsal rudder: this control surface consists mainly of one spar, 10 ribs and riveted Dural skinning. A removable cap is screwed onto Rib 10. A trim tab is located on the trailing edge between Ribs 1 and 6."

The ventral stabilizer was also a two-spar structure. Six ribs provided aerodynamic form and the unit was skinned with Dural sheet. The leading edge was made of wood, with a recess for an antenna attachment point. The rudder consisted of two spars and seven ribs with Dural skinning. Unlike the dorsal rudder, the ventral rudder was fitted with a trim tab which covered the entire trailing edge.

In order to prevent damage to the empennage in the event of inadvertent contact with the ground, a tail skid was installed at the tip of the ventral stabilizer. Attached to an internally-mounted shock absorber, the skid rode on two sliding guides. In order to prevent dirt from entering, the mechanism was covered by a tight fitting slide fairing. The ventral stabilizer was attached to the fuselage by means of explosive bolts, with four attachment points on Frames 21 and 22. The area of the two stabilizers was 3.08 m2. The maximum rudder deflection was 24° to 26°.

This photograph depicts the starboard horizontal stabilizer and elevator. Note the elevator mass balance, which reduced control forces.

1. Flossennase
2. Flossenvorderholm
3. Flosse
4. Flossenhinterkante
5. Seitenruder
6. Ausgleichsruder
7. Unteres Ruderlager
8. Oberes Ruderlager
9. Rumpfanschluß
10. Schmiegungsblech
11. Ruderholm
12. Ausgleichsgestänge
13. Ruderhebel
14. Ruderendkappe
15. Flossenendkappe

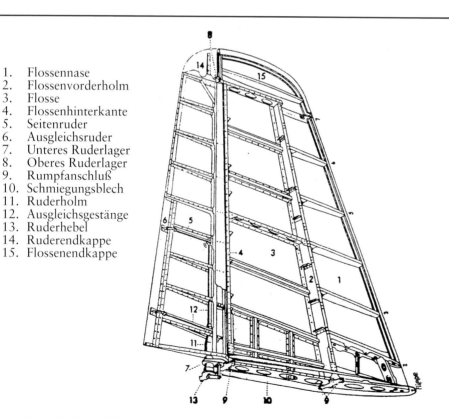

Handbook drawing depicting the structure of the dorsal fin and rudder.

Part 3 of the Do 335 Handbook includes the following description:

"The twin-spar ventral stabilizer, which includes six ribs and metal skinning, is bolted to the underside of the fuselage at four attachment points between Fuselage Frames 21 and 22. It is thus opposite the dorsal stabilizer and has roughly the same dimensions. It, too, may be jettisoned (together with the aft propeller) by means of electrically-operated explosive bolts. Switch in cockpit. The leading edge, which is made of wood, is removable and the leading edge strip is hollow to accept an antenna. Attached to Rib 6 is a skid which conforms to the shape of the fin and rudder…"

"Ventral rudder: the structure of this control surface consists of 2 spars and 7 ribs and is covered with Dural skinning. Of the rudder's two mounts, the upper is attached rigidly to the spar, while the lower is attached to Rib 7. The mounts are bolted to the attachment points on the stabilizer. Mass balancing is provided by a cast iron weight extending the full length of the control surface leading edge…"

Part 2 of the Do 335 Handbook contains the following description of the tail skid:

"The auxiliary skid, which is made necessary by the aircraft's tricycle undercarriage, forms the cap of the ventral stabilizer.

The ventral skid consists of a sturdy cast piece which rides vertically on two guides fore and aft and which is dampened by an oil-air shock absorber (Elma 8-2475 A-1, 75 atm). Shock absorber movement takes place in a sheath-like component attached to the underside of Rib 6 of the ventral stabilizer. Because of the high torsion loads, the two guides are fitted with widened mounting points. The pivoting attachment points are located on the underside of Rib 6 at the forward and rear spars. The shock absorber is contained within the stabilizer and attached to the rear spar. The skid includes a steel cap which may be replaced if damaged."

The Horizontal Stabilizer

The trapezoid-shaped horizontal stabilizer (NACA profile 23012.5) spanned 5.80 meters with an area (free area) of 7.63 m2. The cantilever structure consisted of two spars, twelve ribs and the Dural skinning. Each stabilizer had three elevator attachment points, on Ribs 1, 7 and 12. The elevators consisted of a main spar, an auxiliary spar and eighteen ribs with Dural skinning. The stabilizers were each attached to the fuselage by means of four fittings on Frames 21 and 22. The forward attachment point was adjustable, making it possible to vary stabilizer incidence from 0° to +5°. Stabilizer incidence had to be set manually. Stabilizer dihedral was 2.5°. The range of movement of the elevators was 29° to 31° up, 21° to 23° down.

Structure of a horizontal stabilizer and elevator, taken from the Do 335 handbook.

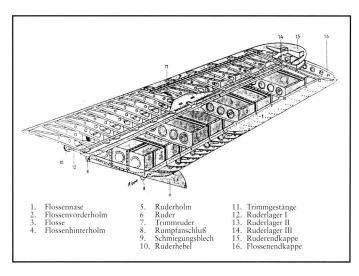

1. Flossennase	5. Ruderholm	11. Trimmgestänge
2. Flossenvorderholm	6. Ruder	12. Ruderlager I
3. Flosse	7. Trimmruder	13. Ruderlager II
4. Flossenhinterholm	8. Rumpfanschluß	14. Ruderlager III
	9. Schmiegungsblech	15. Ruderendkappe
	10. Ruderhebel	16. Flossenendkappe

Horizontal stabilizer, showing details of the attachment rib.

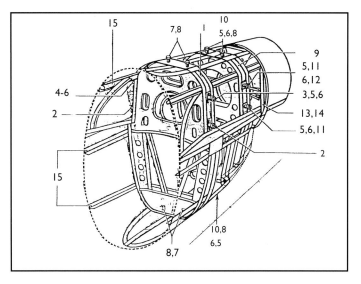

Structure of the tail surface bearer.

Part 3 of the handbook provides the following details:

"The horizontal stabilizer consists of two elements installed left and right of the aft fuselage. The two elements are largely identical and the differences are detailed in the following description.

Horizontal stabilizer: consists of 2 spars with 12 ribs with Dural skinning and fixed leading edge. The stabilizer tip is screwed to Rib 12. Both stabilizer halves are identical and are attached to the fuselage roughly at its mid point between Frames 21 and 22 by means of four flange-type fittings. The incidence of the two stabilizers may be set (manually) from 0 to +5 degrees (trailing edge down). The normal position is +2 degrees.

Three elevator mounts are screwed onto Ribs 1, 7 and 12 of each stabilizer. The stabilizer-fuselage joint is faired. The fairings must be adjusted when the stabilizer incidence is changed. Both stabilizers have 2.5 degrees of dihedral. The stabilizers are equipped with electrical de-icers over almost the entire leading edge."

"Elevators: Consisting of a main and secondary spar with Dural skinning. Within the fuselage the main spar is tubular, control rods are attached by means of control levers, which also serve as travel limiters. The tip of each control surface is attached to Rib 18 by screws and is removable. Deflection is limited by fittings on Frames 22 and 23. Two different types of tabs are fitted to the trailing edge. One version features a balance tab extending from Ribs 11 to 18 with actuator rods within the control surface. There is also a trim tab extending from Rib 9. Its twin actuating rods are contained within the elevator. Attention! Both starboard tabs have been disabled for special reasons! (Actuator rods removed, control surface fixed in place.)

The second version features a balance and trim tab on the port elevator, extending from Rib 11 to 18, while on the starboard elevator a balance tab only occupies the same space. The two balance tab actuator rods are contained within the elevator, the trim tab actuator rods on the port side lead through the hollow elevator shaft into the fuselage. The elevators are mounted at three points per side, rigidly at Rib 1 and loosely at Ribs 12 and 18. The hangers are screwed onto the stabilizer.

The balance tab actuator rods are positioned at elevator mounts 2 and 3. The elevators are balanced by cast weights in the leading edge."

Completed wing halves wait to be fitted with ailerons, flaps and wingtips.

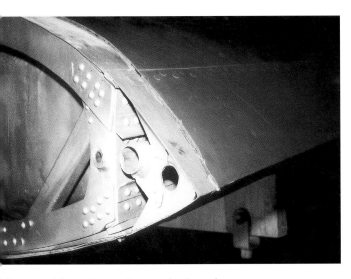
Close-up of the spoiler on the inner leading edge.

Details of a starboard wing without aileron, flap and wingtip.

The landing light was located in the leading edge of the port wing.

The Wing

The Do 335's wing was a trapezoid-shaped cantilever structure with a span of 13.80 m and an area of 38.5m2. The wing's aspect ratio was 5, leading edge sweep was 13° and dihedral was 6°. The backbone of the wing was a box spar, which was attached to the fuselage by means of a wing bearer anchored in the fuselage. The purpose of the wing bearer was to transmit the bulk of the forces exerted on the wing to the fuselage. Each wing was attached to its respective wing bearer by 35 bolts. Dornier abandoned the well-proven dual spar configuration in favor of the box spar. The advantage of this design was that the wing retained its rigidity even when major components, such as the leading edge or parts of the trailing edge, were removed during repairs. Ribs attached to the box spar gave the wing its aerodynamic form and the entire structure was covered with stressed skinning. The wing was based on NACA profile 23012-635. Initial flight trials revealed serious aerodynamic problems. Dieterle reported that the aircraft's stalling characteristics were unpredictable, with no warning of an impending stall. Further flights were made to locate the point at which the

airflow separated. Using the well-proven wool tuft method, it was found that airflow separation occurred between the landing flaps and ailerons. Separation was initially in the direction of the fuselage, but at increased angles of attack the separation moved outward. The solution to the problem was the installation of four spoilers on the leading edge area. The spoilers were strips of metal 67 cm long and 70 mm deep. Though aesthetically unappealing, they were extremely effective. The following is an extract from a report on the subject:

"Behavior is now acceptable in all variations of the stall—climbing, turning and gliding. Based on visual observation of the wool tufts, flow along the leading edge of the profile is sound, even in stalled condition. Without the spoilers airflow separation begins near the fuselage but then moves forward rather suddenly and then moves abruptly along the leading edge of the profile to the outer wing."

This effective solution was later adopted for production aircraft.

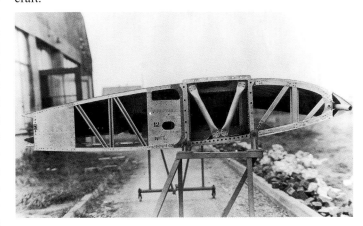
Cross-section of a port wing. Note the location of the main spar and the position of the spoiler on the leading edge.

Wing under construction, depicting the location of the box spar.

The wing attachment point installed in the fuselage.

The Ailerons

The ailerons were all metal structures consisting of a main spar, auxiliary spar and ribs. The ailerons were attached to the wing in three places (Ribs 14, 20 and 26). A trim tab was mounted on the trailing edge of the control surface in the area of Ribs 1 to 11. In addition to their main role of control surface, the ailerons could also be used as landing aids. For this purpose the ailerons could be deflected from 6° to 8°. The maximum allowable difference between the two ailerons was 3°. When used as control surfaces, the ailerons' range of movement was 19° to 21° up and down. The ailerons were activated by control rods. Control surface area was 2.50 m2.

The following description is contained in Part 3 of the handbook:

"Ailerons:
The two flush-mounted ailerons extend from wing ribs 14 to 26. They consist of a main spar, auxiliary spar and ribs and are entirely covered with Dural. The ailerons are hinged at three places:

Another view of the wing attachment point.

Completed box spar.

The internal structure of the box spar.

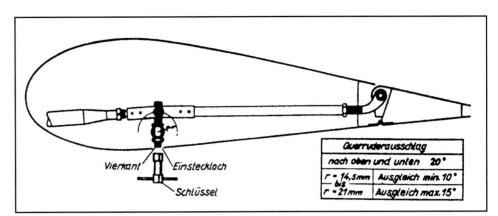

Querruderausschlag

nach oben und unten	20°
r = 14,5mm bis r = 21mm	Ausgleich min.10°
	Ausgleich max.15°

Vierkant   Einsteckloch
Schlüssel

Schematic drawing depicting the aileron balance system.

Close-up of the starboard aileron.

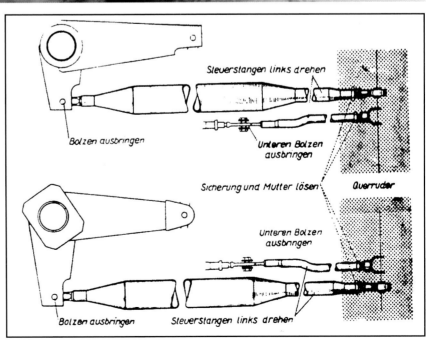

Steuerstangen links drehen

Bolzen ausbringen

Unteren Bolzen ausbringen

Sicherung und Mutter lösen   Querruder

Unteren Bolzen ausbringen

Bolzen ausbringen   Steuerstangen links drehen

Aileron control linkage (Do 335 handbook).

on wing ribs 14, 20 and 26 by means of special mounting arms on the auxiliary spar. Mounts 1 and 3 are loose.

Deflection limiter for the ailerons is located at the bell crank on the rear face of the spar within the fuselage. As they are coupled with the landing flaps, the ailerons may be used as landing and takeoff aids.

A balance and trim tab is located on the aileron trailing edge between aileron ribs 1 and 11. Cast weights in the leading edge of the aileron provide the necessary balance."

The Landing Flaps

The all metal landing flaps (area 3.60 m2) consisted of two spars with attached ribs covered with Dural skinning. The flaps were positioned between the fuselage and the ailerons in the area of Ribs 3 and 14. The flap hydraulic cylinder was electrically actuated. Flap position for takeoff varied from 29° to 31°. For landing the flaps could be set from 49° to 53°. The maximum allowable difference between the two flaps was 3°. As mentioned, the ailerons were coupled with the flaps. This was accomplished by means of a coupling on flap rib 12, which established a connection with the aileron push-rod.

The following appears in Part 3 of the Do 335 handbook:

"Located between the ailerons and the fuselage on the trailing edge of the wing, but extending deeper into the wing, extending from wing rib 3 to 14. The internal structure consists of two spars and attached ribs, completely covered with Dural skinning.

The leading edge is of open design. In general the shape is the same as that of the ailerons. The flap is hinged in three places, within the profile nose, with hinges located on wing ribs 4, 8 and 14 at an auxiliary spar in the wing. The angled pressure-oil control arm is located next to Hinge 2. The flaps are connected to the aileron control rods in such a way that the ailerons may be used as supplementary landing and takeoff aids. The coupling point is located at flap rib 12.

Next to the coupling point is the Start-End switch control for the landing flap system. Hinges 1 and 2 are loose, Hinge 3 is rigid."

Maximum flap angle was 53°. A difference in flap settings of three degrees was tolerable.

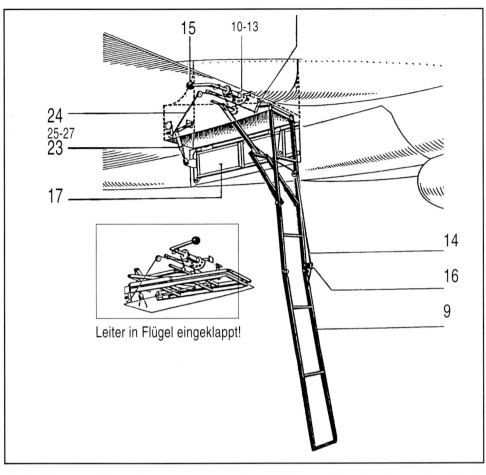

15   10-13

24
25-27
23

17

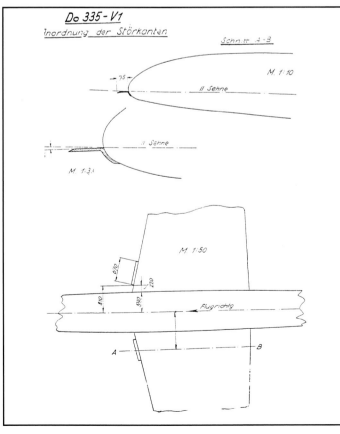

Leiter in Flügel eingeklappt!

14

16

9

Schematic drawing of the retractable entry ladder.

Do 335 - V1
Anordnung der Störkanten

Schnitt A-B

M. 1:10

ll Sehne

75

ll Sehne

M. 1:3.5

M. 1:50

Ø20

220

340

840

Flugrichtg

A

B

Above: The longerons were used to attach the wings to the sides of the fuselage.
Left: Location of the spoilers, using the Do 335 VI as an example.

Concerning the structural strength of the Do 335 airframe, the following information is from Technical Description No. 1582, dated 4 July 1944.

As per the DLA construction regulations dated 6 December 1936 for the stress group H3, printout of the Do 335 structural limits dated 11/2/1943.

- Takeoff weight: 9 600 kg
- Maximum allowable true airspeed in level flight at climb and combat power at ground level = 600 km/h, at height of 8 700 m = 835 km/h
- Maximum indicated airspeed in dive equivalent to speed of 900 km/h at ground level.

Internal and External Fittings

In addition to their main purpose of providing lift, the wings also accommodated some of the aircraft's fuel, the main undercarriage elements and various other accessories as listed below:

- a 20-liter protected hydraulic reservoir in the port wing
- two fuel tanks in the forward wing area
- spherical oxygen bottles for the pilot's oxygen system in both wings (so-called "cannon ball batteries")
- the master compass, located in the outer port wing
- twin landing lights in the leading edge of the port wing
- the pitot tube, positioned on the port wingtip
- control rods for the ailerons and landing flaps
- actuating cylinders for the main undercarriage elements and the undercarriage attachment points
- the folding entry ladder, which was stowed in the port wing root

The Control System

The high speeds attained by the Do 335—it was the fastest piston-engined aircraft operated by the *Luftwaffe*—forced the designers to come up with a control system which could cope with the aircraft's speed range. The solution was a variable input system which could adjust to normal and high-speed flight. The necessary equipment was installed in the forward bomb bay. The following information is from a technical manual for the Do 335 A:

To adjust control forces and displacements to suit the differing control surface forces and displacements in normal and high-speed flight, an electrically-hydraulically-actuated variable input system has been installed on the bell cranks for elevators, rudders and ailerons on Frame 7. The normal control surface forces are set for a speed range of 200-400 km/h. Takeoff and landing in the high-speed position is only permissible in an emergency. The high-speed position is recommended for tight turns, so as to reduce control forces. Selection by means of a toggle switch on the left console. Switch at approximately 400 km/h. In an emergency compressed air (within the pressure-oil system) can be used to switch back to normal flight: third switch from left beneath the main instrument panel.

The following appears in Part 9 of the handbook:

"The purpose of the control changeover is to adjust control forces and displacements to suit the differing control surface forces and displacements in normal and high-speed flight.

The changeover is made at an indicated airspeed of approximately 560 km/h. The changeover is begun by a solenoid-operated switch (HC 10) within the circuit, located on the forward wall of the bomb bay at Frame 7. It is electrically controlled with automatic cutoff provided by two switches at the two end positions of the actuator. The electrical control switch with the position selections "LOW SPEED FLIGHT" and "HIGH SPEED FLIGHT" are located on the port console. No position indicator is planned.

The actuator (Hc 12) is located on the forward end of the bomb bay (rear face of spar). Its piston rod is attached to a connecting rod which, by pushing, moves the control rod attachment point in special links on the rear face of the spar to two end positions which maintain a travel ratio of 1:0.5 for the elevators, 1:0.6 for the rudders and 1:.07 for the ailerons. The actuator piston locks mechanically in the actuator at both end positions. The time required to switch from "LOW SPEED FLIGHT" to "HIGH SPEED FLIGHT" and reverse is approximately one half second.

Operation (see drawing): place selector switch in the "HIGH SPEED" position. The solenoid switch (Hc 10) moves to Position 3. The pressure oil streams to the bottom end (Attachment 2) of the actuator (Hc 11). Within the actuator the piston is unlocked, whereupon it moves upward, taking the switching rod with it. At the same time, the electric end switch drops back down in the cylinder, making it possible to switch back to "LOW SPEED FLIGHT". The pressure oil flushed out by the movement of the actuator piston

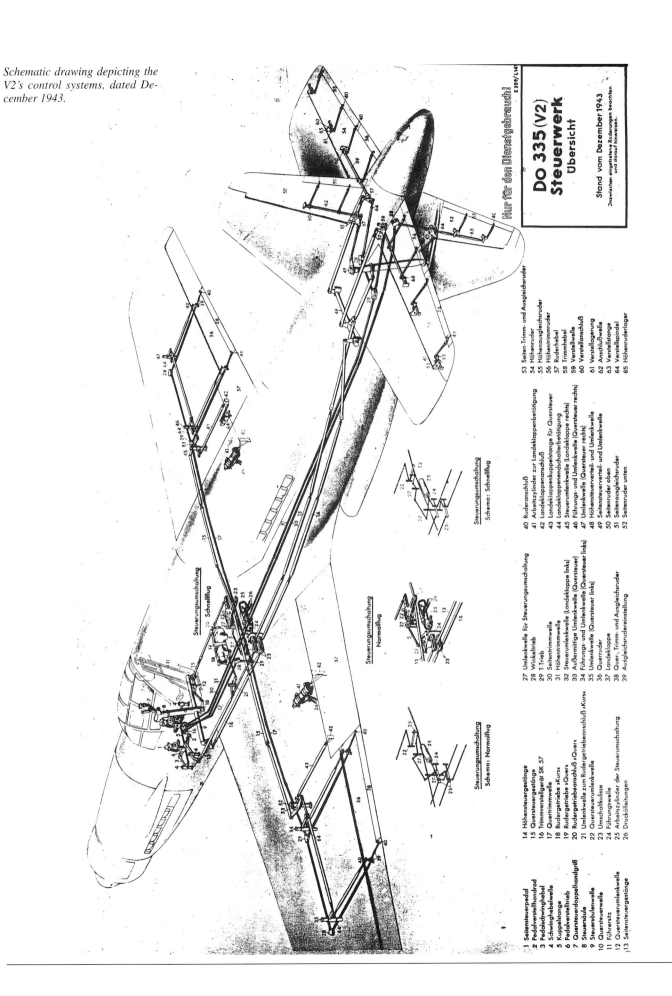

Schematic drawing depicting the V2's control systems, dated December 1943.

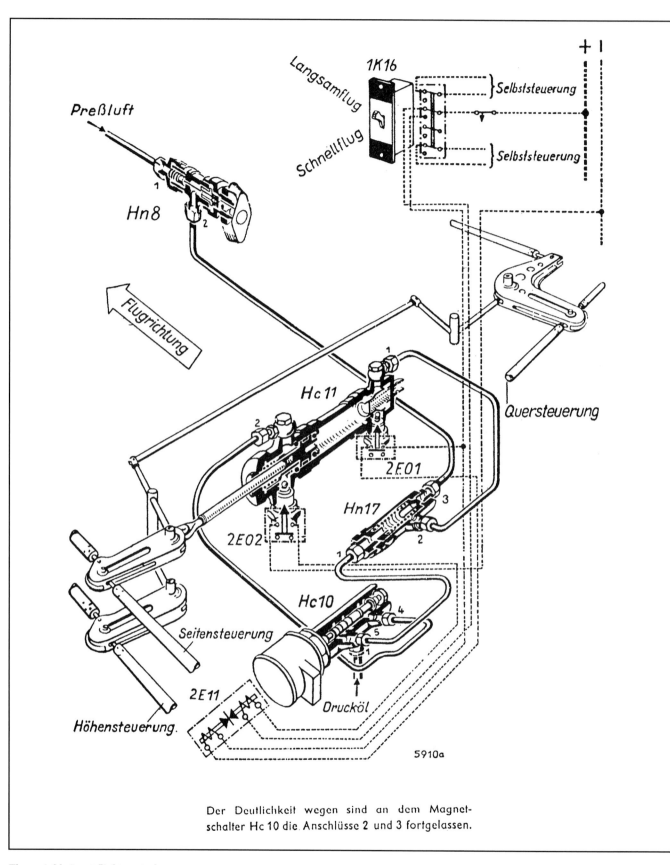

The variable input flight controls system.

flows through the shuttle valve (Hn 17) and the solenoid switch (Hn 10). The piston locks automatically in the end position at the cylinder head. At the same time the electric end switch located there is interrupted, which means that the solenoid switch moves back to Position 1 (circuit position) and the system comes to rest.

Switching from high-speed to low-speed flight: move the selector switch to the "LOW-SPEED FLIGHT" position, whereupon the solenoid switch moves to Position 2 and feeds pressure oil into the top of the actuator cylinder (Hc 11).

Subsequent processes are similar to those resulting from switching from "LOW SPEED FLIGHT" to "HIGH SPEED FLIGHT".

Legend:

- 1K16 = control changeover operating switch
- *2E01 = "HIGH-SPEED FLIGHT" end switch*
- *2E02 = "LOW-SPEED FLIGHT" end switch*
- *2E11 = control changeover solenoid switch*

The manual had the following to say concerning the dual controls of the trainer version:

Complete set of elevator, rudder and aileron controls in the rear cockpit, including trim controls (left console). Rudder pedals not adjustable. Seat to be adjusted according to body size.

A graphic depiction of the control system accompanies this text.

The Main Undercarriage

The main unit consisted of two oil-air oleos which were raised and lowered hydraulically. The oleo pistons were guided in the cylinder by a torque link on the rear of the undercarriage leg. The unusually long oleo travel reached a maximum of 310 mm. The main undercarriage legs were attached to swiveling mounts anchored to the wing spar. Wheel track was 5 584 mm. The undercarriage legs were supported laterally by folding struts. Retraction and extension was hydraulic, electrically-actuated. The hydraulic system was a source of trouble from the beginning. Initially the designers miscalculated the size of the hydraulic cylinder. Tests revealed that the system required an additional twenty bars to ensure certain retraction and locking. Initially it was intended to address this problem by installing a larger hydraulic cylinder, however there was insufficient room. The ultimate solution was two hydraulic cylinders operating in parallel. The second cylinder was used only in the retraction cycle, as less force was required to extend the undercarriage. Attached to the so-called auxiliary cylinder was a pull cable, which led via a guide roller to the retraction mechanism (see drawing for details). The mainwheels were equipped with brakes and in the case of the Do 335 V1, tire size was 935 x 345. Later machines had 1015 x 380 mm tires. In retracted position the undercarriage was entirely hidden within the wheel well, which was covered by undercarriage and mainwheel fairings. The main undercarriage components weighed 485 kg (according to Weights Sheet No. 2881, dated 1/11/1943). Other data sheets, for example in the case of the A-0 (240107), show a weight of 510 kg. The normal retraction time was 18 seconds, extension 12 seconds. Maximum allowable speed

The starboard main undercarriage member and wheel well, photographed looking toward the outer wing.

With the exception of the first prototype, the Do 335's main undercarriage was fitted with 1015 x 380 tires.

36929/

was normally 270 km/h. If the extension-retraction time was extended, maximum allowable speed was increased to 370 km/h. Emergency operation of the undercarriage took a maximum of one minute.

Part 2 of the handbook stated the following about the undercarriage:

"The main undercarriage consists of two identical components, consequently only one unit will be described. The components are designed in such a way that they can be installed on the left or right. The undercarriage is designed as a single-leg unit with one bracing strut aft and a double folding strut towards the fuselage. It is suspended beneath the spar on the underside of the wing and retracts into a well between Ribs 3 and 12.

The powerful air-oil shock absorber (ELMA 8-2386, B-2a or B2b, 32 atm at full pressure, travel 310 mm) is attached by a pivoting mount to a cast piece attached to the main and auxiliary spars at wing rib 12. The wheel bearer is screwed onto the shock strut piston (2 through bolts). The wheel, with its 1015 x 380 tire, turns on an axle attached to the wheel bearer and is equipped with a double brake. The wheel is held in place on both sides by axle flanges. The inner (fuselage side) flange is attached by means of two through bolts (wheel change!), while the outer flange is permanently attached to the wheel bearer. The wheel axle is inserted into the wheel bearer and is secured by a through bolt. Wheel guidance is provided by a rearwards-facing torque link attached to the wheel bearer and the shock strut cylinder. Wheel footprint is approximately 100 mm with the aircraft in flight attitude. Wheel track is 5 584 mm. In the down position the undercarriage leg is braced laterally by the previously mentioned retraction strut and fore and aft by the bracing strut. The two retraction struts lie parallel to one another, are braced laterally at the top, and pivot on pins located on the front and rear of the shock strut cylinder. The retraction struts, which fold upwards at roughly mid-point, are equipped with adjusting screws in order to align the struts for locking. The rear retraction strut and the bracing strut are attached to the same pivot pin. For retraction, the bracing strut is attached to a pivoting mount on Rib 12.

The wheel well is covered by a multi-section undercarriage door. The inner part, which covers the bottom half of the wheel, is attached to the underside of the wing. It closes during the retraction process by means of hooks on the axle flange and rods, and when closed is locked automatically by two spring locks. The main part of the undercarriage door is permanently attached to the undercarriage itself with moving guides on the wheel bearer and closes when the gear is retracted. A smaller three-part, spring-activated door covers the remaining small opening over the undercarriage attachment point. The undercarriage retracts and extends hydraulically by means of an SA hydraulic cylinder 19-2408.325 C (bore 325 mm). It is mounted on the undercarriage attachment point in the wing, while the piston is attached to the undercarriage leg by means of a locking shaft between the two retraction struts. The locking shaft guides the extension and retraction of the retraction struts. With the undercarriage in the extended position the hydraulic cylinder is probably locked automatically, however the retraction struts absorb the forces because of the design of the locking shaft. The locking shaft's stop is adjustable."

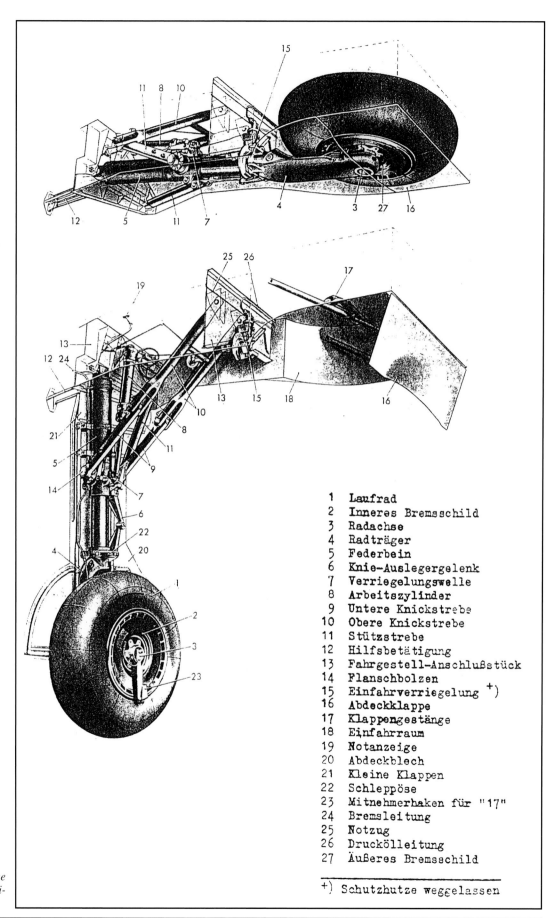

Drawing of a main undercarriage leg in the raised and lowered positions.

1 Laufrad
2 Inneres Bremsschild
3 Radachse
4 Radträger
5 Federbein
6 Knie-Auslegergelenk
7 Verriegelungswelle
8 Arbeitszylinder
9 Untere Knickstrebe
10 Obere Knickstrebe
11 Stützstrebe
12 Hilfsbetätigung
13 Fahrgestell-Anschlußstück
14 Flanschbolzen
15 Einfahrverriegelung +)
16 Abdeckklappe
17 Klappengestänge
18 Einfahrraum
19 Notanzeige
20 Abdeckblech
21 Kleine Klappen
22 Schleppöse
23 Mitnehmerhaken für "17"
24 Bremsleitung
25 Notzug
26 Drucköllleitung
27 Äußeres Bremsschild

+) Schutzhütze weggelassen

1	Radnabe	6	Flanschschraube
2	Achse	7	Bremsanschluß
3	Achsträger		innen
4	Achsschraube	8	Bremsanschluß
5	Vorderer		außen
	Achsflansch		

Abb.21: Radlagerung - Hauptfahrgestell

Drawing illustrating the mounting of the wheel of the main undercarriage.

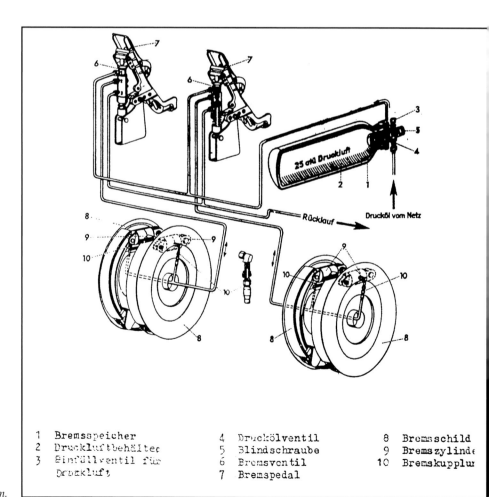

1	Bremsspeicher	4	Druckölventil	8	Bremsschild
2	Druckluftbehälter	5	Blindschraube	9	Bremszylinde
3	Einfüllventil für Druckluft	6	Bremsventil	10	Bremskupplu
		7	Bremspedal		

Schematic drawing of the brake system.

Concerning the so-called "Auxiliary Retraction Mechanism", Part 2 of the handbook states:

"An auxiliary retraction mechanism has been designed to assist the retraction cylinder in raising the undercarriage. This consists of an FO hydraulic cylinder (bore 420 mm) and a pull cable. The cylinder is activated in parallel to the retraction cylinder. It operates only in the direction of retraction and is attached on the outboard side of the undercarriage leg . On the piston is a large compensating roller for the pull cable, which is steered in the necessary direction by two guides. The other end of the cable is attached to the undercarriage leg at the same point as the bracing strut.

When the undercarriage leg is retracted, a locking hook in the roof of the wheel well engages the shock strut piston, locking the leg in place."

The Brake System (From the Do 335 Handbook, Part 2)

"The nosewheel is not equipped with brakes, while the mainwheels have double brakes, meaning backing plates on both sides of the wheels. They are ELMA clasp brakes, held in place by flanges on the wheel axle.

Braking is hydraulic and is part of the general pressure-oil system. It is linked by means of a, pressure 25 atm, installed in the port main undercarriage well.

The Nosewheel Undercarriage

The Do 335's design, with front and rear propellers, made the adoption of a tricycle undercarriage imperative. At that time in Germany the tricycle undercarriage was the exception rather than the rule and was looked down on as too "American". There is no doubt that the tricycle undercarriage was an American domain, and it was used in numerous designs produced in that country. The P-39 Airacobra and its close relative the P-63 Kingcobra were built in the thousands. Both types, which served in large numbers with the Soviet air forces, were equipped with an engine located in mid-fuselage driving a nose-mounted propeller by means of an extension shaft. Other American fighters equipped with a tricycle undercarriage were the Lockheed P-38 Lightning, the Northrop P-61 Black Widow and the Grumman F7F Tigercat. A number of American bomber designs also used a tricycle undercarriage, such as the Douglas A-20 Havoc, the North American B-25 Mitchell, the Martin B-26 Marauder, the Consolidated B-24 Liberator and the Boeing B-29 Superfortress. Also designed with a tricycle undercarriage were the Douglas C-54 Skymaster and the Lockheed C-69 Constellation transports.

Other nations, such as Great Britain, France and the Soviet Union, were slower to adopt the tricycle undercarriage. German designers turned to this advanced configuration later in the war, and it was a feature of such types as the Ta 154, Me 262, Me 264, He 162, He 219 and Do 335.

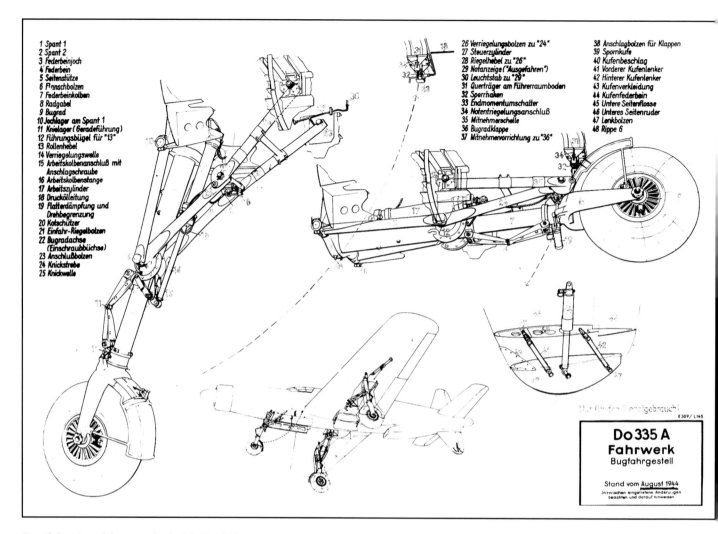

1 Spant 1
2 Spant 2
3 Federbeinjoch
4 Federbein
5 Seitenstütze
6 Flanschbolzen
7 Federbeinkolben
8 Radgabel
9 Bugrad
10 Jochlager am Spant 1
11 Knielager (Geradeführung)
12 Führungsbügel für "13"
13 Rollenhebel
14 Verriegelungswelle
15 Arbeitskolbenanschluß mit Anschlagschraube
16 Arbeitskolbenstange
17 Arbeitszylinder
18 Drucköolleitung
19 Flatterdämpfung und Drehbegrenzung
20 Kotschützer
21 Einfahr-Riegelbolzen
22 Bugradachse (Einschraubbüchse)
23 Anschlußbolzen
24 Knickstrebe
25 Knickwelle

26 Verriegelungsbolzen zu "24"
27 Steuerzylinder
28 Riegelhebel zu "26"
29 Notanzeige ("Ausgefahren")
30 Leuchtstab zu "29"
31 Querträger am Führerraumboden
32 Sperrhaken
33 Endmomentumschalter
34 Notentriegelungsanschluß
35 Mitnehmerschelle
36 Bugradklappe
37 Mitnehmervorrichtung zu "36"

38 Anschlagbolzen für Klappen
39 Spornkufe
40 Kufenbeschlag
41 Vorderer Kufenlenker
42 Hinterer Kufenlenker
43 Kufenverkleidung
44 Kufenfederbein
45 Untere Seitenflosse
46 Unteres Seitenruder
47 Lenkbolzen
48 Rippe 6

Do 335 A
Fahrwerk
Bugfahrgestell

Stand vom August 1944
Inzwischen eingetretene Änderungen
beachten und darauf hinweisen

Detail drawing of the nosewheel of the Do 335 A.

The Do 335's nosewheel unit, which consisted of an oil-air oleo, was changed several times during development of the aircraft. The following description outlines these changes:

- Beginning with the Do 335 V1, the nosewheel was not equipped with brakes and tire size was 685 x 250. The nosewheel was attached to a wheel fork mount. The oleo's range of travel was 400 mm, which was unusually high. The two swiveling undercarriage mounts were attached to Frame 1. The nosewheel was retracted and extended hydraulically. The nosewheel retracted rearwards without rotating 45 degrees as planned for the B-series. The nosewheel bay was positioned beneath the forward engine and was covered by two side-mounted nosewheel doors when the undercarriage was retracted.

- The B-version nosewheel unit differed in a number of respects. The wheel fork was replaced by a single-sided mount, while the nosewheel was equipped with brakes and fitted with a 840 x 300 tire. In both cases the oleo piston was guided by a torque link on the front side of the leg. The B-version also introduced a modified retraction process. During retraction, the nosewheel pivoted 45 degrees, entering the nosewheel bay in a sideways position instead of the vertical as before. The nosewheel leg was actuated by means of folding retraction struts. Impetus was provided by an hydraulic cylinder acting on two intermeshing gear segments.

The Do 335 Handbook, Part 2 described the operation of the undercarriage systems as follows:

Like the main undercarriage, the nosewheel unit, which is located beneath the forward engine, is designed as a single-leg undercarriage. It consists of an air-oil shock absorber (ELMA, 8-2387 A-1, stroke 400 mm) with supports on both sides, a wheel fork with nosewheel and a retraction strut frame.

Oleo charging pressure 13 to 15 atm. The oleo and the bracing struts are attached to Frame 1 and move together. The retraction struts are attached to Frame 2. The nosewheel well is located in the fuselage beneath the cockpit and is covered by folding doors.

The top of the oleo is equipped with a yoke, the ends of which form shafts which pick up the two side bracing struts and form the pivoting mounts right and left on Frame 1.

The side struts and the double retraction struts are both attached to common pivot pins flange-mounted on each side of the lower oleo.

The wheel fork is attached to the bottom of the oleo and is held in place by three cotter-pin bolts. The oleo piston is guided by a torque link on the front side of the oleo.

The two halves of the wheel fork are attached to a freely-rotating ring on the neck of the wheel fork. The freely-rotating wheel fork (piston in shock absorber cylinder) is braced by a spring cylinder which also serves as a flutter damper. This spring cylinder is also movable on the guide ring and is mounted on the port side of the wheel fork. Arc of movement is 38°.

The nosewheel (685 x 250, smooth tire) rotated freely on an axle held in place by bolts on the wheel fork.

Close-up of the nosewheel leg and retraction struts.

A planned locking system is not available at the present time (December 1944—January 1945, the author).

It is equipped with a mudguard, which also houses the retraction locking pins.

The hydraulic cylinder for the nosewheel undercarriage is attached to Frame 1 on a pivoting mount on one end and on the other to the rear of the oleo by way of a locking shaft. During retraction a guide fork on the locking shaft begins the folding of the retraction strut.

On extension the guide causes extension of the retraction strut and causes it to lock in place. In this position the retraction strut absorbs the forces, taking the load off the hydraulic cylinder.

The bracing struts are vee-shaped. The lower parts of the retraction struts are parallel, while the upper parts are vee-shaped with cross braces. They fold downwards when the undercarriage is retracted. The struts are hinged at roughly mid-point and are joined by a shaft on which sits a hydraulic locking mechanism for the undercarriage in the extended position. This consists of a control cylinder with angle levers and tube-guided conical bolts which engage the locking recesses of the retraction struts.

In the retracted position, the nosewheel leg's locking fitting (on the mudguard) is engaged by a locking mechanism on the roof of the nosewheel well and held fast by a locking pin. The load is thus taken off the hydraulic cylinder. For extension the locking mechanism is released hydraulically or by a pull cable operated by the emergency compressed air system.

When the undercarriage is retracted, the nosewheel well is covered by two nosewheel doors split longitudinally. Forks and guides on the doors engage clamp fittings on the retraction struts, causing the doors to close behind the nosewheel leg.

Forward the doors rest on the two stop dogs of the oleo yoke. In the extended position they are held in place by the stop levers of the engaging mechanism and stop forks on the front end which engage the bracing struts.

Extension and retraction hydraulic with electric control. Switch-off automatic after all three undercarriage members have locked. Undercarriage and wheel fairings are mechanically operated. The control switch is located on the left console. Second control switch with neutral position located on left console of rear cockpit of the training version. Control switch in forward cockpit may only be used when the selector switch in the rear cockpit is in the neutral position. Emergency lowering of undercarriage is possible by means of compressed air within the pressure oil system, first switch from left beneath the main instrument panel. In the event of an emergency the undercarriage should be selected first or second (after the bomb doors). A special, compressed-air-operated unlocking system speeds up the emergency procedure.

Indicators: indicator lights for DOWN/UP and LOCKED position for each of the three undercarriage members are in the indicator light panel on the left console. In the event of electrical system failure, flashlight on right side of cockpit floor, or visual indicator on upper surface of wing, left and right.

Table 14:

Component	Do 335 A-0 (to 40th machine) up to the 40th machine	Do 335 A (*Zerstörer*) (from 40th machine) as of the 41st machine
Wing, including ailerons	1 028 kg	1 100 kg
Fuselage	590 kg	620 kg
Empennage, including skid	154 kg	170 kg
Control system	89 kg	95 kg
Engine mounts, nacelle	154 kg	155 kg
Main undercarriage (1015 x 380)	485 kg	495 kg
Nosewheel (685 x 250)	162 kg	180 kg
Paint and putty	51 kg	50 kg
Total Aircraft Weight	2 713 kg	2 865 kg

The History and Configuration of the Daimler-Benz DB 603

The method installation style of this engine helped make possible one of the most unusual aircraft of its day, the Do 335. As related earlier, Dornier had to overcome major hurdles to transport its high-speed aircraft from the years-long planning stage to reality. The front and rear power plants of the Do 335 A were DB 603 twelve-cylinder inline engines each with a maximum output of 2,000 H.P. The A, E and L versions of the DB 603 found use in the Do 335 program. Another version, the DB 603 Q, was under development for use by the Do 335. It was a 2,250-H.P. engine based on the DB 603 EM. The following is a summary of the development of the DB 603.

The engine's beginnings may be traced back to 1936. Daimler-Benz submitted a technical description to the RLM in the autumn of that year. The reaction was positive, however no contract was forthcoming. The RLM merely gave permission for further development of the engine. At that point the target output was 1,500 H.P. In March of the following year DB received a letter which short-sightedly ordered the cancellation of work on the project. In the period that followed, all further development work was paid for by Daimler-Benz itself. Two years passed before the DB 603 made its first bench runs. Toward the end of the first year of the war the RLM received a report concerning the progress of the DB 603. Those responsible were not very impressed and even considering giving Daimler-Benz permission to export the engine. The situation was to change radically in the following year, however: at the begin-

Side view of a DB 603 L.

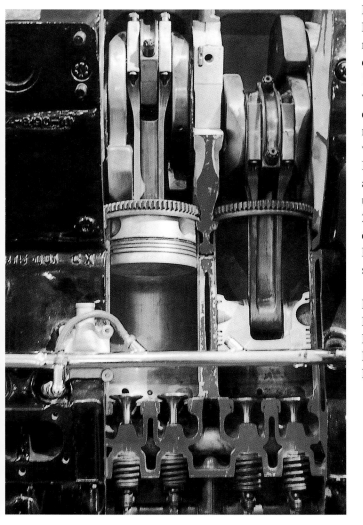

This interior view of the DB 603 illustrates its inverted-vee configuration.

ning of year Daimler-Benz received instructions to begin production as soon as possible. The first order, dated 2 February 1940, covered 120 units.

The DB 603 was one of a family of inline engines. Its design roots were seated in the DB 601, a 33.9-liter engine, more than 19,000 of which were produced in the period 1937 to 1943. During the course of production from 1941 to 1945, there were no less than 36 versions of the DB 603, which were used in the Do 335, Ta 152, He 219 and Me 410. The power plant was also used to power prototypes of the Me 209 and Me 309, the gigantic Bv 238 flying boat and the prototype Blohm & Voss Bv 155, a reworked version of the Me 155. A total of 8,758 examples of the DB 603 was produced. Energy was produced by twelve cylinders (each with a displacement of 3.71 l), with six cylinders in each of two suspended cylinder blocks (60° inverted vee). Bore and stroke were 162 mm and 180 mm, respectively. The total piston displacement of all versions was 44.5 liters. Each cylinder was equipped with two inlet and two exhaust valves. The four-stroke engine (DB 603 A) achieved a maximum output of 1,750 H.P. (2,700 rpm) at ground level. This was reduced to 1,680 H.P. at an altitude of 5 700 m at the same rpm. In the case of the DB 603 E, output was 2,000 H.P. at ground level and 1,740 H.P. at 6 000 meters. The DB 603 LA, which was also used in the Do 335, achieved a maximum output of 2,000 H.P. at 2,700 rpm at ground level. The DB 603 was a so-called quick-change engine, requiring just 20 minutes for an engine change. The following are examples of various versions which were designated standard power plants:

DB 603 A	9-8603 A	(maximum boost altitude 5 700 m)
DB 603 E	9-8603 C	(maximum boost altitude 7 000 m)
DB 603 E	9-8603 B	(maximum boost altitude 9 000 m)
DB 603 LA	9-8603 B-1	(maximum boost altitude 9 000 m)
DB 603 LA	9-8603 E	(maximum boost altitude 9 200 m)

These power plants were equipped as complete units, with all the accessories needed for installation. In addition to the engine, the package included the exhaust system, the cooling system, the propeller pitch control mechanism and the engine cowling. Together with the Jumo 213, the DB 603 LA represented the apex of development of the standard power plant. Deliveries of the DB 603 LA quick-change engine began in 1944 and it was used as the forward engine in the Do 335 B, then in the prototype stage, as well as in the Ta 152 C. The following description of the engine consists of extracts from the Do 335 A-1 Aircraft Handbook, Part 6 (engine installation). It has not been reproduced in its entirety due to the poor state of the original and for reasons of space.

General Description of the DB 603

The front and rear engines of the Do 335 were the Daimler-Benz DB 603 E (the rear engine was assigned the additional letter "Q" to its designation: author's note).

Where this engine is not available, the DB 603 A-2 is being used in its place. The DB 603 is a liquid-cooled inline engine with two blocks of cylinders in an inverted-Vee configuration with 60° between the blocks. The engine is equipped with fuel injection and an automatically controlled supercharger. The amount of fuel mixture injected is controlled by a mixture regulator installed on the injection pump, independent of the supercharger air temperature

The supercharger of the DB 603.

102

Interesting details of a DB 603 mounted in the nose of a Do 335 (also see Appendix, Page 216).

DB 603 nose engine mounted on transport trolley complete with cowlings.

and altitude. Both engines are geared to turn clockwise, however mounting the rear engine in the opposite direction results in the rear propeller turning counterclockwise. The fuel-air mixture is ignited by a ZM 12 CR 8 twin magneto. The entire ignition system is shielded to prevent radio interference. The ignition timing is set automatically, independent of throttle lever position, by means of a cam. The ignition switch for the twin magneto is located on the control panel. For starting, a separate current is generated with the aid of a starter transformer and the twin magneto. At present the starter system for both engines is purely electric (Bosch), but will be changed to gasoline-electric (Viktoria-Riedel). The Bosch starter is equipped with the standard AL SCG 24 DR-2 electric inertia

starter, however this makes it impossible to hand-crank the engines.

The electric starter switches, shielded by a hinged cover, are located on the control panel. Pressing them switches on the starter motor, pulling them engages the starter (with the crank-shaft electromagnetically). The Viktoria-Riedel starter system is equipped with a gasoline-electric starter. The power source is a two-cylinder two-stroke engine which produces 10 H.P. (maximum duration one minute). This engine is itself started by a small electric motor controlled from the instrument panel. The gasoline starter engine is cooled by its own cooling fan. A centrifugal clutch engages when the gasoline engine reaches a certain minimum revolutions. This engages the starter motor with the aircraft engine, causing the latter to turn over.

The purpose of the oil thrower, which is mounted on the right generator drive, is to separate from the oil the oil foam created by the relatively fast oil circulation in the engine. A bell-shaped impeller running at high speed (5,700 rpm at a propeller speed of 2,500 rpm) inside the oil thrower separates the oil and the foam, which have different specific gravities, by centrifugal force. The oil-foam mixture streams into the impeller and is separated, with the oil forced to the outside and the foam to the center. The foam is then directed into a special collector for removal. The oil removed from the circulation system is sucked out by a geared pump in the oil thrower and is redirected through the oil thrower itself and back into the engine. The oil thrower is fitted with another drive, to which the hydraulic system's pressure-oil pump is connected.

The DB 603 E differs from the DB 603 A-2 in that ignition timing and instantaneous stop are controlled by a control lever mounted on the bottom part of the power control unit housing. In its rearmost position the lever activates full premature ignition, at 30° premature ignition (for outside temperatures of -20°) and at 20° premature ignition (for outside temperatures of -10°). For normal ignition the lever is placed in the vertical (downward) position.

The Forward Engine

The front engine is positioned on two triangular engine mounts attached to the forward fuselage bulkhead by ball-and-socket joints.

An annular radiator and oil cooler is installed around the engine's propeller drive housing.

A circular cowling covers the coolers.

Cooling air flows in through the circular area between the spinner and the internal diameter of the cowling. The circular cowling is off-center from the propeller spinner, creating the necessary air intake area for the radiator. Cooling air is directed out through circular guides and adjustable exit gills. The hydraulically-operated gills are activated automatically by thermostats. The actual range of operation of these thermostats can be set from the cockpit. Not only do these controls set the cooling temperature, but the cooling temperature range as well.

The radiator and oil cooler gills are controlled together by thermostats located in the coolant pump intake pipe. Fuselage Frame 1 forms the engine firewall. The emergency fuel shut-off valves for the front engine are located beneath the instrument panel (Frame 4).

The forward engine powered a three-blade VDM propeller with a diameter of 3.5 meters.

An auxiliary drive is bolted to the engine to the right of the drive-shaft. This drives the gun synchronizers and the associated deviation measurement device. The former is mounted on the rear of the drive and the latter on the front.

The Propeller (Front)

The forward propeller has a diameter of 3.5 meters and sits directly on the engine's stub shaft. For the time being a standard VDM propeller is being used, however later, when development is complete, a rapid pitch change propeller (Messerschmitt) is planned (P8 propeller: author's note). With the hand-controlled rapid pitch change it will be possible to position the blades in a special braking position (negative pitch) at a rate of about 60 degrees per second. The process will be ended and limited by a cut-off switch. Moving the switch from "BRAKE POSITION" to "FLIGHT POSITION" places the propeller blades in their former position. The rapid pitch control is combined electrically with the normal electric-automatic and manual pitch control. With the standard VDM propeller now installed, control is automatic based on revolutions after placing the instrument panel switch to "AUTOMATIC". Manual control (pitch change speed approx. 2 degrees per sec.) is also possible by setting the switch to "MANUAL PITCH". An electric propeller gradometer enables the pilot to monitor blade position. Gliding position (propeller feathered) can only be selected with the switch in the "MANUAL PITCH" position.

The following section is from the Daimler-Benz handbook for the DB 603 A engine:

The Reduction and Propeller Pitch Control Drives

Transmission of engine power from the crank-shaft to the propeller occurs by means of a spur-wheel gear. The propeller pitch control drive is mounted over the engine stub shaft and its housing is flange-mounted to the reduction gear housing. The propeller pitch control drive consists of two main components:

- The gearbox, which is spline-mounted on the engine stub shaft and held in place by a nut. Rotating on this gearbox with its fixed sun pinion are the so-called intermediate wheel and the end wheel together with the reduction drive's coupling section.
- The outer drive housing with the planet wheels and planet arms plus spur gearing, driving the rear, rotating planet arm.

When the hub is mounted, the external splines of the propeller shaft engage the internal splines of the hub's end wheel, coupling the pitch drive and the hub. Pressure-oil from the engine housing is fed into the gearbox to the pitch drive. The wheels are oiled from the hollow gearbox by lubricating holes. Running downwards, at the lowest part of the spur gearing the oil is fed back by way of an oil hose socket.

The drive housing is sealed by a special seal at the attachment flange. The elements projecting from the front of the drive are sealed by two piston rings and two felt washers.

As mentioned, it was planned to use the Messerschmitt P 8 propeller in the Do 335 program. The following exchange is from the minutes of an RLM conference held on 30 June 1944:

Feucht: *"The contract for the MP 8 propeller was issued last summer, to the VDM factories in Paris and Messerschmitt. Production was supposed to have started in Paris this fall, however it has been delayed until January 1945..."*

"...It is intended to use the propeller on the Do 335. The numbers are somewhat higher than requirements to allow for setbacks, such as the loss of a production site, perhaps Paris. Unfortunately, there are still technical problems with the propeller. The air raid on VDM in October destroyed all our propellers, unfortunately including those which were there from the E-Stelle for testing. New test propellers will be available for flight trials in the near future. There have also been complaints of vibration..." "The propeller makes its possible to change pitch quickly when landing. It is calculated that the Do 335's landing distance will be reduced to 50% of the value without propeller and nosewheel brakes."

Milch: *"Is the thing foolproof?"*

Feucht: *"One can say that the results are good, but it has not been foolproof. A number of people have been involved in that.*

Two prototypes have been put out of action for certain."

Petersen: *"We especially need the propeller for the 219 and 335, which have tricycle undercarriages, otherwise we will have plenty of crashes because of overruns at night, at night and by day as well..."*

The Exhaust System

The forward engine's exhaust system consists of six ejectors bolted to the exhaust flanges of each cylinder block and the associated hollow cylindrical steel fairing and the spark plug cooling system. The fairing sits on the cylinder block exhaust flanges. The ejector bodies are mounted on top of this, attached to stud bolts on the engine. The ejector fairing is attached to the engine in four places, above on the crankcase and the rear trunnion pin, and below in two places on the camshaft cover. On the interior of the fairing, held in place by two ring clamps, is a ventilation tube which is closed at the rear end. There is an opening over each sparkplug. The cooling air, which is drawn through a special connector on the front bottom of the radiator, flows through the openings above the sparkplug heads and sparkplug wire attachment points, preventing them from overheating or charring. The intake and the ventilation tube are joined by a flexible hose attached to the inner ring of the air flow fairing. The connector on the face of the exhaust fairing serves to cool the exhaust ports. When the aircraft is in flight, air is sucked out of the engine compartment and flows over the ports to the outside, cooling them.

As a result of recent findings, the exhaust system is being fitted with a flame damping installation.

The Engine Mounts (Nose Engine)

"The forward engine is mounted in two triangular bearers, each of which is braced against the firewall by an articulated link strut. The engine's mounting pins are bolted to the attachment castings on the crankcase.

Each engine bearer consists of two hollow pressed components which are welded together.

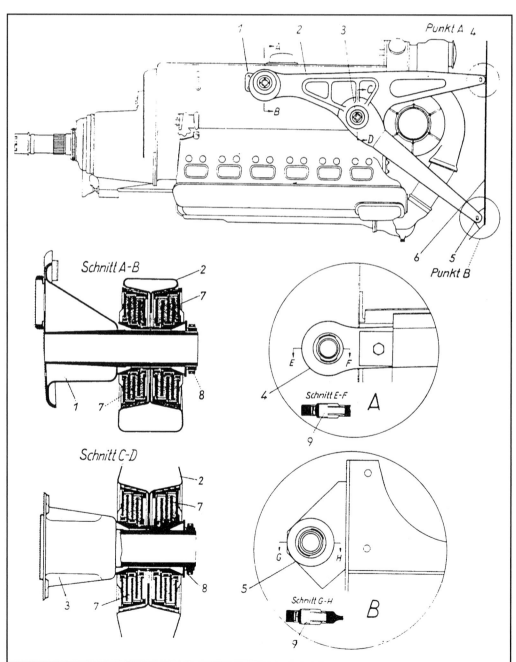

Drawing of the forward engine mounts.

After welding the completed bearers undergo a warm refining treatment.

The engine bearers' eye-shaped hubs accept the vibration-damping metal and rubber mounts. Both eyes and metal-rubber bodies are the same size and are interchangeable.

The engine mounts' firewall attachments are adjustable.

The triangular bearer's bracing strut is mounted articulated at the latter's rear eye and is braced against the lower firewall attachment point. On the new engine bearers these struts are not articulated, rather they are mounted rigidly. The triangular bearers and bracing struts are not adjustable longitudinally."

The Rear Engine

The rear engine with its propeller is mounted counter to the direction of flight and sits between Frames 11 and 17. The associated filter fuel cocks are mounted on the engine side of the firewall. The DB 603 A motor is mounted by means of a ring mounting attached to the propeller drive housing at one end and projecting bearer

Changing the rear DB 603 engine.

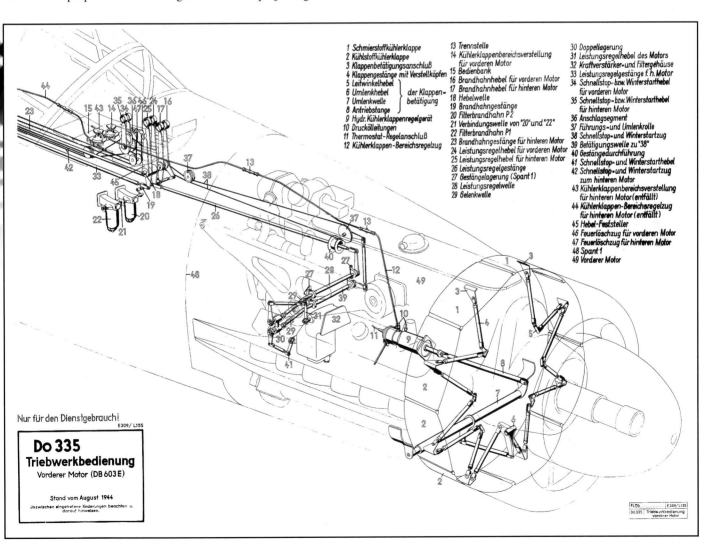

1 Schmierstoffkühlerklappe
2 Kühlstoffkühlerklappe
3 Klappenbetätigungsanschluß
4 Klappengestänge mit Verstellköpfen
5 Leitwinkelhebel
6 Umlenkhebel
7 Umlenkwelle
8 Antriebstange
9 Hydr. Kühlerklappenregelgerät
10 Druckölleitungen
11 Thermostat-Regelanschluß
12 Kühlerklappen-Bereichsregelzug
13 Trennstelle
14 Kühlerklappenbereichsverstellung für vorderen Motor
15 Bedienbank
16 Brandhahnhebel für vorderen Motor
17 Brandhahnhebel für hinteren Motor
18 Hebelwelle
19 Brandhahngestänge
20 Filterbrandhahn P2
21 Verbindungswelle von "20" und "22"
22 Filterbrandhahn P1
23 Brandhahngestänge für hinteren Motor
24 Leistungsregelhebel für vorderen Motor
25 Leistungsregelhebel für hinteren Motor
26 Leistungsregelgestänge
27 Gestängelagerung (Spant 1)
28 Leistungsregelwelle
29 Gelenkwelle
30 Doppellagerung
31 Leistungsregelhebel des Motors
32 Kraftverstärker-und Filtergehäuse
33 Leistungsregelgestänge f. h. Motor
34 Schnellstop- bzw. Winterstarthebel für vorderen Motor
35 Schnellstop-bzw. Winterstarthebel für hinteren Motor
36 Anschlagsegment
37 Führungs-und Umlenkrolle
38 Schnellstop-und Winterstartzug
39 Betätigungswelle zu "38"
40 Gestängedurchführung
41 Schnellstop- und Winterstarthebel
42 Schnellstop-und Winterstartzug zum hinteren Motor
43 Kühlerklappenbereichsverstellung für hinteren Motor (entfällt)
44 Kühlerklappen-Bereichsregelzug für hinteren Motor (entfällt)
45 Hebel-Feststeller
46 Feuerlöschzug für vorderen Motor
47 Feuerlöschzug für hinteren Motor
48 Spant 1
49 Vorderer Motor

Nur für den Dienstgebrauch!

E309/ L155

Do 335
Triebwerkbedienung
Vorderer Motor (DB 603E)

Stand vom August 1944

Inzwischen eingetretene Änderungen beachten u. darauf hinweisen.

Schematic drawing of the engine controls of a DB 603 E in the aft position.

DB 603 engine installed in the aft position between Frames 11 and 17.

off from the main radiator shaft. The air exit from each shaft is regulated by flaps controlled by the existing coolant and oil temperatures (later just the coolant temperature). Control is by means of hydraulic-temperature controlled regulators (VDM).

The Shaft Drive

The rear engine mounted between Frames 12 and 16 drives the rear propeller by means of an extension shaft which is braced in two places and hollow over its entire length to save weight. A steel socket sleeve is slid onto the engine stub shaft and squeezed into a cone by an eye nut. A gear wheel mounted on the end of the extension shaft engages the geared inner face of the free end of the socket sleeve and is held in place by an eye nut, leaving a limited amount of axial play. The gear wheel mounted on the extension shaft has curved teeth to prevent jamming should the shaft wander off center. A rubber sleeve is mounted over the coupling. The rear end of the extension shaft is held in a similar socket sleeve. This may move freely laterally, however, to permit longitudinal movements of the shaft. The rear socket sleeve sits on the actual propeller shaft. The forward race is located behind this sleeve. It is built as a roller thrust bearing sealed by a ring and expander left and right and has lubricating oil feed and discharge. The shaft itself turns in protective sleeve which is riveted to the mount body fore and aft.

arms at the other. The ring mount and bearer arms are attached to the fuselage longerons by metal-rubber bearings. In the case of the DB 603 E, the ring mount is replaced by flange pins bolted directly onto the propeller drive housing.

The radiator and oil cooler are housed in a tunnel-like chamber on the underside of the aircraft. The oil cooler chamber branches

Side view of the installed rear engine with shaft coupling (H. Schuller).

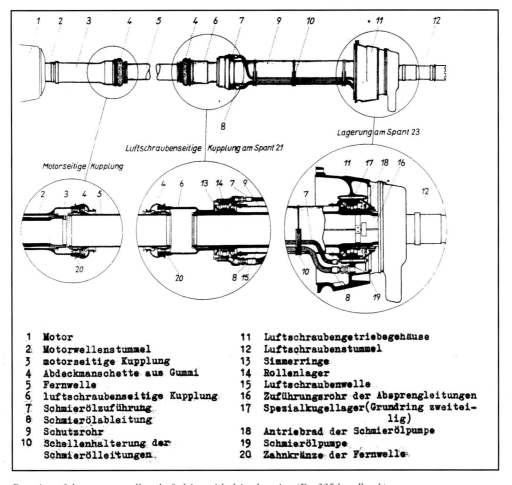

Luftschraubenseitige Kupplung am Spant 21

Motorseitige Kupplung

1	Motor
2	Motorwellenstummel
3	motorseitige Kupplung
4	Abdeckmanschette aus Gummi
5	Fernwelle
6	luftschraubenseitige Kupplung
7	Schmierölzuführung
8	Schmierölableitung
9	Schutzrohr
10	Schellenhalterung der Schmierölleitungen
11	Luftschraubengetriebegehäuse
12	Luftschraubenstummel
13	Simmerringe
14	Rollenlager
15	Luftschraubenwelle
16	Zuführungsrohr der Absprengleitungen
17	Spezialkugellager (Grundring zweiteilig)
18	Antriebrad der Schmierölpumpe
19	Schmierölpumpe
20	Zahnkränze der Fernwelle

Drawing of the rear propeller shaft drive with drive housing (Do 335 handbook).

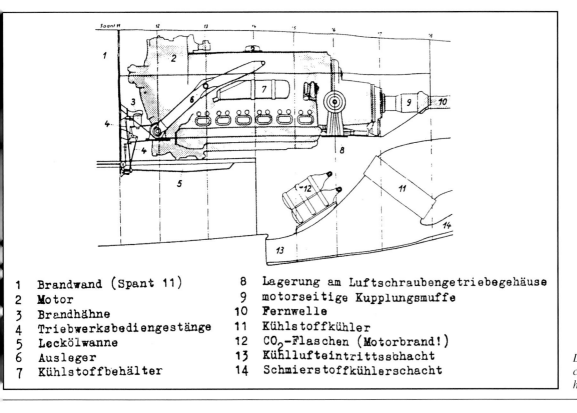

1	Brandwand (Spant 11)
2	Motor
3	Brandhähne
4	Triebwerksbediengestänge
5	Leckölwanne
6	Ausleger
7	Kühlstoffbehälter
8	Lagerung am Luftschraubengetriebegehäuse
9	motorseitige Kupplungsmuffe
10	Fernwelle
11	Kühlstoffkühler
12	CO_2-Flaschen (Motorbrand!)
13	Kühllufteintrittsschacht
14	Schmierstoffkühlerschacht

Drawing of the rear engine compartment (Do 335 handbook).

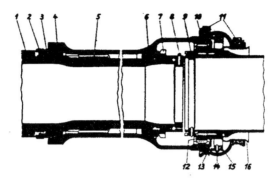

1 Motorwellenstummel	9 Gewindering
2 Gewindering	10 Gummimanschette
3 Konusring	11 Schellenbänder
4 Kupplungsmuffe	12 Innen und aussen verzahnter Ring
5 Verzahnung	13 Bundring
6 Zentrierring	14 Sicherung
7 Wellenmutter	15 Gewindering
8 Sicherungsstift	16 Blechhülse an "13" festgeschweißt

Abb. 36:   Fernwellenkupplung

b. Lagerung am Luftschraubengetriebegehäuse:

Die Lagerung am Luftschraubengetriebegehäuse erfolgt in der Endaus-
führung mit DB 603 E durch zwei Lagerkörper die an den seitlichen Paß-
flächen des Luftschraubengetriebegehäuses befestigt sind.

1 Motor
2 Ringträger
  (DB 603 A-2)
3 Lagergehäuse
4 Metallgummikörper
5 Flanschzapfen
6 Mutter
7 Beilagscheibe
8 Abstützstrebe
9 Querverband am Spant 16
10 Lagerfuß
11 Befestigungsschrauben
12 Spant 16

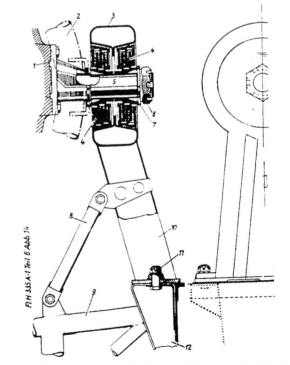

Abb.14:
Lagerung am Luftschraubengetriebegehäuse *(Heckmotor)*

Drawing of the engine mount in the area of the propeller drive housing.

Close-up photo of the extension shaft coupling. (H. Schuller)

The rear fuselage of the Do 335 V1. This photo illustrates the rear propeller drive housing with propeller mounting shaft.

Rear view of a Do 335 A. Propeller diameter was 3.3 meters.

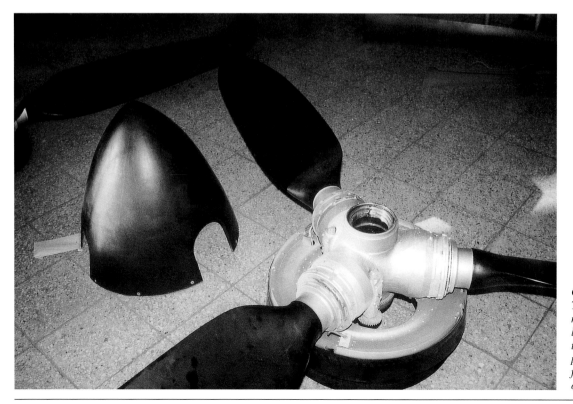

Close-up of the rear propeller. The rear spinner was much more pointed in shape and lacked the circular opening of the forward spinner. The rear propeller was smaller than the forward one, with a diameter of 3.3 meters.

The rear race, attached to Frame 23 in an elastic mount, is a specially designed two-row ball bearing. Both races, fore and aft, are designed as fixed elements, as the rear socket sleeve allows some range of movement of the shaft. Located in the rear race housing are a distributor and a scavenger pump for lubrication of the two bearing sites. They are driven by a gear wheel on the extension shaft. Oil is fed to and from the forward bearing by two hoses attached to the shaft's protective sleeve. The associated electric propeller pitch control powers the propeller pitch setting motor, which is mounted on Frame 20, by means of a Cardan shaft.

The Propeller (Rear)

The propeller is a standard VDM three-blade variable-pitch propeller with a diameter of 3.3 meters. The unit may be jettisoned explosively to enable a safe bail-out. The dorsal or ventral fin may also be jettisoned if required. Like the forward propeller, the rear propeller is regulated automatically based on engine rpm. By operating the selector switch on the instrument panel, the pilot can select MANUAL PITCH. Pitch changes are then effected by means of a toggle switch to the right of the selector switch. Position indication is by means of the previously-mentioned double indicator on the instrument panel. Rapid pitch change for braking purposes is not foreseen for the rear propeller. Gliding pitch can only be selected in the manual position.

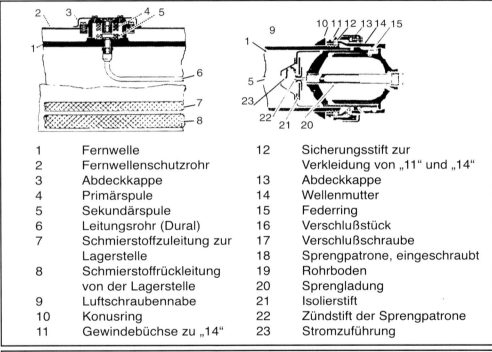

1	Fernwelle	12	Sicherungsstift zur Verkleidung von „11" und „14"
2	Fernwellenschutzrohr	13	Abdeckkappe
3	Abdeckkappe	14	Wellenmutter
4	Primärspule	15	Federring
5	Sekundärspule	16	Verschlußstück
6	Leitungsrohr (Dural)	17	Verschlußschraube
7	Schmierstoffzuleitung zur Lagerstelle	18	Sprengpatrone, eingeschraubt
8	Schmierstoffrückleitung von der Lagerstelle	19	Rohrboden
		20	Sprengladung
9	Luftschraubennabe	21	Isolierstift
10	Konusring	22	Zündstift der Sprengpatrone
11	Gewindebüchse zu „14"	23	Stromzuführung

General arrangement drawing of the rear propeller jettisoning mechanism.

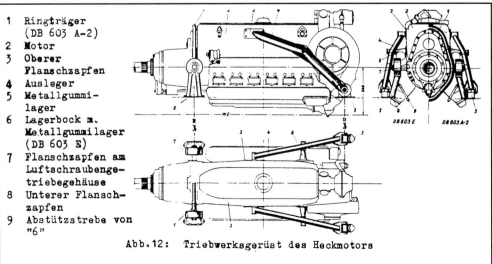

1 Ringträger (DB 603 A-2)
2 Motor
3 Oberer Flanschzapfen
4 Ausleger
5 Metallgummilager
6 Lagerbock m. Metallgummilager (DB 603 E)
7 Flanschzapfen am Luftschraubengetriebegehäuse
8 Unterer Flanschzapfen
9 Abstützstrebe von „6"

Abb. 12: Triebwerksgerüst des Heckmotors

The rear engine mounts from several angles, showing differences in the installation of the DB 603 A and E engines (Do 335 handbook).

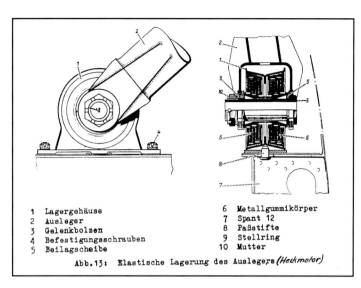

1	Lagergehäuse	6	Metallgummikörper
2	Ausleger	7	Spant 12
3	Gelenkbolzen	8	Paßstifte
4	Befestigungsschrauben	9	Stellring
5	Beilagscheibe	10	Mutter

Abb.13: Elastische Lagerung des Auslegers *(Heckmotor)*

Illustration of the elastic mounting of the rear engine (Do 335 handbook).

The Rear Propeller Jettisoning System

The rear propeller explosive jettisoning system is housed in the end of the extension shaft. It consists of an electrically-ignited explosive cartridge (18) (see illustration below: author's note) and a current feed (23). The current is fed by induction through two coils (4, 5) into the interior of the shaft, where it is carried through a Dural tube (6) to the explosive cartridge. The latter is screwed into a socket (19) inserted into the end of the drive shaft. Together with the cover (16), which is held in place by a shaft nut (14) and spring washer (15), this forms the actual charge chamber. One of the two coils (4) sits on the fixed shaft protective tube (2), while the other is attached to the drive shaft (1), inducing the necessary current when the jettison switch (either on the port console or electric switchbox) is activated. Gas pressure created by the exploding cartridge forces the cover outwards, shearing off the safety pins (12) as a result of its attachment to the shaft nut (14). The safety pins serve as break point between the shaft nut (14) and its threaded sleeve (11). When the rear propeller is jettisoned, the threaded sleeve is separated by the conical collar (10) and the air pressure on the stationary propeller and is subsequently screwed from the shaft. The propeller is thus released from its mount and falls away (see drawing for details).

The Engine Mount

The rear engine is mounted on two cantilever bearers right and left and, depending on the engine type, two bearing brackets on the front of the propeller drive housing (DB 603 E) or a ring mount on the face of the propeller drive housing.

The cantilever bearers were bolted to flange trunnions attached to each side of the engine. The lower arms of the bearers curved outwards and were braced against the base of the engine by resilient metal-rubber bodies (Frame 12). See drawing.

The DB 603's supercharger.

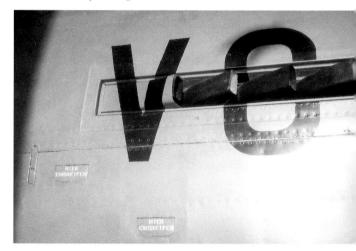

The ejector exhausts provided additional thrust (H. Schuller).

In the final version with the DB 603 E, mounting on the propeller drive housing was by means of two bearing boxes attached to the sides of the propeller drive housing (see illustration). These side castings are absent on the DB 603 A and therefore a ring mount is attached to the flange of the propeller drive housing using the existing screws. The ring mount is oval in shape, consisting of two tubes of differing diameters welded together. Shins are welded to the inner side of the ring for attachment to the housing flange, with holes to match the flange screws. Two bearing tubes with U-shaped supports of flat steel are welded to the two narrow sides of the ring and these are mounted in bearing boxes with metal-rubber bodies.

The Exhaust System

The rear engine's exhaust system is largely similar to that of the forward engine. The exhaust ports, which are produced as ejectors, sit on the steel fairing, which lies flat on the exhaust flanges. Both are secured in place by the exhaust flange stud bolts. A ventilation tube provides cooling air to the sparkplugs. The fresh air is taken in the radiator shaft in front of the radiator and passes through a tube to the actual ventilation tube on the motor. Cooling air for the exhaust ports is provided by a header on the face of the exhaust port fairing. Pressure differential causes the cooling air to be sucked of the engine compartment. As a result of recent findings the exhaust system is being fitted with flame dampers.

This concludes the extracts from the aircraft handbook concerning the engine systems. Space limitations have made it necessary to limit reproduction of the original, which exceeded sixty pages, to the most relevant sections.

The Supercharger

First an extract from the DB 603 A handbook concerning the design and mode of operation of the supercharger:

"The purpose of the supercharger is to increase the specific gravity of the supercharger air and thus increase the filling of the cylinders. This results in a significant increase in engine performance, especially at higher altitudes, where air density normally causes engine performance to fall off rapidly. The supercharger is designed as a single-stage centrifugal blower and basically consists of impeller, supercharger cover and housing. The impeller is powered by the accessory drive by means of an auxiliary shaft and hydraulic coupling (pressure-oil). The purpose of the hydraulic coupling is to slowly accelerate the supercharger, which runs slowly on the ground (supercharger switched off), to the highest speed (supercharger switched on) with altitude. This increase in supercharger speed is variable, so that supercharger speed can best match engine requirements at all altitudes. The supercharger is equipped with a

The rear engine supercharger. Visible above is the channel leading to the air intake. In front is the engine bearer. (H. Schuller)

connecting flange to allow air to be bled off for special purposes (for example to pressurize tanks or for ventilation). Pressure-oil for the hydraulic coupling is provided by a feeder pump which is barometrically controlled independent of altitude. The boost pressure produced by the blower is controlled up to maximum boost altitude* by means of a boost pressure regulator gill, which it located in the boost pressure line just behind the supercharger and actuated by the boost selector by means of a push-rod. This ensures that the selected boost pressure always prevails in the line in front of the valves. In production series 1 and 2 engines (A-1/A-2, author's note) an air pressure relief valve is installed at the bend in the pressure pipe between the regulating and power bleed flaps. If an excessively high boost pressure is reached because of supercharger overspeeding in a dive or rapid descent, this valve opens automatically until the allowable boost pressure is achieved."

Concerning the boost pressure selector: "The boost pressure selector is located between the throttle lever and the boost pressure control flap. Its purpose is to set a certain boost pressure for any throttle lever position and hold it constant in any flight attitude to maximum boost altitude."

Various types of supercharger were installed in the course of DB 603 A development. The spectrum ranged from single-stage superchargers, which were used on the DB 603 A, D, E and G variants. Two-stage superchargers were used to increase the performance of the DB 603 N and L.

A turbo-supercharger, which unlike a mechanical supercharger is driven by the energy of exhaust gases streaming through it, was fitted to the DB 603 R and U engines.

The DB 603 L production engine, equipped with a two-stage mechanical supercharger, supercharger air cooler and intake guide unit for air capacity control, made it possible to raise maximum boost altitude to 9 200 meters. Under ideal conditions this could be

Table 15: DB 603 A, E and LA (quick replacement engine 9-8603 B1)

Technical Data	DB 603 A	DB 603 E	DB 603 LA (9-8603) B1*
Cylinder Data			
Number of cylinders	12	12	12
Cylinder arrangement	60° inverted vee	60° inverted vee	60° inverted vee
Bore	162 mm	162 mm	162 mm
Stroke	180 mm	180 mm	180 mm
Displacement (per cylinder)	3,71 l	3,71 l	3,71 l
Displacement (total)	44,5 l	44,5 l	44,5 l
Compression**	1: 7,5 / 1.7,3	1:7,5 / 1:7,3	1:7,5 / 1:7,3
Gear reduction	1 : 1,93		
Intake and exhaust valves	two each	two each	two each
	DW 250 ET 7/1	DW 250 ET 7/1	DW 250 ET 7/1
Sparkplugs	two per cylinder	two per cylinder	two per cylinder
Ignition sequence	1-11-2-9-4-7-6-8-	1-11-2-9-4-7-6-8-	1-11-2-9-4-7-6-8-
	5-10-3-12-1	5-10-3-12-1	5-10-3-12-1
Ignition system	Bosch ZM 12 CR 8	Bosch ZM 12 CR 8	Bosch ZM 12 CR 8
Starter	data not available	Bosch AL-SGC 24 DR 2	Bosch AL-SGC 24 DR 2
Mode of operation	four-stroke	four-stroke	four-stroke
Supercharger type	single-speed gear-driven	single-speed gear-driven	two-speed gear-driven
Direction of rotation (crankshaft)	counter-clockwise	counter-clockwise	counter-clockwise
Direction of rotation (propeller)	clockwise	clockwise	clockwise
Performance Data			
Maximum output (ground level) PS = H.P. U/min = rpm	1750 PS (2700 U/min)	2000 PS (2700 U/min)	2100 PS (2700 U/min)
Maximum output	1680 PS in 5700 m (2700 U/min)	1740 PS in 6000 m (2700 U/min)	1760 PS in 9000 m (2700 U/min)
Short duration output (ground level)	1590 PS (2500 U/min)	1710 PS (2500 U/min)	1800 PS (2700 U/min)
Short duration output	1540 PS in 5700 m (2500 U/min)	1550 PS in 6400 m (2500 U/min)	1500 PS in 9000 m (9000 U/min)
Continuous output (ground level)	1390 PS (2300 U/min)	1540 PS (2500 U/min)	1500 PS (2300 U/min)
Continuous output	1450 PS in 5500 m (2300 U/min)	1300 PS in 6400 m (2300 U/min)	1240 PS in 8600 m (2300 U/min)
Output per unit of displacement	39.3 PS/l	44.97 PS/l	47.2 PS/l
Output per cylinder	145.7 PS	166.6 PS	166.7 PS
Maximum boost altitude	5700m	6400 m	9000 m

	Fuel, Oil and Cooling Systems		
Fuel type	B 4		
Fuel consumption (short duration output)	220 g/PSh	220 g/PSh	220 g/PSh
Fuel consumption (continuous output)	205 g/PSh	205 g/PSh	205 g/PSh
Injection pumps	Bosch PZ 12 HP 120/22	Bosch PZ 12 HP	Bosch PZ 12 HP
Mixture control	EP/HB 52/9		
Fuel pump type	Ehrich & Graetz ZD 500 B od. -E-2 (A-0 u. A-1), ZD 1000 B für A-2	Ehrich & Graetz ZD 1500 A	Ehrich & Graetz ZD 1500 A od. W
Capacity (per pump half)	500l/h (ZD 500 B u. E-2) 1000 l/h (ZD 1000 B)		
Fuel pressure	1.3 - 1.8 kg/cm"		
Oil consumption	5-8 g/PSh	5-8 g/PSh	5-8 g/PSh
Oil pump	DB gear pump	DB gear pump	DB gear pump
Capacity	47 kg/min at 2,500 rpm and 75° inlet temperature		
Main oil scavenge pump	DB double gear pump (collector tank to cooler)		
Capacity	ca. 68 kg/min (2,500 rpm)		
Secondary oil scavenge pumps (2)	DB double gear pump (cylinder covers to collector tank)	no information	no information
Capacity	7 kg/min per cylinder cover at 2,500 rpm		
Gear oil pump	DB gear pump	DB gear pump	DB gear pump
Capacity	50 kg/min (2,500 rpm)		
Fuel pump	DB centrifugal pump		
Capacity	57 m³ at 2,500 rpm		
Propeller pitch control system	VDM 9-9538 V3E (A-0) VDM 9-14502 A-1 (A-1/A-2)		
	Dimensions and Weights		
Engine length	2680 mm	2705 mm	2740 mm
Engine height	1167 mm	1167 mm	1203 mm
Engine width	830 mm	830 mm	1008 mm
Dry weight	910 kg	950 kg	990 kg
Installed weight	1040 kg	1080 kg	1120 kg
Weight to power ratio	0.52 kg/PS	0.47 kg/PS	0.47 kg/PS
Weight to capacity ratio	20.42 kg/l	21.30 kg/l	22.20 kg/l

*Further information on the quick-replacement engine may be found in the chapter on the Do 335 B.

** The cylinder banks had different sealing values to compensate for differences in boost pressure. Pressure differences resulted from the one-sided installation of the supercharger (values with 87 octane fuel).

increased even further, to 11 000 meters. The single-stage mechanical superchargers of the DB 603 A and E enabled maximum boost altitudes of 5 700 and 7 400 meters, respectively.

In relation to this theme there follow definitions of the terms "maximum boost altitude" and "boost pressure".

The term "maximum boost altitude" refers to the maximum achievable altitude at which a prescribed boost pressure, without consideration of the dynamic pressure produced by flight, can be maintained at a specific rate of revolution.

The term "boost pressure" defines the pressure in an engine's supercharger induction pipe, measured by the boost pressure instrument at a point determined for a specific type of engine.

The following extracts from the handbook describe the fuel, lubrication and cooling systems. These descriptions are supported by schematic drawings of the systems, which are also taken from the Do 335 handbook (valid for the Do 335 A-0, A-1 and A-10).

The Fuel System

Total of three tanks:

- 1 main fuselage tank, 1 230 liters (protected)
- 1 main fuselage tank, 355 liters (two-seaters only)
- 2 wing leading edge auxiliary tanks, each 375 liters

Removal and transfer (combat aircraft): removal to engines only from the main fuselage tank, with two lines to each engine, as well as at filler and auxiliary tank caps. Electric tank pumps in the feed lines at the auxiliary tank cap to assist the engine supply pumps (always switched on). Tank pumps transfer fuel from the leading edge tanks to the main tank. Both transfer pumps deliver approximately twice the rate of engine consumption at normal rpm. Pump switch on the right side of the main instrument panel, transfer limiter.

Training aircraft: removal only from the main fuselage tank cap, otherwise as above. Pump switch in front cockpit only.

Non-usable remnant amounts: main tank (1 230 l), approximately 15 l, auxiliary tanks, approximately 5 l.

Fuel type: aviation gasoline type B4 (87 octane) or C3 (97 octane).

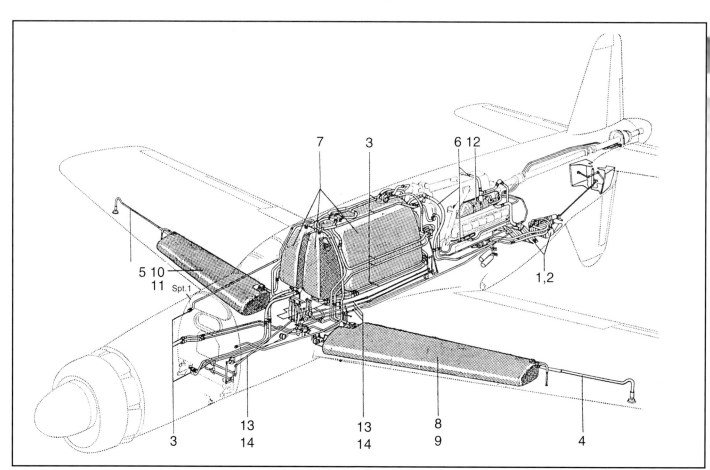

Schematic drawing of the fuel system of the Do 335 V2 (handbook).

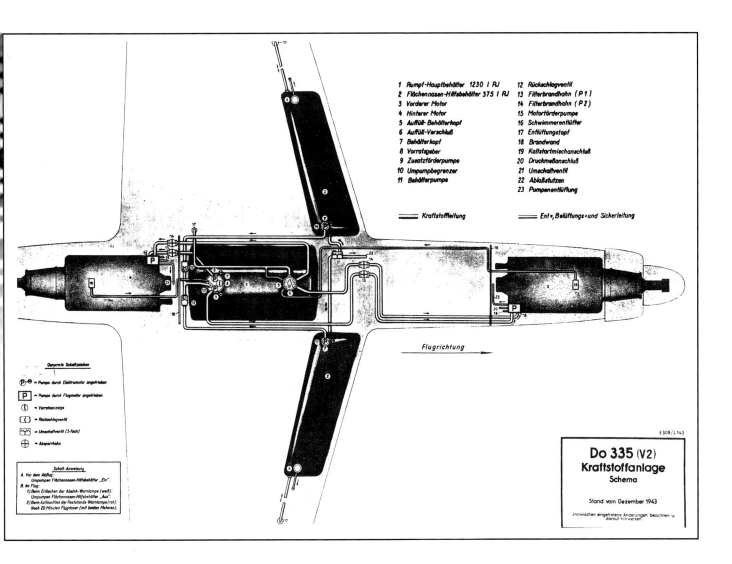

Do 335 (V2)
Kraftstoffanlage
Schema

Stand vom Dezember 1943

Jnzwischen eingetretene Änderungen beachten u. darauf hinweisen.

1 Rumpf-Hauptbehälter 1230 l RJ
2 Flächennasen-Hilfsbehälter 375 l RJ
3 Vorderer Motor
4 Hinterer Motor
5 Auffüll-Behälterkopf
6 Auffüll-Verschluß
7 Behälterkopf
8 Vorratsgeber
9 Zusatzförderpumpe
10 Umpumpbegrenzer
11 Behälterpumpe

12 Rückschlagventil
13 Filterbrandhahn (P1)
14 Filterbrandhahn (P2)
15 Motorförderpumpe
16 Schwimmerentlüfter
17 Entlüftungstopf
18 Brandwand
19 Kaltstartmischanschluß
20 Druckmeßanschluß
21 Umschaltventil
22 Ablaßstutzen
23 Pumpenentlüftung

▬▬ Kraftstoffleitung   ▬▬ Ent-, Belüftungs-und Sickerleitung

Flugrichtung

Genormte Schaltzeichen

Ⓟ = Pumpe durch Elektromotor angetrieben
[P] = Pumpe durch Flugmotor angetrieben
Ⓘ = Vorratsanzeige
[I] = Rückschlagventil
= Umschaltventil (3-fach)
= Absperrhahn

Schalt-Anweisung
A. Vor dem Abflug:
    Umpumpen Flächennasen-Hilfsbehälter „Ein".
B. Im Flug:
    1) Beim Erlöschen der Absink-Warnlampe (weiß):
        Umpumpen Flächennasen-Hilfsbehälter „Aus".
    2) Beim Aufleuchten der Reststands-Warnlampe (rot):
        Noch 20 Minuten Flugdauer (mit beiden Motoren).

According to the technical description, none of the tanks had provision for fuel jettisoning (author's note).

The Lubrication System

Two tanks each with a capacity of 95 liters* are installed side by side behind the pilot's seat. The extension shaft bearings (own fuel pump in rear bearing) are also lubricated with engine oil. System monitored by temperature and pressure indicators (main instrument panel, right). Temperature regulated by automatic cooling flap adjustment (thermostatic), controlled by coolant system. Fuel mixture for cold start (thinning of oil). Introduction into the supply lines at the tank bottom plug. Mixture cock on the rear wall of the nosewheel well.

Lubricant: INTAVA "Rotring".

*It should be noted that the A-0/A-1 technical description dated 4/7/1944 lists two unprotected aluminum tanks, each with a volume of 102 liters.

Each filled with 70 liters of oil and 15 liters of fuel (for thinning for cold starts).

No oil level indicator was planned. The forward engine's oil cooler was designed as an annular cooler. (frontal area 9.9 dm2, with a depth of 250 mm).

An aluminum oil tank. Two of these tanks were located behind the cockpit.

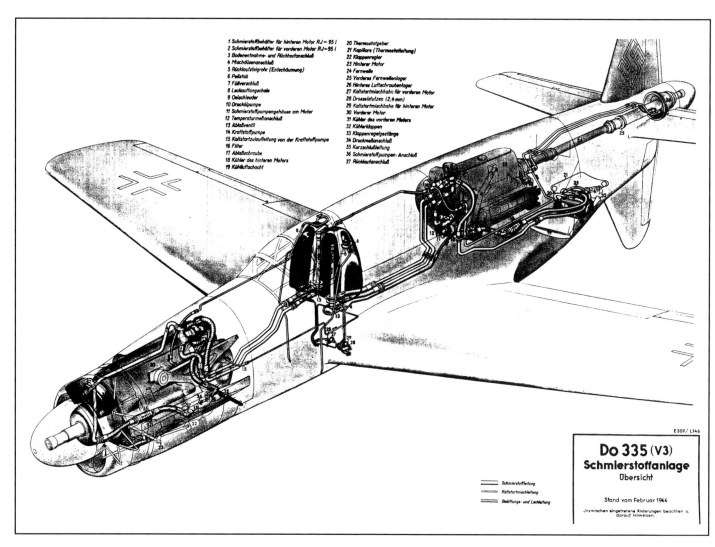

1 Schmierstoffbehälter für hinteren Motor RJ = 95 l
2 Schmierstoffbehälter für vorderen Motor RJ = 95 l
3 Bodenentnahme- und Rücklaufanschluß
4 Mischdüsenanschluß
5 Rücklaufsteigrohr (Entschäumung)
6 Peilstab
7 Füllverschluß
8 Leckauffangschale
9 Oelschleuder
10 Drucköpumpe
11 Schmierstoffpumpengehäuse am Motor
12 Temperaturmeßanschluß
13 Ablaßventil
14 Kraftstoffpumpe
15 Kaltstartzulaufleitung von der Kraftstoffpumpe
16 Filter
17 Ablaßschraube
18 Kühler des hinteren Motors
19 Kühlluftschacht
20 Thermostatgeber
21 Kapillare (Thermostatleitung)
22 Klappenregler
23 Hinterer Motor
24 Fernwelle
25 Vorderes Fernwellenlager
26 Hinteres Luftschraubenlager
27 Kaltstartmischhahn für vorderen Motor
28 Drosselstutzen (2,4 mm)
29 Kaltstartmischhahn für hinteren Motor
30 Vorderer Motor
31 Kühler des vorderen Motors
32 Kühlerklappen
33 Klappenregelgestänge
34 Druckmeßanschluß
35 Kurzschlußleitung
36 Schmierstoffpumpen-Anschluß
37 Rücklaufanschluß

E 309/ L146

Do 335 (V3)
Schmierstoffanlage
Übersicht

Stand vom Februar 1944

Inzwischen eingetretene Änderungen beachten u.
darauf hinweisen.

Schmierstoffleitung
Kaltstartmischleitung
Belüftungs- und Leckleitung

General arrangement drawing of the Do 335 V3's lubrication system (February 1944).

The Coolant System

Closed cooling system with two equalizing tanks, separated, for each engine. Filling and topping up in each starboard tank only (filler point). Tank capacity approximately 15 liters. Total coolant volume: forward engine approximately 90 liters, rear engine approximately 93 liters. Monitoring by temperature gauge (right side of main instrument panel). Temperature regulated by automatic cooling gill adjustment (thermostatic).

The coolant consisted of water (47 parts) and Glycol (50 parts), with the remainder *Schutzöl 39* anti-corrosive. The front engine was equipped with an annular radiator with two 25.5 dm2 frontal areas (depth: 135 mm). The rear engine was cooled by a ventral radiator with a frontal area of 46 dm2 and a depth of 135 mm. (Author's note).

Details of the annular radiator. (H. Schuller)

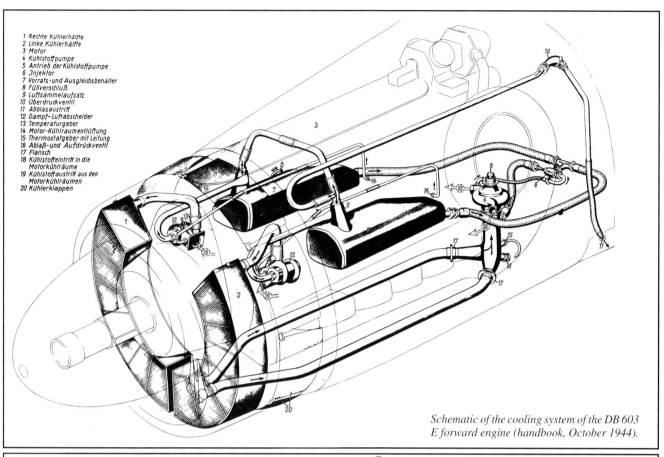

1 Rechte Kühlerhälfte
2 Linke Kühlerhälfte
3 Motor
4 Kühlstoffpumpe
5 Antrieb der Kühlstoffpumpe
6 Jnjektor
7 Vorrats- und Ausgleichsbehälter
8 Füllverschluß
9 Luftsammelaufsatz
10 Überdruckventil
11 Abblasaustritt
12 Dampf-Luftabscheider
13 Temperaturgeber
14 Motor-Kühlraumlüftung
15 Thermostatgeber mit Leitung
16 Ablaß- und Aufdrückventil
17 Flansch
18 Kühlstoffeintritt in die
   Motorkühlräume
19 Kühlstoffaustritt aus den
   Motorkühlräumen
20 Kühlerklappen

Schematic of the cooling system of the DB 603 E forward engine (handbook, October 1944).

The cooling system of the rear engine (handbook, October 1944).

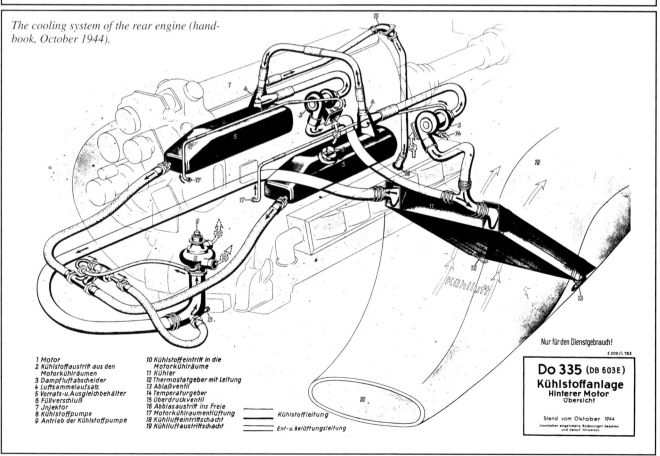

1 Motor
2 Kühlstoffaustritt aus den
   Motorkühlräumen
3 Dampfluftabscheider
4 Luftsammelaufsatz
5 Vorrats-u. Ausgleichbehälter
6 Füllverschluß
7 Jnjektor
8 Kühlstoffpumpe
9 Antrieb der Kühlstoffpumpe
10 Kühlstoffeintritt in die
   Motorkühlräume
11 Kühler
12 Thermostatgeber mit Leitung
13 Ablaßventil
14 Temperaturgeber
15 Überdruckventil
16 Abblasaustritt ins Freie
17 Motorkühlraumlüftung
18 Kühllufteintrittschacht
19 Kühlluftaustrittschacht

—— Kühlstoffleitung
—— Ent-u.Belüftungsleitung

Kühlluft

Nur für den Dienstgebrauch!

E 309/L 153

Do 335 (DB 603 E)
Kühlstoffanlage
Hinterer Motor
Übersicht

Stand vom Oktober 1944

Jnzwischen eingetretene Änderungen beachten
und darauf hinweisen.

The radiator intake of the rear engine.

Table 16:

Engine System	Do 335 A-0 (to 40th machine)	Do 335 A (*Zerstörer*) (from 41st machine with GM-1)
Engine, including extension shaft and VDM drive	2090 kg	2090 kg
Engine control system	20 kg	20 kg
Ignition system	49 kg	50 kg
Fuel system	276 kg	305 kg
Oil system	102 kg	100 kg
Cooling system	225 kg	230 kg
Exhaust system	45 kg	45 kg
Propeller 3.3 m/3.5 m	440 kg	440 kg
Coolant	175 kg	180 kg
Unusable fuel	90 kg	90 kg
Estimated reserve	35 kg	35 kg
GM-1 system	———	140 kg
Engine installation (total)	3547 kg	3725 kg

The Hydraulic System

The aircraft was equipped with a common pressure-oil net which actuated the following systems:

- undercarriage
- landing flaps
- variable controls
- bomb doors
- cooling gills
- wheel brakes

The first four of the above-named systems are normally controlled electrically, in an emergency by compressed air. The cooling gills are controlled by thermostats, the undercarriage brakes by the rudder pedals. The maximum operating pressure (during activation) is approximately one hundred atmospheres, circulating pressure approximately thirty atm. The various systems are connected to the circulation system of the pressure-oil net, which is pressurized by two pressure-oil pumps driven by the aircraft engines. These draw the pressure-oil (12 or 18 l/min. with engines at approximately 2,000 rpm) through a filter from the protected tank (18 l) and transfer it to the four solenoid-operated pilot valves arranged one behind the other. The first four of the named systems are attached to these.

Cooling gill actuation and the brake system are connected directly to the circulatory system (before the pilot valves). Various float, bleed and pressure relief valves are installed in the circulation system, and the system's external attachment points are located where the two lines meet. A pressure indicator is also attached to the system. It is located in the on the right side of the cockpit floor. The four solenoids cannot be switched on simultaneously and must be selected individually. No particular order.

Cooling gill actuation is constant while the engines are running. Their regulators, which are set for various temperature ranges, are controlled by coolant temperature.

The regulating range for the forward engine may be adjusted from the instrument panel.

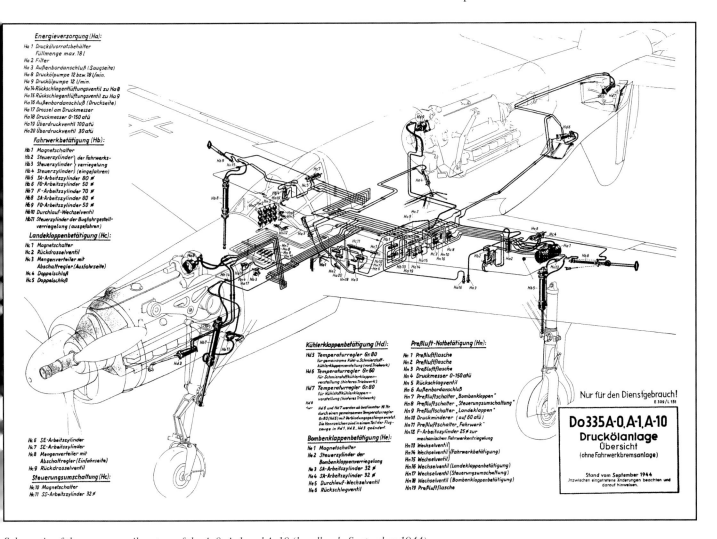

Schematic of the pressure-oil system of the A-0, A-1 and A-10 (handbook, September 1944).

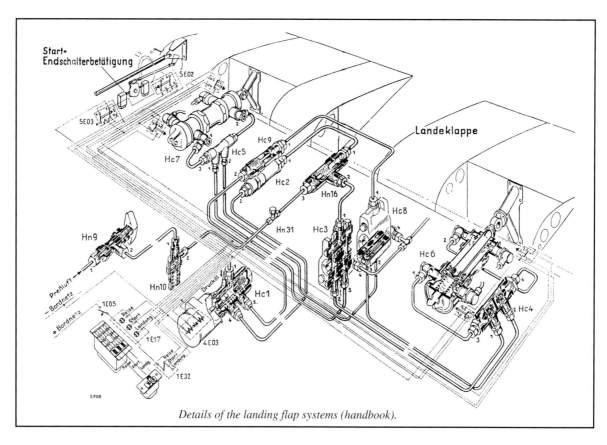

Details of the landing flap systems (handbook).

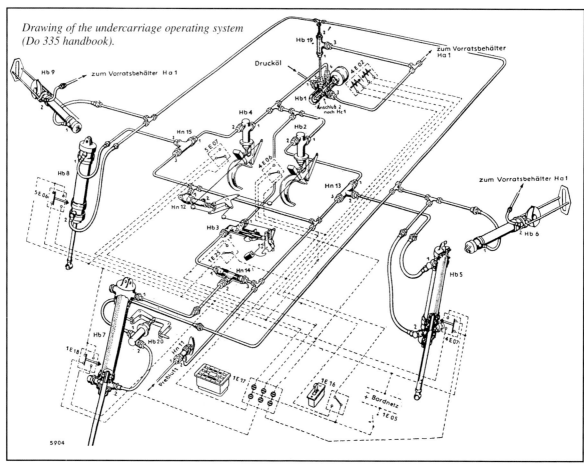

Drawing of the undercarriage operating system
(Do 335 handbook).

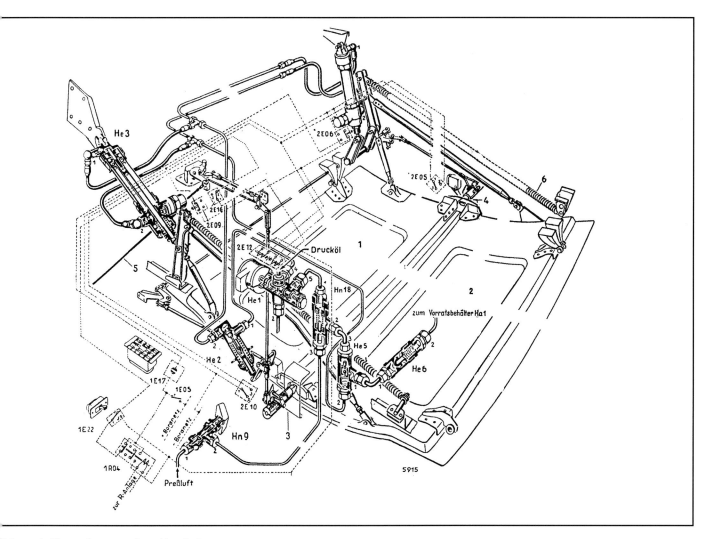

Schematic illustrating operation of bomb doors.

The brake system is also under pressure at all times. With the help of an accumulator, maximum pressure is maintained with the assistance of compressed air (25 atm). Allocation to the brakes by brake valves attached to the rudder pedals.

In an emergency undercarriage, landing flaps, variable controls and bomb doors can be operated by compressed air from the compressed air net. This enables:

- bomb doors to be closed
- undercarriage to be lowered
- landing flaps to be extended
- controls to be switched to "NORMAL FLIGHT"

The above sequence is to be followed unless the undercarriage is already down, in which case no particular sequence is required.

Permanent Equipment	Do 335 A-0 (to 40th machine)	Do 335 A (*Zerstörer*) (from 41st machine with GM-1)
Flight and navigation instruments	8 kg	8 kg
Engine instruments	20 kg	20 kg
Equipment mountings	40 kg	40 kg
Safety equipment	2 kg	2 kg
Installation	50 kg	50 kg
Hydraulic system (pressure-oil)	70 kg	70 kg
Permanent Equipment (total)	190 kg	190 kg
All positions added to empty weight of:	6540 kg*	6780 kg*

*Sum of airframe, engine systems and permanent equipment.

The Electrical System

Power supply: direct current electrical system, rated voltage 24 Volts. Two generators (type LK 2000/24 R 15) each with 2,000 Watts on the engines. System storage battery on cockpit floor. External access point on right side of fuselage between Frames 5 and 6. Switchbox on right side of cockpit.

Both generators are connected to the main bus bar by remote automatic switches (emergency switch on the instrument panel).

For special systems three-phase alternating current 36 Volts, 500 Hz (own transformer). Army Group Center voltage from the generators approximately 29 Volts from 1,900 engine rpm.

Military Equipment

The Do 335's armament varied quite considerably from one version to another. Initially it was armed with the MG 151/15 (15-mm), which in the course of development became the MG 151/20 (20-mm). Later the type's armament was bolstered by the addition of an engine-mounted MK 103 cannon (30-mm). The *Zerstörer* (heavy fighter) version was also equipped with two wing-mounted MK 103s. The Do 335 was also provided with a bomb bay. Internal stowage of bombs avoided drag-producing external racks. The bay could also be used to house extra fuel tanks.

Mauser MG 151/15 and MG 151/20

The history of these weapons began in 1934, when the Mauser company of Oberndorf received a contract to develop a super-heavy machine-gun with a caliber of 15 mm. Development of the weapon was headed by Dir. von Lossnitz and Dr. Doerge. Production began in 1938, even though there were fears that wear would result in the weapon having a short service life. These fears were based on the high performance figures for the MG 151, which made it appear superior to the MG 131. The MG 151 was a fully automatic recoil-operated weapon with a fixed lockable breech. Ammunition could be fired either by firing pin or electrically and was fed by disintegrating belts from the right (MG 151 A) or left (MG 151 B). Spent casings were ejected from the bottom of the weapon. The MG 151 was the first weapon to use the so-called "increasing twist"*, however this feature and the hard chromium plating of the barrel did little to reduce wear. The use of increasing twist did, however, improve accuracy, which resulted from the increased rate of rotation of the projectile. Firing the weapon produced recoil forces of approximately 430 kg. Even in extreme flight attitudes, with the resulting centrifugal forces, rate of fire was 450 rounds per minute. Normal rate of fire was 700 rounds per minute. International developments in aircraft design resulted in a requirement for heavier armaments. The RLM issued a basic requirement for a weapon which

*Increasing twist: initial angle of twist of 0° or 0°30', then increasing to a maximum of 9°30' at the muzzle.

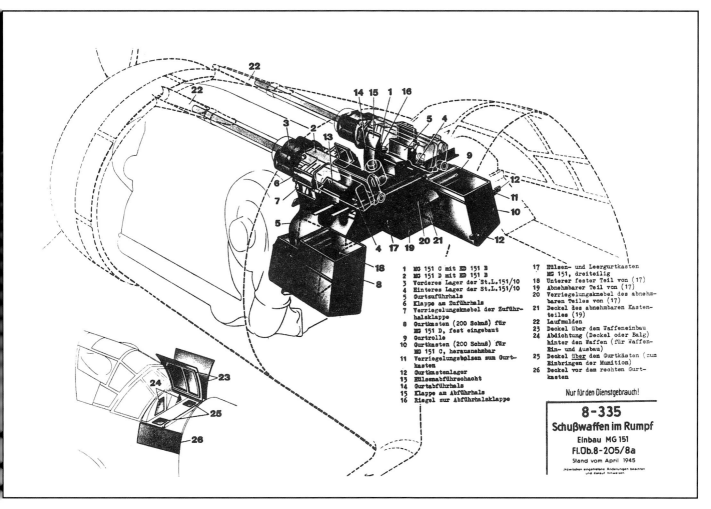

Installation schematic of two MG 151 cannon.

1 MG 151 C mit ED 151 B
2 MG 151 D mit ED 151 B
3 Vorderes Lager der St.L.151/10
4 Hinteres Lager der St.L.151/10
5 Gurtzuführhals
6 Klappe am Zuführhals
7 Verriegelungsknebel der Zuführhalsklappe
8 Gurtkasten (200 Schuß) für MG 151 D, fest eingebaut
9 Gurtrolle
10 Gurtkasten (200 Schuß) für MG 151 C, herausnehmbar
11 Verriegelungsbolzen zum Gurtkasten
12 Gurtkastenlager
13 Hülsenabführschacht
14 Gurtabführhals
15 Klappe am Abführhals
16 Riegel zur Abführhalsklappe
17 Hülsen- und Leergurtkasten MG 151, dreiteilig
18 Unterer fester Teil von (17)
19 Abnehmbarer Teil von (17)
20 Verriegelungsknebel des abnehmbaren Teiles von (17)
21 Deckel des abnehmbaren Kastenteiles (19)
22 Laufmulden
23 Deckel über dem Waffeneinbau
24 Abdichtung (Deckel oder Balg) hinter den Waffen (für Waffen-Ein- und Ausbau)
25 Deckel über den Gurtkasten (zum Einbringen der Munition)
26 Deckel vor dem rechten Gurtkasten

Nur für den Dienstgebrauch!

8-335
Schußwaffen im Rumpf
Einbau MG 151
Fl.Ob.8-205/8a
Stand vom April 1945

Inzwischen eingetretene Änderungen beachten und darauf hinweisen

Two Mauser MG 151/20 cannon were mounted above the forward engine. They were synchronized to fire through the propeller disc.

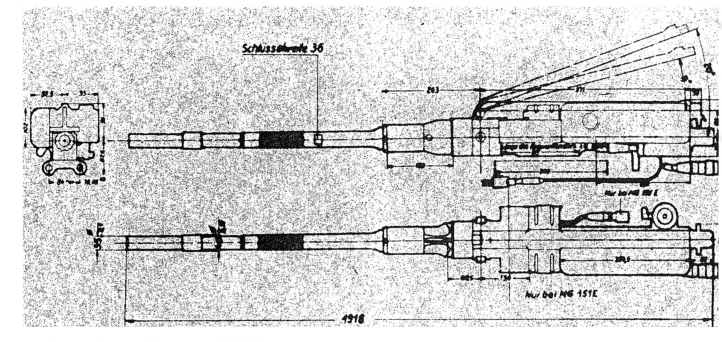

Manufacturer's drawing of the Mauser MG 151/15.

could fire at least one kilogram of ammunition in one second. Mauser responded by developing a 20-mm barrel for its proven MG 151/15 cannon. At 1104 mm, the barrel of the 20-mm weapon was slightly shorter than the 1254-mm barrel of the MG 151/15. All other components were largely similar to those of the original. This was one of the reasons why the 20-mm weapon was able to go into production so quickly.

Designated the MG 151/20, Mauser's new cannon entered the test phase in 1938. 39,500 examples of the weapon were produced from 1940 to 1945, with an average price of RM 787. In *Luftwaffe* service it was used in a wide variety of roles. Galland estimated that 20 to 25 hits were required to bring down a heavy bomber. Given a probability rate of 97%, this required 275 rounds to be fired from a range of 500 meters. From 1 000 meters this rose to 840 rounds. At a distance of 1 500 meters, 3,000 rounds were required to achieve this result.

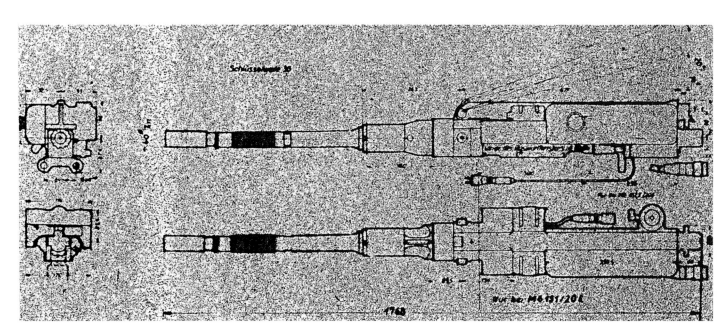

Manufacturer's drawing of the Mauser MG 151/20.

Table 17:

Technical Data	Mauser MG 151/15	Mauser MG 151/20
Caliber	15 mm	20 mm
Weapon weight	42.7 kg	42.5 kg
Length (with barrel)	1916 mm	1766 mm
Height	195 mm	195 mm
Width	190 mm	190 mm
Barrel length	1254 mm	1104 mm
Weight (barrel)	10.33 kg	10.50 kg
Rate of fire	660-700 rounds per minute (depending on type of ammunition)	630-720 rounds per minute (depending on type of ammunition)
Muzzle velocity	850-1020 m/sec (depending on type of ammunition)	695-785 m/sec (depending on type of ammunition)
Gas pressure	3000 atm	2900 atm
Shell weight /velocity H.E. L	151 g / 960 m/Sec	205 g / 705 m/Sec
Shell weight / velocity A.P. L	165 g / 850 m/Sec	205 g / 705 m/Sec
Shell weight / velocity H.A.P.	151 g / 1025 m/Sec	183 g / 810 m/Sec
Shell weight / velocity Incend. L	151 g / 1010 m/Sec	207 g / 695 m/Sec
Weight of fire	0.665 kg/Sec	1.08 kg/Sec M.Gr.9
Weight of explosive	0.033 kg/Sec(Spr.Gr.)	0.224 kg/Sec
Belt link with 100 links	3310 mm	3310 mm

The following excerpt from a Dornier company technical description details the installation of the MG 151 in the Do 335:

Guns: two MG 151s above the forward engine, installed between Frame 1 and Frame 2, synchronized to fire through the propeller arc. Number of rounds: 200, ammunition box, spent belt and casing collector box. Firing button on front of right control horn.

Rheinmetall MK 103

As the war progressed, increased demands were made in all areas of technology. This was also the case in the field of aircraft armaments. It became necessary to increase the caliber of aircraft weapons in order to inflict the level of damage required to bring down enemy aircraft. In response to this situation a contract was issued to Rheinmetall, which in 1941 began development of the MK 103. The design was based on the already obsolescent MK 101, and after a relatively brief development period, the MK 103 became available in 1942.

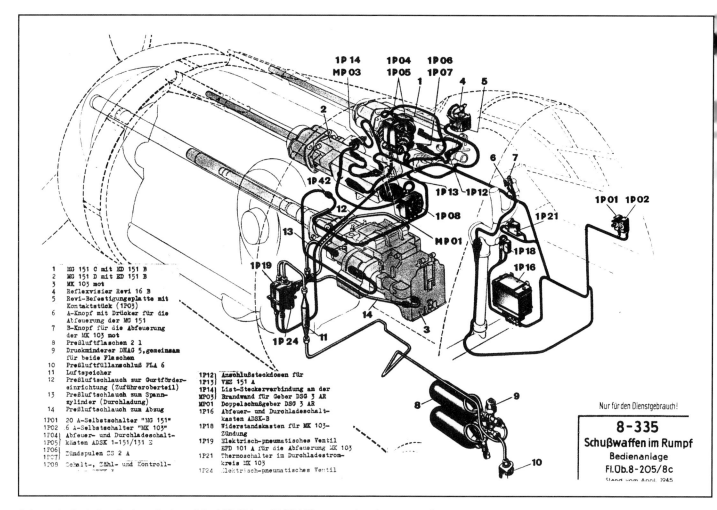

Schematic depicting the installation of the MG 151 and MK 103 cannon (engine-mounted).

The MK 103 differed from the MK 101 in the following areas:

- method of operation: blowback operated weapon
- weight reduced by 40 kg
- installed length (reduced by 400 mm)
- belt feed (instead of drum feed used by MK 101)
- rate of fire nearly doubled
- strengthened recoil springs and friction brakes
- potential installation as engine-mounted weapon

Ammunition could be fed from the left or right by disintegrating belt. The ammunition was fired electrically. In the beginning the housing was still forged, however as production progressed this was changed to stamped metal technology. The result was an increase in the rate of production, and the change also reflected the growing shortage of skilled labor. Initially the firing unit was served electrically, later a more reliable electro-pneumatic system was introduced for cocking and firing.

The MK 103 was fitted with additional friction brakes to absorb the immense forces generated by recoil. With a muzzle brake installed, recoil forces were 2 000 kg. Without the muzzle brake a figure of 3 000 kg was reached.

In the case of the Do 335, the MK 103 was installed as an engine-mounted weapon and, in the case of the *Zerstörer* variants, as a wing-mounted weapon. In contrast to the MG 151, which required 20 to 25 hits to bring down a heavy bomber, the MK 103 required just three hits on average to achieve the same result. With a firing probability of 95%, it was calculated that 76 rounds would have to be fired from a range of 500 meters to achieve the desired three hits. This figure rose to 203 rounds from one-thousand meters and 650 rounds from 1 500 meters.

Introduced into service in 1943, the MK 103 could also be used against hardened ground targets. The MK 108, on the other hand, was a specialized weapon for use against enemy bombers.

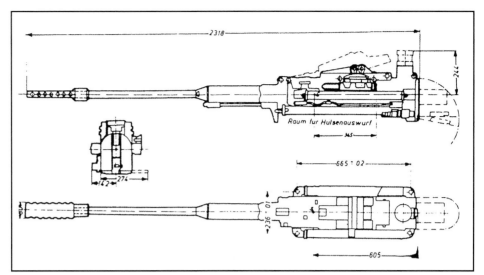

Manufacturer's drawing of the MK 103 as a wing-mounted weapon, fitted with the so-called "Strainer-Hole Muzzle Brake".

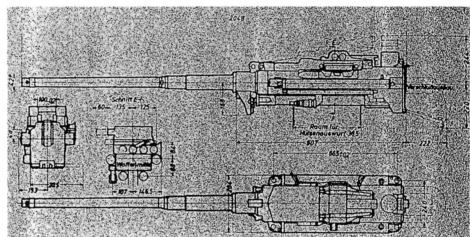

Manufacturer's drawing of a Rheinmetall MK 103 engine-mounted cannon.

In the case of the Do 335 B the MK 103 was employed as a wing-mounted weapon. Note the muzzle brake.

Table 18:

Technical Data	MK 101	MK 103	MK 108
Caliber	30 mm	30 mm	30 mm
Weapon weight	139 kg	145 kg	58 kg
Length (with barrel and muzzle brake)	2586 mm	2335 mm	1050 mm
Barrel length	1350 mm	1338 mm	545 mm
Rate of fire	220-260 Sch/min	380/min (H.Pzgr.L´spur) 420/min (Minengesch.).	ca. 600 Sch/min, später bis zu 850 Sch/min
Muzzle velocity	700-960 m/sek (je nach Munitionsart)	940 m/sek (Pzgr.) 860 m/sec (Minengr.)	520 m/sec
Velocity of explosive round		860 m/sec	520 m/Sec
Weight of fire, explosive round	1.278 kg/Sec	2.310 kg/Sec	3.575 kg/Sec
Weight of high-explosive, explosive round	0.416 kg/Sec	0.525 kg/Sec	0.812 kg/Sec
Gas pressure		3300 at	3100 at
Installed weight (engine-mounted)	-	165 kg	73 kg
Installed weight (nose-mounted)	-	199 kg	88 kg
Penetrative ability	75 mm auf 300 m (Stahl) m.H.Pzgr.L´spur	110 mm auf 300 m (Stahl) m.H.Pzgr.L´spur	Daten nicht verfügbar
Flight Path Deviations Flugz. = flight time)			
Range 500 m	0.58 m	1.9 m (Flugz. 0.66 Sec)	6.0 m (Flugz. 1.13 Sec)
Range 1000 m	2.74 m	9.4 m (Flugz. 1.5 Sec)	29.1m (Flugz. 2.65 Sec)
Range 1500 m	7.68 m	26.3 m (2.6 Sec)	78.3 m (Flugz. 4.37 Sec)

The Dornier technical description stated the following on the installation of the MK 103:

"One MK 103 in Mol 103/1A engine mount in forward engine, firing through the hollow propeller shaft. Rate of fire: sixty-five rounds per minute.

Ammunition box between Frame 1 and Frame 2, also belt and spent casing collector.

Firing button on top of right control horn."

The Gunsight

There is conflicting information in this regard.

The Do 335 A-0 and A-1 pilot manual lists the gunsight as a Revi 16 D, while Part 8A of the aircraft handbook specifies a Revi 16 B. The EZ 42 gunsight was evaluated during development.

The Bomb Bay

As the Do 335 was designed as a high-speed bomber, the aircraft was equipped with an internal bomb bay for the carriage of air-dropped weapons. The area could also be used to carry additional fuel. A number of bomb racks were installed in the bomb bay, making possible the carriage of various combinations of weapons, of which the following are several examples:

- 8 x SD 50 (fragmentation bomb, length 1 090 mm, diameter 200 mm)
- 8 x SD 70 (fragmentation bomb, length 1 090 mm, diameter 200 mm)
- 1 x SD 500 (fragmentation bomb, length 2 022 mm, diameter 447 mm)
- 2 x SC 250 (high-explosive bomb, length 1 640 mm, diameter 368 mm)
  later versions with ring tail
- 1 x SC 500 (high-explosive bomb, length 2 007 mm, diameter 396 mm)
  SC 500 K with cruciform tail, SC 500 J with ring tail
- 2 x AB 250 (bomb dispenser)
- 2 x AB 500 (bomb dispenser)

Bomb rack variants (choice of):
- 3 x Schlosslafetten 500/1000/XI B
- 1 x Schloss 2000/XIII
- 2 x Schloss 500/XII/C
- 4 x Träg.Schloss 50/X (Rüstsatz)

Camera installation in the bomb bay of a Do 335.

The following information is taken from the Do 335 handbook:

Air-Dropped Weapons: bomb racks in bomb bay for 250-kg or 500-kg bombs. Loading with heating accessories and block and tackle possible. ASK 335 bombing switchbox with SWA 10 B switch mechanism for single, stick or multiple drops; bomb release switch on left control column horn. ZSK 246 arming switchbox with Zu 21 arming transformer and control equipment for time and impact fuses.

Bomb Bay Doors: Beneath the bomb bay between Frame 7 and Frame 14, split longitudinally and folding to the sides. Hydraulically-operated. Controlled electrically, either automatically by the ZSK (arming switchbox), thus independent of the bomb-dropping system, or manually by means of a toggle switch on the right side of the nosewheel well, used on the ground for loading.

The following table lists additional equipment, which was also part of the weapons system. The weights of the various components are also listed and these are added to other figures to give the aircraft's equipped and gross weights for two different versions of the Do 335. (Type Sheet dated 1 November 1943).

The final part of the technical description deals with the cockpit and pilot escape system.

The Cockpit in Detail

The following depiction of the Do 335's "nerve center" consists of photographs and technical drawings. The cockpits of the various versions of the Do 335 differed in detail, and this description applies to the A-version.

The bomb bay could be used to carry bombs of various sizes, reconnaissance equipment or extra fuel.

Bomb in the bomb bay of a Do 335. A wide variety of stores could be carried internally.

Table 19:

Additional Equipment and Loads	Do 335 A-0	Do 335 A (*Zerstörer*)
Additional flight and navigation equipment	62 kg	48 kg
Additional safety and rescue equipment	33 kg	33 kg
Electrical equipment and radio gear	186 kg	186 kg
Signals and flare equipment	3 kg	3 kg
Additional installations	5 kg	5 kg
Guns	330 kg	720 kg
Bombs*	145 kg	30 kg
Armor	16 kg	250 kg
Additional equipment (total)	780 kg	1275 kg
All Positions Added to Equipped Weight of:	7230 kg	8055 kg
Fuel (including 40 kg for engine warm-up)	1500 kg	1150 kg
Oil	110 kg	90 kg
Crew	100 kg	100 kg
Bombs	500 kg	340 kg
Ammunition	160 kg	455 kg
Oxygen	10 kg	10 kg
Load (total)	2380 kg	2145 kg (inclusive GM-1)
All Positions Added to Gross Weight of:	9610 kg**	10200 kg**

*   Equipment for their mounting and release.

**   Including 40 kg of fuel for warming up the engines.

The teardrop-shaped bulges on both sides of the canopy were combined with mirrors. The rearwards-folding canopy was a feature of the V2 and V3 only and cost test pilot Altrogge his life.

Cockpit of a Do 335 A. Note the differences in instrumentation compared to the smaller photo (next page).

Here a compass has taken the place of the Revi gunsight.

The standard canopy, attached on the right and folding sideways.

The Pilot Escape System

The ejection seat is another form of "life insurance" for the pilot of modern day aircraft. In the 1940s, however, it was a rather rare piece of equipment. The modern ejection seat has saved the lives of thousands of pilots. During the Second World War, ejection seat technology, like the turbojet, was in its infancy.

Increasing speeds made it increasingly dangerous for pilots to abandoned crippled aircraft. An American study in 1943 revealed that a high percentage of pilots sustained injuries or were killed in the process of baling out. Of the pilots who baled out, 12.5% did not survive, while 45.5% sustained injuries. The situation in Germany was much the same. Approximately 6% of all crew members of Ju 88s failed to survive a bale-out. For the Fw 190 this figure was 28%. These statistics were based on 2,500 bale-outs in the period 1939 to 1944. The logical consequence of this was the development of a suitable escape system.

The ejection seat of the Do 335. Now commonplace, ejection seats were a novelty in 1944.

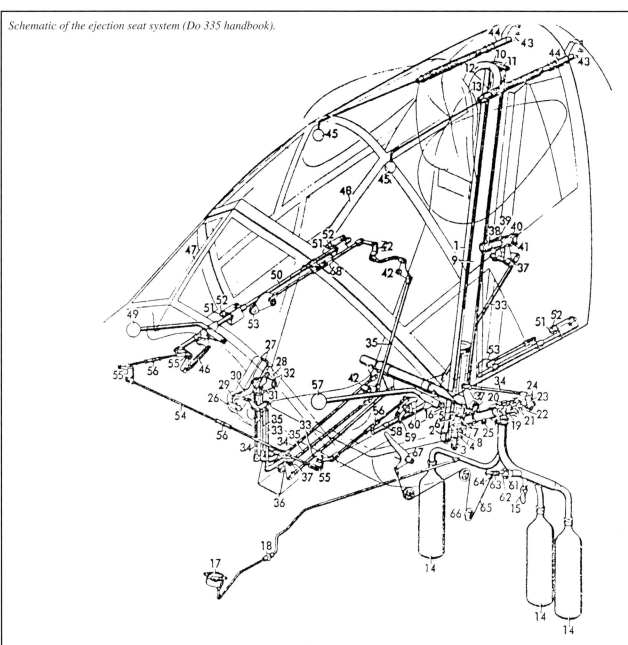

Schematic of the ejection seat system (Do 335 handbook).

1 Schleuderzylinder
2 Zylinderabschluß und- Befestigung
3 Befestigungsmutter
4 Zylinderbodenstuck
5 Kolbendorn
6 Verriegelungskolben
7 Verriegelungskugeln
8 Verriegelungsfeder
9 Schleuderkolben
10 Sitz Anschlußlasche des Schleuderkolbens
11 Anschlußbolzen
12 Sitz Anschlußbügel
13 Führersitz
14 Druckluftflasche (2 Liter)
15 Druckluft Fullventil

16 Schlüsselloch (zum Öffnen der Dachhaube von außen)
17 Druckmesser
18 Trennstelle
19 Schnelloffnungsventil
20 Ventilkegel
21 Ventilstift
22 Ventilnocke
23 Nockenhebel
24 Nockenriegel
25 Druckluft Ablaßschraube
26 Schaltkasten
27 Schleuder-Entriegelungshebel
28 Verriegelungshebel zu „27"
29 Mitnehmer zu „27"
30 Schleuderhebel
31 Schleuderzwischenhebel

32 Spannfeder
33 Entriegelungsgestange
34 Schleudergestange
35 Sicherungsgestange
36 Weitenlagerung
37 Umlenkwelle
38 Verriegelungsbolzen
39 Verriegelungsgehouse
40 Entriegelungsmuffe
41 Bolzenspannfeder
42 Umlenkwinkelhebel
43 Kippnocke
44 Halteriegel
45 Riegelzug
46 Ruckzugfeder
47 Dachhaube (fester Teil)
48 Dachhaube (abwerfborer Teil)
49 Abwurfhebel fur Dachhaube

50 Abwurfgestange fur Dachhaube
51 Halte- und Drehbolzen fur Dachhaube
52 Anschluß der Dachhaube
53 Abwurfhebel fur Dachhaube
54 Verbindung zwischen Abwurf- und Schließgestange
55 Umlenkwinkelhebel dazu
56 Spannschloß
57 Schließhebel fur Dachhaube
58 Schließgestange fur Dachhaube
59 Abwurfmitnehmer
60 Oeffnungsanschlag
61 Schlagblatchen
62 Schlagbolzen
63 Schlagbolzenventil
64 Verriegelungshaxen
65 Spannschloß
66 Seilrolle
67 Druckluft-Ablaßhebel
68 Mitnehmeraestange

With a maximum speed in the 800 km/h range, very close to that of its turbojet competitors, the Do 335 was an ideal candidate for the ejection seat. Extensive research was required, however, including a determination of the maximum forces the human organism could tolerate. Technically, a loading of 26 g was required for a successful ejection. The physicians determined that the absolute maximum the human body could tolerate was 28 g, or twenty-eight times the force of gravity. Many concentration camp inmates lost their lives in live tests.

The *Luftwaffe* maintained a test facility at the Dachau concentration camp where, for example, inmates were immersed in ice-cold water to determine how long crews could survive in the event of a ditching. There were also experiments with pressure chambers, which often resulted in the death of the test subject. Barbaric experiments in the name or research were standard practice in the Germany of that time.

Heinkel began experimenting with ejection seats at the beginning of the 1940s. In the course of development the Heinkel engineers developed two different operating systems. One was the cartridge system, in which the pilot was ejected explosively from the cockpit. The second system operated on compressed air. The latter was adopted for the Do 335. Working pressure was 120 to 140 atm, sufficient to eject a pilot clear of an aircraft. The energy produced was also enough to clear the tail surfaces and rear propeller if these failed to jettison.

Two two-liter compressed air bottles served as the system accumulator. Initial fears that combat damage might explode the bottles and damage the aircraft were later dispelled by experiments. Another source of concern was inadvertent firing of the seat. On several occasions vibration nearly caused such an incident, as the safety mechanism consisted merely of a raster. Technology in its infancy is always good for surprises.

The following is from the Dornier directive concerning the ejection seat:

Emergency escape by means of ejection seat (no seat provided for the second pilot of the training aircraft).

The pilot's seat is ejected by compressed air, and the pilot achieves sufficient clearance of the tail surfaces and rear propeller. Sufficient height is achieved to clear the tail surfaces at an operating pressure of 120 atm and airspeed of 900 km/h.

The ejected seat is lowered by a special parachute to prevent injury to the pilot. A special release valve for the compressed air is planned, control lever above the instrument panel (safety measure for forced landings).

Method of Operation:

1. Jettison the canopy with the hand lever on the front right of the canopy (ejection seat operating rods are locked when the canopy is closed, preventing the ejection rods from being activated).

2. Pull recessed ejection seat lever in the ejection control box on the right side of the cockpit all the way up: this causes the ejection release lever inside the recessed ejection seat lever to spring up, while the recessed lever itself releases the ejection piston's locking rod.

3. Fold the release lever extension upwards and pull the lever back to the stop, which opens a quick-release valve in the compressed air line and causes compressed air from the three compressed air bottles to stream into the ejection cylinder. The inrushing compressed air first releases the piston's ball lock at the bottom of the cylinder and then ejects the piston along with the attached seat, which rides on rails, and the pilot.

In addition to the regular escape system, consideration was given to an extremely unconventional solution. It was a parachute escape system designed specially for the Do 335, which was to slow the aircraft and allow the crew to exit the aircraft with minimal risk. The system was designed to reduce the Do 335's speed in a dive from 1 050 km/h to a relatively low 500 km/h.

The *E-Stelle Rechlin* was charged with carrying out the necessary tests. Rechlin worked closely with Dornier and the parachute maker Kostelezky as well as the Graf Zeppelin research group. Test drops were conducted during the period from 25 March to 9 May 1944, when six-ton weights were dropped from the Me 323 V18. The experiments were carried out from altitudes in the 4 000 to 6 000 meter range. Six drops were made, with the parachute opened by delayed action once the weight had reached the desired speed. Further tests were conducted by Zeppelin, with the Me 323 V16 carrying 7-ton weights to the necessary height. On 30 September 1944 the *Gigant* and its crew were lost during one such test. It is not known if testing was resumed at a later date.

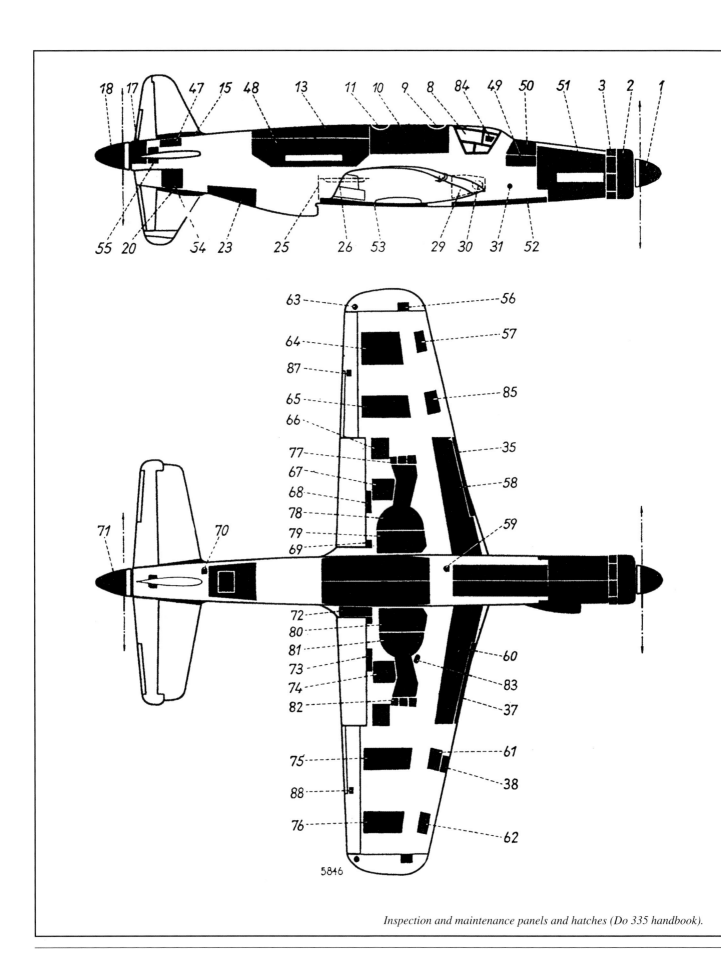

Inspection and maintenance panels and hatches (Do 335 handbook).

5846

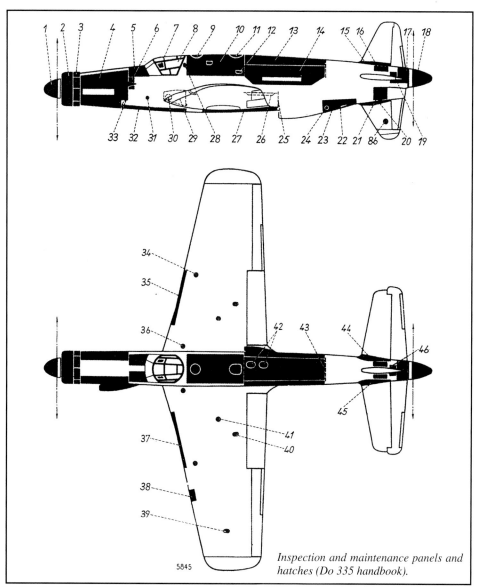

Inspection and maintenance panels and hatches (Do 335 handbook).

5845

Lfd. Nr.	Stück			Benennung und Ort	Zweck
	li	mi	re		
1	—	1	—	Luftschraubenhaube am E-Triebwerk	Verkleidung
2	—	1	—	Strömungshaube am E-Triebwerk	Verkleidung
3	—	1	—	Spreizklappe am E-Triebwerk	Regelung der Kühlluft
4	1	—	—	Haubenteil links für E-Triebwerk	Verkleidung
5	1	—	—	Oberer Deckel zw. Spt. 1 u. 2 links	Waffenwartung
6	1	—	—	Seitl. Deckel zw. Spt. 1 u. 2 links	Wartung
7	1	—	—	Klappfenster in der abwerfbaren Haube links	Sicht bei Schlechtwetter
8	—	1	—	Abwerfbare Haube	Verkleidung
9	—	1	—	Auffülldeckel	über Auffüllkopf
10	—	1	—	Haube über Behälter	Verkleidung
11	—	1	—	Deckel über Nebenbehälterkopf	Zugang
12	2	—	—	Griffklappen	Einstieg
13	—	1	—	Haube über Heckmotor	Verkleidung
14	1	—	—	Seitl. Verkleidung zum Heckmotor	Verkleidung
15	—	1	—	Verkleidung zw. Rumpf u. Seitenflosse oben	Verkleidung
16	1	—	—	Seitl. Deckel zw. Spt. 21 und 22 links	Steuerungswartung

Lfd. Nr.	Stück			Benennung und Ort	Zweck
	li	mi	re		
17	—	1	—	Abschlußhaube hinter Spant 23	Verkleidung
18	—	1	—	Hint. Luftschraubenhaube	Verkleidung
19	1	—	—	Seitl. Deckel zw. Spt. 22 und 23 links	Steuerungswartung
20	—	1	—	Verkleidung zw. Rumpf- u. Seitenflosse unten	Verkleidung
21	1	—	—	Kühlerklappe links	
22	—	1	—	Kühlerklappe zum Ölkühler	Regelung der Kühlluft
23	—	1	—	Schwenkbare Ölkühlerverkleidung	Regelung der Kühlluft
24	1	—	—	Handlochdeckel bei Spt. 18	Verkleidung
25	—	1	—	Mannlochdeckel bei Spant 14	Wartung
26	—	1	—	Abdeckung unter Heckmotor zw. Spt. 11 u. 14 mit Deckel	Gerätewartung Zugang zum Motor
27	1	—	—	Bombenklappe links	
28	1	—	—	Handlochdeckel	
29	—	—	1	Deckel in der Bugradnische	Verkleidung Schmierstoffauffüllung
30	—	—	1	Handlochdeckel in Pos. 29	Wartung
31	1	—	1	Deckel bei Spant 2 links und rechts	Wartung

Lfd. Nr.	Stück			Benennung und Ort	Zweck
	li	mi	re		
32	1	—	—	Bugradklappe links	Verkleidung
33	—	1	—	Deckel über Bugrad-welle	Verkleidung
34	1	—	1	Deckel über dem Auffüllkopf	Auffüllen
35	—	—	1	Abnehmbare Nase zw. Aufmaß 4 u. 14 rechts	Verkleidung
36	1	—	1	Deckel über Neben-behälterkopf	Zugang
37	1	—	—	Abnehmbare Nase zw. Aufmaß 4 u. 14 links	Verkleidung
38	1	—	—	Deckel über Schein-werfer	Verglasung
39	1	—	—	Deckel über Mutter-kompaß	Zugang
40	1	—	1	Handlochdeckel	Hydraulik-behälter
41	1	—	1	Handlochdeckel	Kontrolldecke
42	—	—	2	Deckel in der Motor-haube	Motorwartung
43	—	1	—	Deckel an Spant 18	Geräte-wartung
44	—	—	1	Verkleidung zw. Höhenflosse und Rumpf	Verkleidung
45	1	—	—	Verkleidung zw. Höhenflosse und Rumpf	Verkleidung
46	—	1	—	Oberer Deckel zw. Spt. 22 und 23	Steuerungs-wartung
47	—	—	1	Seitl. Deckel zw. Spt. 21 u. 22 rechts	Steuerungs-wartung
48	—	—	1	Seitl. Verkleidung zum Heckmotor	Verkleidung
49	—	—	1	Seitl. Deckel zw. Spt. 1 u. 2 rechts	Wartung
50	—	—	1	Oberer Deckel zw. Spt. 1 u. 2 rechts	Waffen-wartung
51	—	—	1	Haubenteil rechts über E-Triebwerk	Verkleidung
52	—	—	1	Bugradklappe rechts	Verkleidung
53	—	—	1	Bombenklappe	Verkleidung
54	—	—	1	Kühlerklappe rechts	Regelung der Kühlluft
55	—	—	1	Seitl. Deckel zw. Spt. 22 u. 23 rechts	Steuerungs-wartung
56	1	—	1	Deckel im Randbogen	Montage und Wartung
57	—	—	1	Deckel in der Nase zw. Aufmaß 22 u. 24 rechts	Wartung
58	—	—	1	Deckel unter Kraft-stoffbehälter rechts	Zugang
59	—	—	1	Deckel zw. Spt. 6 u. 7	Außenbord-steckdose u. Kennlicht
60	1	—	—	Deckel unter Kraft-stoffbehälter links	Zugang
61	1	—	—	Deckel in der Nase zw. Aufmaß 16 u. 18 links	Wartung
62	1	—	—	Deckel in der Nase zw. Aufmaß 22 u. 24 links	Wartung
63	1	—	1	Deckel im Randbogen	Montage
64	—	—	1	Deckel zw. Aufmaß 21 und 24 rechts	Montage
65	—	—	1	Deckel zw. Aufmaß 16 und 18 rechts	Montage
66	1	—	1	Deckel zw. Aufmaß 12 und 14	Montage
67	—	—	1	Deckel zw. Aufmaß 8 und 10 rechts	Behälter-einbau
68	—	—	1	Deckel im Flügel-abschluß rechts	Montage
69	1	—	1	Deckel im Flügelab-schluß bei Aufmaß 4	Montage
70	—	—	1	Deckel am Spant 20	Kennlicht
71	—	1	—	Unterer Deckel zw. Spant 22 und 23	Steuerungs-wartung
72	1	—	—	Deckel am Flügel	Einsteigleiter
73	1	—	—	Deckel am Flügel-abschluß links	Montage
74	1	—	—	Deckel zw. Aufmaß 8 und 10 links	Behälter-einbau
75	1	—	—	Deckel zw. Aufmaß 16 und 18 links und 18 links	Montage
76	1	—	—	Deckel zw. Aufmaß 22 und 24 links	Montage
77	—	—	1	Fahrgestellabdeckung bei Aufmaß 12 rechts	Verkleidung
78	—	—	1	Abdeckung der Fahr-gestellnische rechts	Verkleidung
79	—	—	1	Abdeckung am Rad-schacht v. Aufmaß 3 bis 5 rechts	Verkleidung
80	1	—	—	Abdeckung am Rad-schacht v. Aufmaß 3 bis 5 links	Verkleidung
81	1	—	—	Abdeckung der Fahr-gestellnische links	Verkleidung
82	1	—	—	Fahrgestellabdeckung bei Aufmaß 12 links	Verkleidung
83	1	—	—	Handlochdeckel zw. Aufmaß 7 u. 8 links	Drucköl-auffüllung
84	—	—	1	Klappfenster in der abwerfbaren Haube rechts	Sicht bei Schlecht-wetter
85	—	—	1	Deckel in der Nase zw. Aufmaß 16 u. 18 rechts	Wartung
86	1	—	—	Deckel an der unteren Seitenflosse	Wartung des Federbeines
87	1	—	—	Deckel am Querruder zw. Aufmaß 9 u. 10	Lagerzugang
88	—	—	1	Deckel am Querruder zw. Aufmaß 9 u. 10	Lagerzugang

Table 20: Technical Data in Detail – Dornier Do 335 A

1. Fuselage	
Overall length	13.85 m
Maximum fuselage height (nose)	4.30 m (tip of propeller blade)
Maximum fuselage height (tail)	5.00 m
Number of frames	24
Construction	all-metal stressed skin with Z, U and L profiles
Skin thickness	nose engine firewall to forward firewall of rear engine: 1.8 mm
Skin thickness	rear engine firewall to rear radiator housing: 1.3 mm
Skin thickness	from area behind rear radiator to rear propeller: 1 mm
Hoist points:	left and right at Frames 5 and 11
Jacking point:	Frame 20, also Frame 1

2. Wing	
Profile	NACA 23012-635
Overall span	13.80 m
Wing area	38.50 m^2
Maximum depth	3.77 m
Aspect ratio	5.0
Wing loading (at maximum gross weight)	249.3 kg/m^2
Trailing edge sweep	6°
Leading edge sweep	13°
Number of ribs	26 ribs each wing
Spar	box spar
Type of skinning	Dural skinning 1.5 mm thick (forward of spar), wingtips 0.9 mm
De-icing System (electric)	Leading edge and propeller de-icing not installed initially. Pitot de-icing only. (not planned until production aircraft)

3. Ailerons	
Area (both ailerons)	2.50 m^2
Hinges	three
Location	between Ribs 14 and 26
Number of spars	2
Skinning	Dural
Operating range (takeoff and landing assist)	6°-8°
Operating range (up and down)	19° und 21°
Balance deflection	13° - 15°
Trim setting	4° - 6°

Table 20: Technical Data in Detail – Dornier Do 335 A

4. Landing Flaps	
Hinges	three
Location	between Ribs 3 and 14
Area (both flaps)	3.60 m²
Number of ribs	2
Number of spars	-
Skinning	Dural, 0.5 mm
Operating range (takeoff)	29° - 31° (Limit 340 km/h. 30°)
Operating range (landing)	49° - 53° (Limit 270 km/h. 50°)
Actuation	electric-hydraulic in 3 positions

5. Tailplane	
Profile	NACA 23012.5
Wingspan	5.80 m
Area	7.75 m² with fuselage filet, free area 7.63 m²
Number of ribs	12
Number of spars	2
Type of skinning	Dural, 0.9 mm thickness
Incidence range	0 to +5° (set on ground)
Dihedral	2.5°
Elevator	-
Spars	2
Ribs	18
Attachment	3 attachment points
Type of skinning	Dural
Operating range	29-31° (up), 21-23° (down)
Trim tab	9° (up), 11° (down)

6. Fin and Rudder	
Dorsal fin	jettisonable
Profile	NACA 23012.5
Number of ribs	7
Number of spars	2
Type of skinning	Dural skinning, thickness 0.9 mm (wooden nose strip)
Rudder (dorsal)	jettisonable
Attachment	2 attachment points
Number of ribs	10
Number of spars	2
Type of skinning	Dural skinning
Operating range	24-26°
Operating range (rudder balance tab)	15-17° (normal flight

Table 20: Technical Data in Detail – Dornier Do 335 A

Fin area (both fins)	3.08 m² (without root filet)
Ventral fin	jettisonable, with sprung skid
Profile	NACA 23012.5
Number of ribs	6
Number of spars	2
Type of skinning	Dural skinning
Rudder (ventral)	jettisonable, with sprung skid
Attachment	2 attachment points
Number of ribs	7
Number of spars	2
Type of skinning	Dural skinning
Operating range	24-26°
Trim tab	15-19° (normal flight

7. Undercarriage

Main undercarriage wheels (size)	1015 x 380 mm
Oleo (each unit)	1 oil-air shock strut (travel 310 mm, operating pressure 30-34 atm)
Track	5584 mm
Nosewheel	685 x 250 (B-Serie. 840 x 300 mm)
Oleo	oil-air shock strut (shock absorber ELMA 8-2387 A-1, travel 400 mm, operating pressure 13-15 atm)
Range of travel	38° both sides
Wheel base	4.00 m
Cycles	retraction time 18 seconds
	extension time 12 seconds
	emergency activation: max. 1 min.
Tail skid	operating pressure 72-78 atm

8. Oxygen System	1 Type 41 m, 4 spherical bottles (2 in each wing), capacity for ca. 2.5 hours

9. Radio Equipment	FuG 16 Z(Y) with ZVG 16 homing unit, FuG 125 (between Frames 15 and 16, antenna in ventral fin), FuG 25A (between Frames 15 and 16) Training aircraft equipped with EiV 7 intercom

10. Armament

Engine-mounted cannon	1 Rheinmetall MK 103 with 70 rounds (possibly 65 rounds) (between Frames 1 and 2)
Synchronized guns	2 Mauser MG 151/15 (200 rounds per gun) or 2 MG 151/20 (200 rounds per gun) (between Frames 1 and 2)
Internal payload	50-kg, 70-kg, 250-kg or 500-kg bombs (see text (between Frames 7 and 14) for details)
Gunsight	Revi 16 D, other accounts say Revi 16 B and EZ 42 (B-version)

Table 20: Technical Data in Detail – Dornier Do 335 A

11. Armor	two-piece armored ring behind the front propeller, armored boxes for ammunition, 2 armor glass panels in windscreen, 2 armor plates behind and beneath the oil tanks, also 1 armor plate beneath the rear oil cooler
12. Power Plants	
Engines Do 335 A	Daimler-Benz DB 603 A, E, LA, Q
Configuration	12-cylinder inline engine (quick change engines)
Cylinder arrangement	60°, inverted vee
Power and dimensions	see data table for DB 603
Mounting of forward engine	firewall, Frame 1
Mounting of rear engine	between Frames 12 and 16
Oil cooling, forward engine	integrated into annular radiator (9.9 dm2 surface area, later 12 dm2, cooler depth 175 mm)
Oil cooling, rear engine	tunnel cooler with 8.85 dm2 surface area, cooler depth 250 mm (location: Frame 19)
Coolant cooling, forward engine	Integrated in annular radiator (2 x 25.5 dm2, depth 135 mm)
Coolant cooling, rear engine	tunnel cooler with 46 dm2 surface area, depth 135 mm (location: Frame 17)
Coolant volume	nose (90 l), rear (ca. 93 l)
Starter system	Bosch AL SGC 24 DR-2 electric inertia starter
Starter system (later)	gasoline-electric system by Viktoria-Riedel (two-stroke, 10 H.P.)
Ignition system	ZM12 CR 8 twin magneto
Electrical system	24 V, external access between Frames 5 and 6
Power source	one LK 2000/24 R15 generator per engine
Battery	12 GL 3 storage battery (fuselage), all users ca. 6000 Watts (without starter)
13. Fuel System	**no fuel jettisoning**
Type of fuel	B4 aviation gasoline (87 octane) or C3 (96 octane)
Fuselage tank (protected)	1230 l (location: Frame 6 to 11)
Fuselage tank (two-seater)	355 l (protected)
Leading edge tanks (2)	375 l each (aluminum), protected 310 l each

Table 20: Technical Data in Detail – Dornier Do 335 A

Long-range tanks (bomb bay)	volume not known
Long-range tanks (two beneath wings)	in planning only
Type of oil	INTAVA "Rotring"
Tanks 1 and 2 (fuselage)	95 l each (details see text)
	(location: between Frames 6 and 7)

14. Propellers	
Manufacturer	Vereinigte Deutsche Metallwerke
Type	three-blade variable-pitch propeller
Diameter	nose (3.50 m, clockwise rotation), tail (3.30 m, counterclockwise rotation, jettisonable)
Propeller	pitch drive (rear) location: near Frame 20
End limit (gliding position)	nose (8°), rear (7° 15')
End limit (shallowest climb)	nose (12° 25'), rear (12° 25')
Pitch change speed	ca. 2°/sec
Extension shaft (length)	3 m
Extension shaft (mounting)	Frames 21 and 23

15. Weights	design
Equipped weight	7230 kg (8500 kg ab 41. Do 335)
Fuel	1500 kg (1150 kg ab 41. Do 335)
Oil	110 kg (90 kg ab 41. Do 335)
Payload	500 kg (140 kg GM1 ab 41.Do 335)
Crew	100 kg (1 Man)
Ammunition	160 kg (455 kg ab 41. Do 335)
Takeoff weight	9610 kg (10200 kg ab 41. Do 335)

Weights of Various Components from Disassembled Transport Plan for Train and Truck Transport	
Fuselage, without equipment	630 kg
Fin (dorsal)	17 kg
Fin (ventral)	27 kg
Rudder (dorsal)	13 kg
Rudder (ventral)	10 kg

Table 20: Technical Data in Detail – Dornier Do 335 A

Tailplane halves (2)	26 kg
Elevators (2)	11 kg
Wing with undercarriage	840 kg
Main undercarriage halves (2)	255 kg
Nosewheel	150 kg
Power plants (2)	forward 1400 kg, rear 1150 kg
Propellers (2)	each 170 kg (despite different diameters)
16. Performance Data	
Maximum allowable speed with flaps extended	takeoff: 340 km/h
	landing: 270 km/h
Maximum allowable speed with undercarriage lowered	normal extension and retraction times 270 km/h, longer duration 340 km/h
Maximum allowable horizontal speed	climb and combat power at ground level 600 km/h, at altitude of 8700 m 835 km/h
Maximum indicated airspeed in dive	equivalent to 900 km/h at ground level
Maximum speed (ground level)	580 km/h (combat power)
Maximum speed (7000 m)	700 km/h (combat power)
Maximum speed (ground level)	550 km/h (continuous power)
Maximum speed (6600 m)	703 km/h (continuous power)
Time to climb to 1000 m	1.3 minutes
Time to climb to 2000 m	3.0 minutes
Time to climb to 4000 m	6.0 minutes
Time to climb to 6000 m	10 minutes
Time to climb to 8000 m	14.5 minutes
Service ceiling (at 9.5 tons)	9500 m (two engines), 4500 m (one engine)
Service ceiling (at 8.3 tons)	10 700 m (two engines), 6800 m (one engine)
Range	cruising speed of 703 km/h at 6600 m and 500 kg payload: at least 1380 km (with 1350 kg of fuel)
Range	cruising speed of 750 km/h at 8000 m and 500 kg payload: at least 500 km penetration range
Range	at economical cruise of 460 km/h at 6000 m and 500 kg payload: 2150 km (with 1350 kg of fuel)
Landing speed	190 km/h
Takeoff distance	630 m
Landing distance	470 m (with P8 propeller), normal 700 m
Escape system	ejection seat with operating pressure of 120-140 atm, produced by three pressure bottles each with capacity of 2 liters
Crew	1 man (two-seater also 1 student or radar operator)

Camouflage

The topic of camouflage schemes applied to German aircraft of the Second World War is an often contentious one. The information in this chapter was provided by Michael Ullmann, who has conducted extensive research on the subject supported by official documents. His work is therefore among the most credible on the subject and his findings have been compiled in a book by Bernhard & Graefe.

Four different camouflage schemes were used during the course of Do 335 production. These are listed below along with the variants of the Do 335 on which they were used.

- RLM 71 upper surfaces, 65 under surfaces, applied to the Do 335 V1 and V2 prototypes
- RLM 70/71 upper surfaces, 65 under surfaces, applied in splinter scheme to the Do 335 V3, V5, V6, V7 and V8 prototypes.
- RLM 81/82 upper surfaces, 65 under surfaces. This was an interim scheme pending the introduction of the final camouflage scheme and may have been applied to the Do 335 V4. The V9, V11 and V13 were finished in these colors as were the first pre-production (A-0) and production aircraft.
- RLM 81/82 upper surfaces, 76 under surfaces. This camouflage scheme was applied to pre-production aircraft (A-0), production machines (A-1) and various prototypes such as the V10 and V16.

The interim scheme of RLM colors 81 and 82 upper surfaces with 65 under surfaces was definitely non-standard. The use of RLM 65 may have been due to a shortage or because the manufacturer was directed to use up stocks of existing paints.

It should be mentioned that there were two versions of the color RLM 65. One was the classic pale blue color, while the other, seen in 1941, was a more grayish tone. Which was used on the Do 335 has become a subject of much discussion.

The under surface color normally combined with RLM 81/82 upper surfaces was RLM 76. Page 13 of the Do 335 A-0/A-1 handbook specifies colors and the camouflage pattern to be used. Propellers and spinners were painted in the prescribed color of RLM 70. The restored "102" deviates from this standard.

National insignia were applied in a variety of sizes. White *Balkenkreuze* with bar lengths of 1 000 mm were painted on the fuselage of the V1 and V2 prototypes. The V13 prototype and subsequent machines received white *Balkenkreuze* with bar lengths of 1 250 mm. Simplified white *Balkenkreuze* were applied to the upper surfaces of all aircraft. In contrast white-outlined black crosses were applied to the under surfaces of the prototypes with bar lengths of 1 525 mm. A dimension of 1 000 mm was decided upon for pre-production and production aircraft.

Swastikas were applied in white outline form on both sides of the dorsal fin. The bar length of these unpopular symbols was 535 mm.

The so-called *Stammkennzeichen*, or manufacturer's code, was applied in the form of four letters, two in front of the fuselage cross and two behind. One such sequence was VG+PH (240 102). The sequence of letters was applied from left to right. The *Stammkennzeichen* was repeated beneath the wings. There is no reliable information concerning the size and spacing of the letters.

The last three digits of the aircraft serial number were applied on both sides of the dorsal fin in white characters 315 mm high.

The following remarks concern the RLM colors 81 and 82. The aircraft manufacturers received paints from different suppliers, which resulted in different designations for the same RLM color numbers. Messerschmitt designated RLM 81 "brown-violett". Dornier called the color "dark green" while Blohm & Voss described it as "olive-brown".

The terminology applied to RLM 82 was equally confusing. Blohm & Voss and Messerschmitt referred to the color as "light green", while Dornier designated it "dark green" like RLM 81.

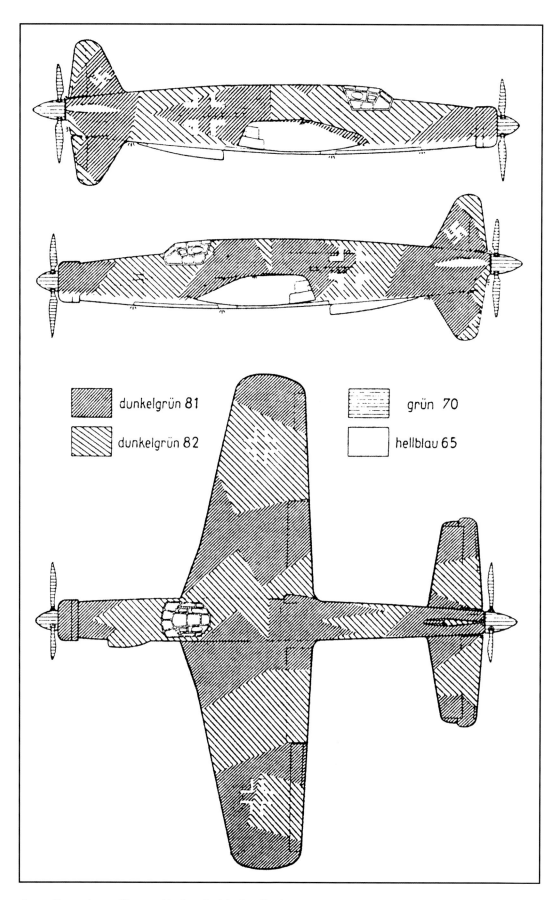

Camouflage scheme, illustrated in Part 0 of the handbook.

dunkelgrün 81

dunkelgrün 82

grün 70

hellblau 65

10. Evolution

The Do 335B Series: Prototypes and Planned Production Versions

A series of prototypes, from the V13 to the V22, was planned for use in the Do 335 B test program. In fact, however, only a few of these machines were completed. Researching this topic proved extremely difficult because of extremely contradictory sources. The following description was compiled using information from the Deutsches Museum.

The B-Series Prototypes

The **Do 335 V13** (*Werknummer* 230 013) served as the prototype for the planned Do 335 B-2 *Zerstörer*. Dimensions were similar to those of the A version with a fuselage length of 13.85 meters and a wingspan of 13.80 meters. Other changes included the instal-

lation of an EZ 42 gunsight, a servo brake system and a modified windscreen. The V13 achieved a maximum speed of 760 km/h. Range was 1 400 km and service ceiling was 11 400 m. The aircraft's maiden flight was scheduled for 31 October 1944, however this was delayed on account of a problem with the main undercarriage. Its participation in the test program was initially limited to taxiing and braking tests. Flight trials began in November and in mid-December 1944 the aircraft began extensive armament trials using the EZ 42 gunsight. The V13 returned to Mengen sometime around mid-March 1945.

The main change compared to the earlier A-series was the addition of two MK 108 cannon installed in the wings. These MK 103s were mounted forward of the main spar with ammunition feeds

The V13 prototype was powered by two DB 603 E engines. The most obvious differences from the Do 335 A were the wing-mounted cannon and revised nosewheel undercarriage.

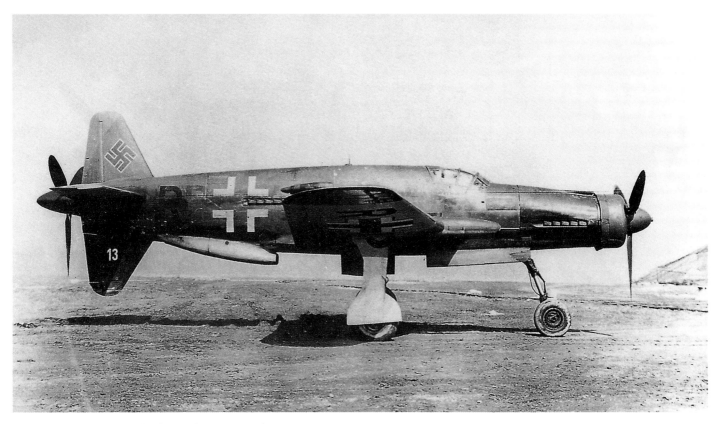

Side view of the Do 335 V13 a few weeks prior to its destruction.

Overall view of the Do 335 V13. The aircraft's extended wing is apparent in this photograph.

Front view of the Do 335 V14, which flew in French colors.

from the fuselage. Fitting these large weapons inside the wing posed a problem which was solved by adopting fork-shaped gun mounts. These enabled the bulk of the weapon to be outside the wing while providing the necessary stability.

The parts of the cannon forward of the leading edge were enclosed in streamlined conical fairings with just the seven-hole muzzle brake visible. Installation of these weapons plus the required ammunition feeds resulted in the deletion of the leading edge fuel tanks. Each MK 103 was provided with 70 rounds of ammunition. A third MK 103 was installed as an engine-mounted cannon firing through the propeller hub.

The next prototype was the **Do 335 V14** (Werknummer 230 014), which largely resembled its predecessor the V13. The increased armament resulted in a reduction in fuel capacity and therefore range. Mounting the weapons in the leading edge of the wing eliminated two 375-liter fuel tanks which had been installed in the wings of A-series aircraft. Each tank was replaced by an ammunition box for seventy rounds of 30-mm ammunition and the associated ammunition feeds. No information has come to light concerning the timing of the aircraft's first flight or the duration of testing. At a later date the aircraft came into possession of the French. It was ferried to Lyon still wearing German markings. The V14 underwent limited testing in French hands, during which it was involved in a landing accident. The aircraft was scrapped in 1949.

The Do **335 V15** was a prototype of the Do 335 B-6 night fighter version. Work on the aircraft, which under construction in Oberpfaffenhofen, was not completed.

The **Do 335 V16** was a prototype of the Do 335 B-1 and B-2. Regrettably little is known about this aircraft. Details concerning its armament and power plants are not known with certainty. The ultimate fate of the V16 is likewise uncertain.

Much more is known about the Do 335 V17. The aircraft bore the *Werknummer* 240 313 and represented the Do 335 B-6, the night fighter variant, whose most obvious feature was the second cockpit for the radar operator. The aircraft's forward power plant drove a Messerschmitt P8 propeller.

The prototype was still under construction when the war ended, however work continued in Mengen under French supervision. The V17 flew for the first time on 2 April 1947, almost two years after the end of the war. Initial results were encouraging and preparations were made to ferry the aircraft to France. Problems with the engines delayed the flight until 29 May 1947. In 1949 the V17 was scrapped.

The **Do 335 V18** was similar to the V17 and was also a prototype of the B-6 night fighter. It is not known if the aircraft was completed by the end of the war.

The **Do 335 V19** was a prototype of the Do 335 B-3 *Zerstörer* version. The aircraft was never completed. The B-3 was to have been powered by two DB 603 LA engines.

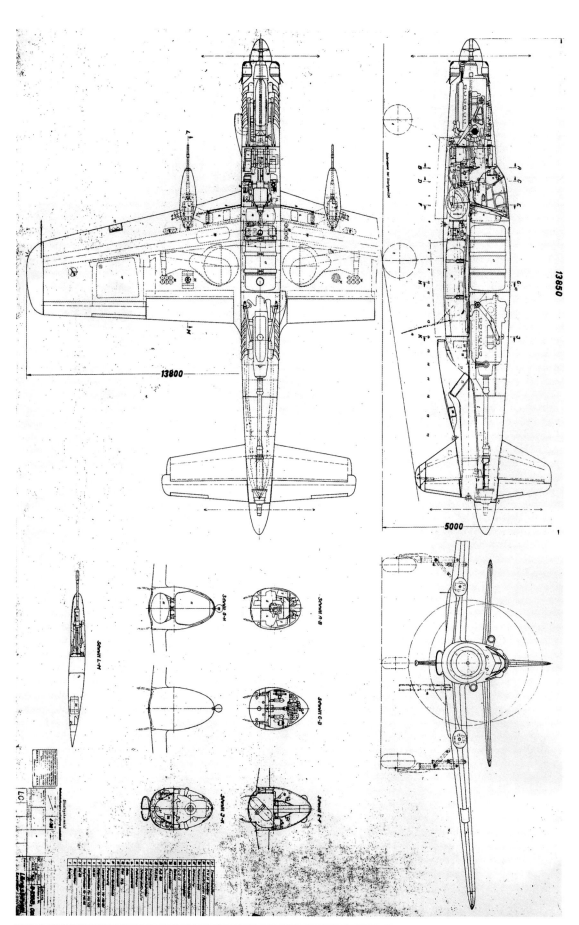

Do 335 B with 13.80-meter wing.

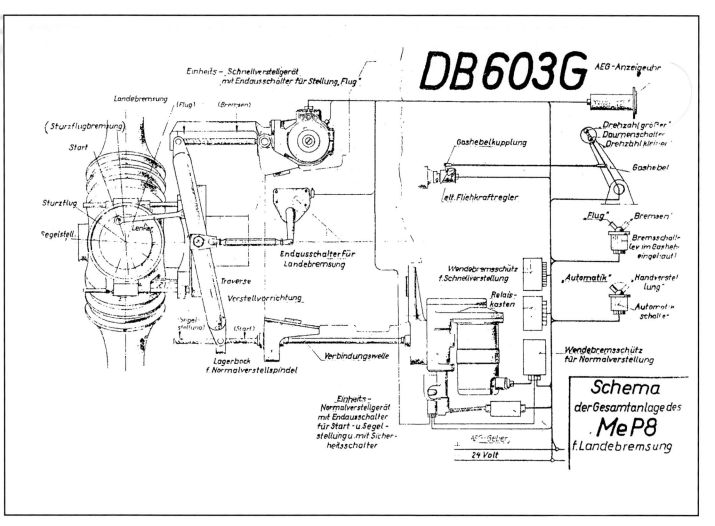

Systems drawing of the P8 propeller.

The **Do 335 V20**, which proceeded no farther than the planning stage, was to have been the prototype of the B-7 night fighter. The V20 was to have been fitted with a wing of increased span of laminar profile. Proposed power plants were two DB 603 LA engines.

The **Do 335 V21** was similar to the V20 but featured a further increase in wing span. It was to have been the prototype for the projected Do 335 B-8.

The **Do 335 V22** was to have been built in the same configuration as the V21. It, too, remained a project only.

As this summary shows, only a few examples of the V13-V22 series of prototypes were in fact completed. Plans to build the Do 335 B in quantity also went unfulfilled. Like so many other promising designs produced by the German aviation industry, the Do 335 never proceeded beyond the experimental stage. Many authors have suggested that this or that weapon could have altered the military situation in Germany's favor, however this is mere wishful thinking. The events in the final act of the chaotic and bloody drama of the Second World War also affected the Do 335, which was represented by only by prototypes, pre-production aircraft and a few examples of the A-1, the first production version. These few machines were used for test purposes and saw no operational service. As described in the preceding account, adverse conditions prevailing in Germany late in the war prevented the aircraft from quickly entering production. This of course affected the Do 335 B program as well. The Dornier company conceived ten versions of the Do 335 B with configurations to meet a wide spectrum of operational roles.

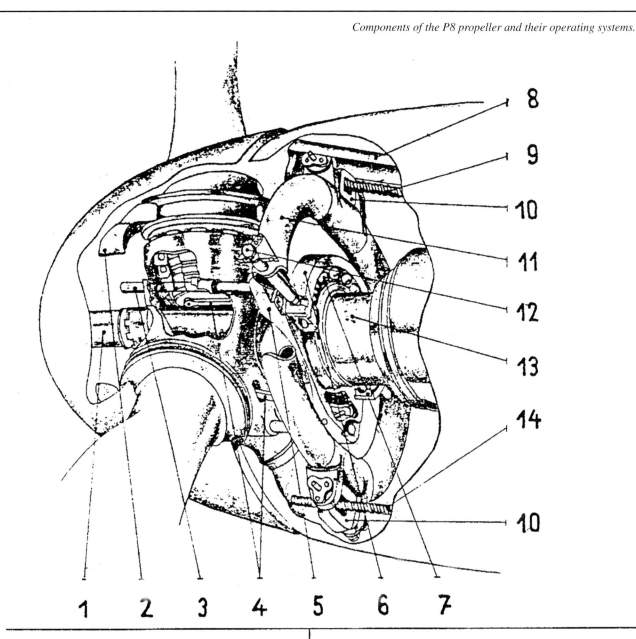

8
9
10
11
12
13
14
10

1 2 3 4 5 6 7

Zur Luftschraube gehörig:	Zur Bedienanlage gehörig:
1 Panzerrohr (Falls Durchschuss)	8 Spindelabstützung
2 Gewichtsausgleich	9 Schnellverstell-Spindel
3 Führungsstangen	10 Spindelmutter mit Kardanlagerung
4 Lenker	11 Traverse
5 Verstellmuffe	12 Traversenbolzen mit Sicherung
6 Verstellring	13 Gleitbuchse
7 Ringschräglager	14 Normalverstell-Spindel

(3-7) Verstellvorrichtung

Do 335 B-0

Designation for the pre-production series of the *Zerstörer* version.

Do 335 B-1

This version was designed as a *Zerstörer*. Standard armament was initially one MK 103 and two MG 151/20 cannon. Later this was increased to three MK 108 and two MG 151/20 cannon. The wing cannon were mounted at a distance of 4 260 mm from the center of the propeller disc. The intended power plants were two DB 603 E-1 engines. The B-series featured a revised nosewheel member, which rotated 45 degrees during retraction into the nosewheel bay. Nosewheel dimensions were 850 x 300.

A total of 25 examples of this type was supposed to be produced by September 1945.

Do 335 B-2

This variant was also a *Zerstörer* powered by two DB 603 E-1 engines. The corresponding prototypes were the Do 335 V13 and V14. This version also carried the heavy-caliber armament consisting of three MK 108 and two MG 151/20 cannon. Seventy rounds were provided for each wing cannon. The ammunition was housed in boxes in the leading edge area of the wing which replaced the auxiliary fuel tanks located there in previous versions.

Do 335 B-3

This was another *Zerstörer* version, of which the Do 335 V19 was the intended prototype. The B-3 was to have been the first to be powered by two DB 603 LA engines. Armament was similar to that of the B-1.

Do 335 B-4

Especially interesting is this projected high-altitude reconnaissance version powered by two DB 603 LA engines. In keeping with its high-altitude role, the B-4 was to be fitted with a wing of increased span developed by Heinkel (18.40 m). Compared to the original wing, a segment 2.30 meters in length was added to each side, increasing wing area to 43 m2. Reconnaissance equipment consisted of two cameras mounted in the bomb bay. Production plans called for 1,866 examples to be completed by May 1946.

Do 335 B-5

This proposed weapons trainer was supposed to be built with the extended wing of the B-4. It was to be powered by two DB 603 E-1 engines. The aircraft was to carry the standard Do 335 armament of one MK 103 and two MG 151/20 cannon.

Do 335 B-6

This was a two-seat night fighter variant with a wingspan of 13.80 m. Compared to the A-6 night fighter, the B-6 was to have a strengthened airframe and a redesigned nosewheel member. Armament of the Do 335 B-6 series was one MK 103 and two MG 151/20 cannon. The selected radar equipment was the FuG 218 G/R Neptun, which was built by Siemens/FFO in various versions. The G/R version combined an air intercept radar and a tail warning radar. The system had a power output of 30 kW (later 100 kW) and six frequencies could be selected in the 158-187 MHz range. The FuG 218 G/R used so-called "Antler" antennas. Other features of this version included a shallower canopy over the radar operator's position and DB 603 E-1 engines with flame-dampers. The Do 335 V17 and V18 were the designated prototypes for this version.

Do 335 B-7

In terms of equipment, this version was largely similar to the Do 335 B-6. The most significant differences were its DB 603 LA power plants and revised wing. The latter was of laminar profile with increased span. The proposed Do 335 V20 was to have been the prototype of the B-7.

Do 335 B-8

This two-seat night fighter was designed with the extended wing with a span of 18.40 meters and area of 43 m2. The B-8 series was also supposed to be equipped with DB 603 LA engines. The designated prototypes for this version were the Do 335 V21 and V22.

Do 335 B-12

This projected version was to have been a two-seat trainer. While in terms of equipment it was based on the A-12, as its designation suggests it was to have used the airframe of the Do 335 B.

The B-series in all its versions would undoubtedly have benefited the units of the *Luftwaffe* greatly. In particular, it would have given the *Luftwaffe* an aircraft which could finally match the performance of the British Mosquito. The A-2 and A-3 could have entered service much earlier, however this did not happen because of the emphasis placed on the Do 335 B program.

11. Production Planning - Illusion and Reality

Optimistic Plans

Like many production plans, in the case of the Do 335 intentions and reality bore little resemblance to one another. The company had to clear many hurdles before large-scale production could begin. Many factors determined whether such an industrial undertaking was a success. The most important points in this regard were the worsening raw materials situation in Germany and the growing shortage of skilled workers, who were being pulled from the factories to be replaced by women, forced laborers and concentration camp inmates. As well there was the growing problem of the Allied bombing offensive, which quickly made drastic inroads into production. Thousands of workers, buildings and installations fell prey to enemy bombs. In spite of all this, in 1944 German aircraft production reached an all-time high as a result of Speer's thorough reorganization of production capacities. The German aircraft industry produced 40,593 aircraft of all types under adverse conditions. Another 7,539 machines were built from January 1945 until the end of the war.

One of Speer's recipes was decentralization, the splitting up and dispersal of existing production facilities. Production went underground in the truest sense of the word. Manufacturers produced their products in inhuman conditions in caves and mines. As well,

companies which had never been involved in the building of aircraft were brought into the organization. Huge bunker factories were in the plans or under construction. All of these ambitious plans were doomed, however, as soon as the Allied air forces began attacking the German transportation system. Strikes against this Achilles heel caused the nation's industrial system to collapse. The situation was further exacerbated by the Allied bombing campaign against the hydrogenation plants and other fuel targets. This was a death blow to the Luftwaffe, which was unable to halt the attacks even with its modern new aircraft.

Of course the situation just described also affected the Do 335 program. Production of the aircraft was slow beginning. Construction work on the original "Anteater", the Do 335 V1, began in spring 1943 in an unspectacular location, a wooden hut in the Manzell factory complex. The aircraft's wings were built in a small town southwest of Ravensburg. Other prototypes were subsequently built in the Dornier-Werk in Friedrichshafen. Definitive examples were the V3 and V6, which were constructed at the Löwental airfield. An unidentified prototype was assembled in a hangar in Lindau-Siebertsdorf. Other prototypes were assembled in a woodworking plant in Ummendorf.

According to an industry delivery plan valid at the beginning of November 1944, production of the Do 335 was to take place in the following stages:

The production pool was to include a total of six factories. To these were added a not inconsiderable number of subcontractors, all of which cannot be identified due to gaps in the records. The following production facilities are known to have been associated with production of the Do 335:

Bad Schachen, Bregenz, Konstanz, Langenargen, Manzell, Meersburg, Mengen, Ravensburg, Risingen, Seeblick, Strohmeyersdorf, Ummendorf and the Enzisweiler Reithalle near Wasserburg, Lake Constance. Fuselage Frames 20, 21, 22 and 23 were produced in Strohmeyersdorf.

For reasons of security, in 1940 the Army High Command introduced a system which assigned a one- to three-letter code to each arms manufacturing plant. This "List of Production Codes for Weapons, Munitions and Equipment" listed all firms involved in war production up to and including 1945.

hmv – Dornier Friedrichshafen
hmw – Dornier Wismar
jbo – Dornier Oberpfaffenhofen
mch – Dornier repair facility Oberpfaffenhofen
jhf – Heinkel Oranienburg

Programs and Planned Numbers

The "Hermann Göring Program", which was created with much effort and soon proved impractical, was adopted toward the end of May 1944.

On 25 October 1944 the armaments staff worked out a new program. In addition to the Do 335, Ta 152 and Ju 388, it contained the jet-powered He 162, Me 262 and Ar 234 plus the rocket-powered Me 163 "Power Egg". This so-called "ideal program" comprised no less than 9,000 units per month.

The "real program" was rather more modest, calling for the production of 5,700 to 6,700 aircraft per month. The difference between the two numbers was due to the individual suitability of the aircraft.

If the He 162 proved a success, the rate of production was to be increased by 1,000 machines per month. Aircraft types and numbers were as follows:

Do 335 (300), Ta 152 (1,500), Ju 388 (200), Ar 234 (300), Me 262 (2,000), He 162 (1,000 – 2,000) and 400 training versions of these types.

In November 1944 the "emergency program" was adopted, this calling for the production of 5,400 units per month. The plan included the Do 335, production of which was to continue into 1946. In detail, the emergency program encompassed the Bf 109 and Fw

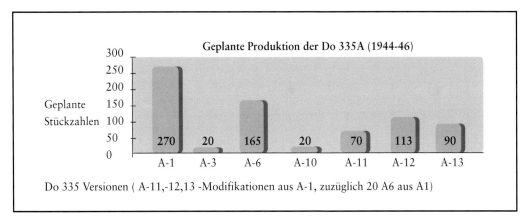

Diagram 1 (planned production of the Do 335 A).

190 (production to continue as a stop-gap measure, after which it would run down), Do 335 (200 Zerstörer and night fighters), Ta 152 (1,000), Ju 388 (200 Zerstörer and night fighters), Ar 234 (200), Me 262 (1,500), He 162 (1,000 to 2,000 for the reasons explained). To these numbers would be added 300 training aircraft. The Me 163 was not included in the program. Officers were appointed to oversee the start of production and deal with production problems as soon as they arose. In the case of the Do 335, Major Bauer was assigned this undoubtedly complex task.

The following is a breakdown of planned deliveries of the Do 335:

• Dornier, Friedrichshafen (1943 to September 1945).
It was anticipated that just 85 aircraft would be produced in the named period.

• Dornier, Munich
From October 1944 to December 1946, a period of 27 months, an average of 86 Do 335s was to be produced.

• Heinkel, Oranienburg
Heinkel's show factory, or at least what was left of it, was to be associated with Do 335 production in a large way. This affected the period from January 1945 to March 1946 with a planned production of 82 Do 335s per month.

• Luther Factory, Brunswick
Production of the Do 335 was planned there from February 1945 to March of the following year. An average output of 54 machines per month was planned.

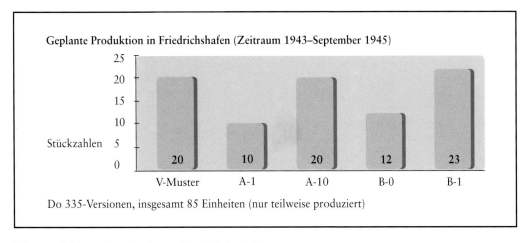

Diagram 3 (planned production at Friedrichshafen).

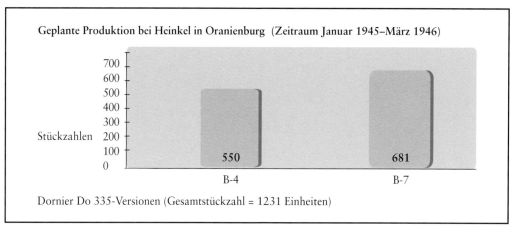

Diagram 5 (planned production by Heinkel in Oranienburg).

The monthly figures named here are of course averages. Production output would have been low at first and then increase. Definitive monthly figures for the various plants are not available and the monthly figures cited here do not take modifications into account. The following graphic illustrates the production plans, arranged by manufacturer.

The Dornier facility at Friedrichshafen would have played the smallest role in production of the Do 335. A much greater role would have been played by Dornier's Munich facility, which was expected to produce 2,313 examples of the Do 335 in five versions.

It should be noted that final assembly of Do 335 A aircraft was done at Oberpfaffenhofen . The Aubing factory (Munich) built fuselages, while the wings came from Ravensburg.

Some production was also to have taken place in Landsberg. An intermediate depot for DB 603 engines and their extension shafts was set up in Weilheim. All components were shipped by rail to Oberpfaffenhofen for final assembly.

Heinkel was also included the production organization. Its Oranienburg facility was scheduled to produce large numbers of B-series aircraft in the period from January 1945 to March 1946. Heinkel's Vienna plant was also supposed to have built twenty examples of the Do 335 A-6, modified from A-1s.

The Luther Werke in Brunswick was supposed to join the production program in February 1945, producing no less than 1,031 A- and B-series aircraft in the period until March of the following year.

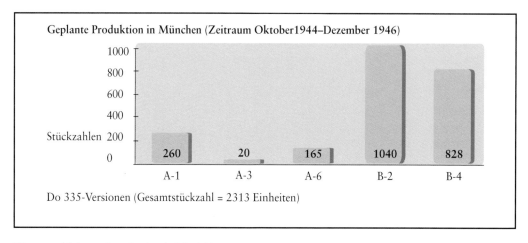

Diagram 4 (planned production in Munich).

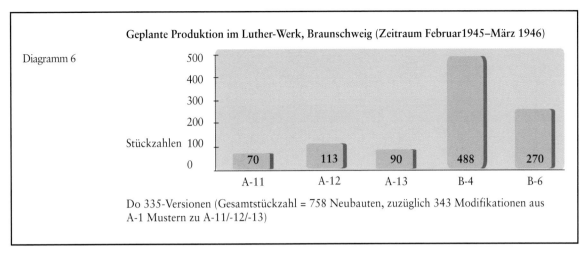

Diagram 6 (planned production in the Luther-Werk, Brunswick).

There were also plans to modify numbers of Do 335 A-1 series aircraft to the standard of the A-11, A-12 and A-13 two-seaters.

One other firm was associated with the Do 335 program. Bachmann and Blumenthal of Fürth was primarily a repair facility, however it was assigned the task of converting 210 examples of the B-2 to B-6 standard. Work was to have taken place from March to August 1945.

Germany's surrender on 6 May 1945 put an end to all of these ambitious plans.

Production – The Reality

Adherence to the production plan was extremely limited in scale. The actual results, a mere handful of "Anteaters", were out of proportion to the amount of work devoted to the type's development, testing and production preparation.

This was due in large part to the course of the war, but also to frequent changes in priorities by the Reichsluftfahrtministerium. *The RLM's indecisiveness affected many programs adversely, including Messerschmitt's Me 262 jet fighter, however that it another story.*

Major *Schreiweis described the working situation at Dornier:*

"One other thing strikes me as worthy of mention: the emergency fighter program, which demanded a supreme effort from the industry, had just been announced, bringing with it a significant increase in the work week. When my men went to work on the production line, I felt that I had to urge them on to perform well as an example to the civilians, telling them that things would not be as easy as they had been in the unit. I was soon told by many of the men that they had never led such a cushy life in the Geschwader as was being led by the Dornier people. The entire subject of the emergency fighter program was shrugged off as mere propaganda."

As to what extent this attitude prevailed in the production centers is a subject for discussion. Many workers had undoubtedly realized the pointlessness of their efforts given the war situation, resulting in little motivation and unsatisfactory results. In addition, the foreign workers and concentration camp inmates were turning to sabotage on a growing scale. Filed hydraulic lines, stripped bolts or metal shavings in the oil system were all effective means. If these went unnoticed, the result could be fatal for an unsuspecting pilot.

Herr Schliebner wrote of the situation at that time:

"The manufacture of aircraft components was scattered all over the Lake Constance area. All of the parts had to be transported to Oberpfaffenhofen. Much materiel had already been destroyed there. The main factory in Manzell was destroyed. In my opinion, it was impossible to restore a normal level of production. The rest and the end are well known."

Three-view drawing.

12. War Prizes

The Do 335 Under Test by the Allies

The Americans

Peace returned when the Americans occupied Oberpfaffenhofen airfield at the end of April 1945. The site's new masters soon began to show an interest in the unusual aircraft they found at the wrecked facility. One GI asked why the aircraft also had a tail propeller, whereupon some joker replied: "Sot it can fly backwards too". In an effort to bring some semblance of order to the devastation inflicted by their bombs, the Americans ordered all remaining Do 335s brought to a central point regardless of their state of construction. This has been documented in a well-known photograph.

"Hour Zero" at Oberpfaffenhofen. Soon after the end of the war these "Anteaters", in various stages of construction, were assembled at a central point.

121 in the company of other uncompleted Do 335s. In the foreground are two American soldiers.

American technical personnel soon began restoring the intact Do 335s to flying condition. Technical problems hampered the effort, as did the American aviation gasoline, which was not to the Dornier's "taste". In June 1945 several experienced German mechanics were placed in charge of the operation under American supervision. There were plenty of aircraft on the field, however only a few proved to be usable. The selection therefore concentrated on a handful of machines whose subsequent histories will be described. Among the survivors was VG+PH, the second pre-production machine, which Hans-Werner Lerche had flown from Rechlin. Also among the aircraft selected was a two-seater bearing the number 112 on its tail. Another machine, which was transferred to the British, was assembled from components and replacement parts. This "Anteater" was to have a very short life in the hands of the RAF, as it was destroyed in a crash in the United Kingdom. The aircraft destined for America had a very different fate. They included the Do 335 flown by Lerche and an example with the Werknummer 241 101*, whose identity cannot be confirmed. This aircraft's trail subsequently disappeared in the USA.

The captured aircraft had to travel a great distance before they were given the opportunity to show what they could do. The first stage of the journey saw them flown from Oberpfaffenhofen via Neubiberg to Cherbourg. The French port was the collecting point for captured aircraft destined for the United States. 240 101 ar-

An "Anteater" next to the remains of an Me 262 and an He 162. Now bearing American markings, its previous identity is hidden by a coat of paint. According to Butler, 240 101 and the positively-identified 102 were shipped to the USA. Other sources claim that the aircraft's Werknummer was in fact 240 161. This discrepancy is most likely due to a printing error.

A Do 335 is lowered onto the deck of the aircraft carrier "Reaper". Note the absent cowling panels over the rear engine.

rived there on 17 June 1945, flown by Flugkapitän *Padell. Standing by to transport the captured enemy aircraft to the USA was the escort carrier* Reaper. *Assembled on deck was the cream of German aviation development.*

The two Do 335s found themselves in good company. The carrier's cargo consisted of 40 German aircraft of every description. On the deck of the escort carrier were four Ar 234 Bs, ten Me 262s, one Ju 88 G, one Ju 388, three He 219s, four Fw 190 Ds, five Fw 190 Fs, one Ta 152 H, three Me 109s, two Bü 181s, one Doblhoff WNF 342, two Flettner Fl 282 helicopters, one Bf 108 and the two Do 335s, Werknummer *240 101 (Reaper No. 8) and 240 102 (Reaper No. 35).*

The aircraft were covered in a protective layer of sealant for their sea voyage. This method or protecting aircraft from the effects of salt water was frequently used in the transport of aircraft to distant theaters.

Once in the USA the captured machines were taken to Newark Army Air Field and transferred to the US Material Command. There the protective cocoons were removed and the aircraft were test flown. Do 335 Werknummer *240 101 was flown from Newark. Jack Woolams, Bell's chief test pilot, encountered problems soon after takeoff. The temperature gauge indicated that the rear engine was*

overheating. Woolham succeeded in getting the German machine back on the ground before the engine caught fire. A report dated May 1946 placed 240 101 at Freeman Army Air Field. The aircraft was 75% repaired there. Work on the engine proceeded through the summer of 1946, however it cannot be determined if the work was completed and further test flights made. Like countless thousands of other aircraft, the "Anteater" was scrapped.

Unfortunately it has not been possible to determine this aircraft's identity with certainty. According to Buttler in War Prizes, it bore the Werknummer *240 101. Smith, Creek and Hitchcock reached a very different conclusion. It is their opinion that the aircraft was* Werknummer *240 161. The confusion may have been due to a printing error, with a zero appearing as a six.*

One of the aircraft's features was a paint scheme of RLM 81/ 82 upper surfaces and RLM 65 under surfaces. The unpainted natural metal panel on the cowling had been mounted in Oberpfaffenhofen. The aircraft's Stammkennzeichen *was VG+PG. German nationality markings were replaced with American stars and the registration FE-1012, which later gave way to T2-1012. The first named prefix stood for "Foreign Equipment". Following a reorganization of American test stations this was changed to "Technical Data Laboratory T-2 Intelligence". Many German air-*

A cocoon of preservative protected the captured aircraft from the effects of salt water while on the deck of the "Reaper". Which of the two "Anteaters" is seen here suspended from a hook will probably never be known.

craft, including Ar 234 and Me 262 jets and Fw 190 D piston-engined fighters were registered for various destinations. The new and often final home for aircraft assigned to the USAAF was Freeman Field of Wright Field.

Others were sent to the US Navy facility at Patuxent River. Among the various German aircraft sent there was Werknummer 240 102. *The "Arrow" was assigned the US Navy registration Bu No 121447.*

Very soon, however, the Do 335 had become "old hat". Retired on 31 August 1947, it languished at Naval Air Station Norfolk until 1961. An entire chapter will be dedicated to this last surviving Do 335. On the subject of ferry flights, Hans Padell wrote of his experiences 29 years later:

"Yes, the war was lost. I had made my way from Berlin to join my wife in Munich. In the morning during breakfast there was a knock at the door. There stood two American MPs. `Come on!' they said. They had caught me, I was a prisoner of war.

But they wanted me for a very different reason. They had discovered that I had been a test pilot on the Do 335. There was only one such machine left. The fastest propeller-driven aircraft in the world.

The bird was at Nuremberg (Roth: the author). I was supposed to fly it to Cherbourg, France for the Amis.

The Captain said to me, 'To prevent you from doing anything stupid, we have removed the compass and two Mustangs will escort you.' That was the fastest American aircraft at the time. A vi-

This photograph was taken at Roth, just prior to the aircraft's flight to Cherbourg. Posing in front of the aircraft are Herr Santer (engine mechanic), Padell and an unidentified Dornier employee. In the background is a huge four-engined Ju 290.

sual flight of 400 kilometers the Captain told me. I laughed out loud. 400 kilometers? The Do 335 could do 700 easily. I brashly offered a wager: 'I can fly faster than you on one engine!'

The Captain said, 'OK, 20 cartons of Camels.' I needed both engines to get airborne. But then, at a height of 500 meters, I switched off the rear engine. After half an hour both Mustangs were nowhere to be seen. I had lost them!

It took me 1 hour and 40 minutes to cover the 900 kilometers. I never had any idea of trying to escape, I just wanted to show them. When I arrived at Cherbourg I had to wait twenty minutes for my Captain to arrive.

He clapped me on the shoulder and said, 'OK, you won.' Then he gave me the cigarettes, a treasure at that time. A cigarette cost up to 6 Marks."

*Major Albert Schreiweis (*Kommandeur *of EK 335) wrote:*

"Padell was my Leutnant, engineer, an expert in aircraft construction. He was assigned to me for testing and development of the Do 335, which meant that he remained at the Mengen testing station when we went to the night fighters. He flew the Do 335 to Cherbourg in preparation for shipping to the USA. We were very much offended by that at the time."

This previously unpublished photograph was taken n Roth near Nuremberg. Hans Padell and an American captain pose in front of the Do 335. Roth was an en route stop on the way to Cherbourg.

Werknummer 240 112, a Do 335 A-12, in British markings at Farnborough.

Do 335 240 112 shortly after its completion in February-March 1945. Assembled in front of the aircraft are the men who built it plus Hans Padell (wearing hat).

The British

The British also came into possession of a significant amount of captured equipment. Most of the captured German aircraft were extensively tested at the British experimental station at Farnborough. The following examples of the Do 335 were flown there:

Do 335 A-12, Werknummer 240 112

The Do 335 A-12 was a two-seat training variant and this example was captured by American forces at Oberpfaffenhofen. German personnel restored the aircraft to flying condition. Then, on 7 Sep-

tember 1945, a crew from the Royal Air Force took charge of 240 112. At that time the machine wore American insignia. The only reminder of its former owners was its German camouflage finish. The nose cowling, a replacement unit, was natural metal. The Dornier was flown from Oberpfaffenhofen to Reims via Neubiberg and Strasbourg. Final checks were carried out and the next day Squadron Leader McCarty took off for Farnborough. After its arrival, the aircraft was given a complete overhaul and British markings were applied.

Testing of "112" by the British did not commence until 1 October. The aircraft then formed part of a display of captured Ger-

Another photo of 112 at Oberpfaffenhofen. The aircraft now wears British roundels and the registration AM 223.

112 after the end of the war. Note the start trolley on rims with no tires. (A. Schliebner)

man equipment. Testing resumed on 15 January 1946, however two days later the aircraft was destroyed in a crash. The reason for the crash was severe overheating of the rear engine, which led to an engine fire. The aircraft's pilot, Group Captain Alan F. Hards, died in the crash.

Do 335 A-1 (British Serial AM 225)

This "Anteater" is believed to have been an A-1. Like the above-described two-seater, it was captured by the Americans at Oberpfaffenhofen. The aircraft was unpainted except for areas of the cowling and tail.

On 7 September 1945 the aircraft was ferried to Neubiberg by an American pilot. There a British pilot took charge of the machine and flew it to Reims. There it was grounded by technical problems. After the completion of repairs and the necessary maintenance test flights, on 9 and 12 December 1945, the Dornier took off for Merville.

Further problems developed en route and the pilot made a wheels-up landing at Merville which resulted in structural damage. The pilot was not hurt.

This Do 335 A-1 bears the markings of the Royal Air Force plus the registration AM 225. In the background is a Piper L-4 of the American armed forces. It is not known for certain where this photograph was taken. (A. Schliebner)

This photograph depicts an aircraft allocated to the British during an en route stop at Neubiberg. The engine cowling is finished in a splinter camouflage scheme. The tail area is also camouflaged. Most of the rest of the aircraft, however, is unpainted. The machine wears American insignia. Visible in the background is the tail of a Mustang.

Each enemy aircraft captured by the British received British nationality markings and an Air Ministry number.

Examples:

AM
AIR MIN (plus three-digit registration number)
AIR MINISTRY

The French

Even the "poor relative" among the Allies, recently liberated France, made use of the technology of its defeated foe. A considerable number of aircraft which had formerly served with the Luftwaffe *were taken on strength by the new French Air Force. As well, the French used German-designed aircraft built in France during or after the war. Most common were the Arado Ar 96, Fieseler Storch, Siebel 204 and Junkers Ju 52. The latter was produced in France as the A.A.C. 1. More advanced German types such as the Ar 234, Heinkel He 162 and Messerschmitt Me 262 were used for test purposes. Dornier's contribution to this research effort was two Do 335s.*

Do 335 V14 (Werknummer 230 014)

The war ended in Mengen toward the end of April 1945. French units occupied the airfield and among other types of aircraft discovered several examples of Dornier's "Anteater".

The fourteenth prototype was among the Do 335s captured at Mengen. It was subsequently restored to flying condition by German and French personnel. A French pilot was then ordered to fly the machine to Lyon. The aircraft still bore full German war paint and photographs prove that it bore the code RP+UQ.

In Lyon the aircraft was checked over and then repainted overall in an olive gray color. French roundels were applied on the wings and fuselage, while the French flag was applied on both sides of the vertical fin.

On 8 August 1945 the aircraft was involved in a landing accident. Colonel Badré was on approach in the V14 when the aircraft began to vibrate badly and smoke filled the cockpit. Badré immediately shut down both engines and put the machine down hard. The right main tire blew and the aircraft, now without hydraulics or brakes, slid down the runway. To make matters worse, Badré collided with a parked B-26, resulting in damage to the airframe. The Do 335 underwent a lengthy spell of repairs, after which it was

The V14 during testing in Brittany.

destined for the test center in Brittany. Prior to handover, however the aircraft underwent ground checks by SNCASO. Based on the results of these, the test center took charge of the aircraft on 3 June 1946. In Brittany the machine was once again checked out carefully. Taxiing trials did not begin until 24 February 1947.

Technical problems delayed the first flight until 13 March 1947. In may of the same year the V14 completed further test flights, which resulted in further repair work. Not until 21 November 1947 were the tests resumed. These continued until January 1948, when testing was again interrupted for repairs.

The "Anteater" took off on its last flight in June 1948. Altogether the machine had logged just 11 hours and 25 minutes in French hands. The following year the Do 335 V14 was scrapped.

Do 335 V17, Werknummer 240 313*

This Do 335 was also captured by French troops in Mengen and was completed under their supervision. Not until 2 April 1947 was the aircraft reported flyable. It was supposed to be flown to France two days later, however mechanical trouble prevented this.

German personnel replaced the engine which was the source of the problem, however the second engine also failed. Not until it, too, had been replaced did everything function smoothly.

On 29 May 1947 Capitane Roger Receveau took off from Mengen in the V17. Forty-five minutes later he landed at the Brittany test center. Following a mechanical inspection of the aircraft. Tests began immediately, however this machine also suffered problems. On 27 November 1948 the right main undercarriage collapsed while taxiing and the rear fuselage sustained considerable damage. This Do 335 subsequently suffered the same fate as the V14.

There is also some question concerning the aircraft's Werknummer. *According to Butler, author of* War Prizes, *it was 240 017.*

Herr Stemmer, an eyewitness from that time, wrote of this:

"At that time we were just a handful of specialists from the prototype construction department. We therefore had to support and assist one another in all our activities and everyone had to share in the responsibilities. My special field was undercarriage and power plant. Final checks were made by myself and a colleague who had experience in this area.

The initial flights were not made by our pilots, on account of insurance concerns and the imminent change from the Reichsmark to the Deutschmark.

At the Mengen airfield our pilots briefed the French pilots and us on takeoff and landing maneuvers. We still had problems, especially with the rear engine, caused by faulty installation in those confused times.

We were no longer able to obtain special tools from Daimler-Benz, which meant an engine change. The engines were handled gingerly and we slowly worked our way up to rated power. We had to overcome considerable difficulties with the aircraft at that time. Difficult to imagine today.

Special attention had to be paid to the barometrically-controlled large spring-mounted impeller for the supercharger drive. The Do 335 was heavily damaged while under test and the maintenance team was not required to move to the Brittany test field in France."

Herr Stemmer also described a very interesting apparatus associated with the Do 335:

"At that time they carried out the first installation of a flight vibration system. A unbalance shaft with drive was installed in mid-fuselage, then a shaft extension to the outer wings, left and right, to the outermost wing rib, and to an unbalance shaft which terminated at the wingtips. When the system was started up on the ground it caused the experts great concern, as they feared that in flight the aircraft might have to be sacrificed in an extreme case. The system was removed and was later supposed to be installed in a production aircraft of another type."

Tests in the Soviet Union?

This is a question which may yet be answered as the archives of the former Soviet Union are opened. At present there is no proof that examples of the Do 335 were captured and tested by the Soviets. It is known, however, that the Soviets did come into possession of a wide range of German aircraft, which they tested extensively, both propeller-driven and jet types.

The only published reference to the Do 335 appears on Page 45 of Under the Red Star *by Carl-Frederick Geust. According to Geust, two Soviet officers named Ankudinov and Tishenko discovered a Do 335 in a hangar at Oranienburg in April 1945. The aircraft was apparently a night fighter as it had wing-mounted radar antennas. Regrettably this information cannot be confirmed, not is it known for sure whether a flyable example of the Do 335 fell into Soviet hands at Rechlin.*

13. Look Back - The Life Story of an Aircraft

Do 335 A-0, Werknummer 240 102

Do 335 A-0, Werknummer 240 102

This chapter concerns itself with the last survivor of an otherwise extinct species of aircraft, one whose survival is due to good fortune. The subject is Werknummer 240 102, the second pre-production machine, which left the assembly line in the summer of 1944. The date of its first flight is unclear, however it is known that Hans Dieterle began flight testing 240 102 on 30 September.

In the month that followed the aircraft completed several flights. After completion of acceptance tests Dornier was instructed to ferry 240 102 to the E-Stelle Rechlin. The first official mention of the aircraft there is in a weekly report dated 20 November 1944. After initial tests the machine was assigned to Department E4 for radio signals technology. Similar trials had been carried out with the Do 335 V3 until that aircraft was damaged in a crash-landing in No-

vember 1944. The third prototype was capable of being repaired, however 240 102 took its place in the test series, as confirmed by several weekly reports from the period 18 November to 23 December. The report for the period 4 to 9 December reported that repairs to the V3 were not yet complete. This reference was to the removal of the loop antenna and its installation in "102". The next report (11/12 – 16/12/1944) reported satisfactory ground readings for the loop antenna of the FuG 16. Readings for the antenna placed in the dorsal fin were less satisfactory. As well, there were still reports of the DF loop (FuG 16 Z) "squinting" rearwards. This earned the makers of the FuG 25 a radio system harsh criticism.

Quote: "It is incomprehensible that a leading firm should dare offer such a design." Two further reports (18/12 – 23/12/1944) reported the following incidents. One spoke of a delay in testing caused by a nosewheel repair and compass swing. The master compass

102 with both engines running. (A. Schliebner)

was relocated from its usual and largely trouble-free position in the wing to the area of the rear engine. This location contained more interference-causing metals than the port wing, which affected readings.

Another report in the same period spoke of the ending of ground measurements with the loop antennas and DF loop. The latter was certified with a "squint error" of 30° to the rear. The report attributed this to the proximity of the air intake. VG+PH was last mentioned in the weekly reports toward the end of December 1944. The war had ended its final, bloody stage. It was now just a matter of weeks before the Soviets took Rechlin. In the face of this hopeless situation, Rechlin became a beehive of activity in an effort to leave as little as possible to the enemy. These efforts undoubtedly resulted in much valuable material being irretrievably lost to historians. By April 1945 the situation had become acute. The evacuation of men and materiel to the west was in full swing. This atmosphere of departure also affected the fate of 240 102, resulting in efforts which ultimately saved the aircraft and possibly its pilot. He was Hans Werner Lerche, a Rechlin test pilot who specialized in evaluating enemy aircraft. This was a difficult task, as the Germans had no pilot's notes for or experience with these machines. A pilot who had successfully flown no fewer than 125 German and Allied aircraft types was undoubtedly the right man to ferry this exotic aircraft home. Lerche was ordered to deliver Do 335 A-0 240 103 to Oberpfaffenhofen in Bavaria. A flat tire prevented this, however.

240 102 was serviceable and took its place. The aircraft's odyssey began on the evening of 20 April 1945, when VG+PH lifted off from Rechlin's runway for the last time.

Using the state autobahn as a reference point, Lerche initially flew over Berlin, then destroyed Dresden, to Prague, where he landed at approximately 2020 hours. On the airfield Lerche found he had two obstacles to overcome: the Do 335 had developed an undercarriage problem and the necessary high octane fuel was in short supply. Hard to find luxury items smoothed the way. Lerche used cigarettes to motivate the ground personnel to take care of the undercarriage problem. The precious fuel was also forthcoming. Then the "weather god" intervened, initially preventing Lerche from continuing his flight home. After two days of tense waiting, on the morning of 23 April Lerche was able to take off in conditions of rain and low cloud. His route took him over occupied Czech territory and the Bavarian Forest. Suddenly tracers reached out for his machine. Lerche could not tell for sure where the fire was coming from. Whether he was fired on by light flak or an enemy aircraft will never be known. Lerche applied full power and took evasive action. Soon afterwards Munich, the "Capital of the Movement", came into sight. He flew over the city at high speed and headed for the nearby towns of Augsburg and Fürstenfeldbruck. Lerche began an approach to land at Lager Lechfeld, but he could not have chosen a more inopportune time, as an air raid warning had just been

This photo of 102 was taken on the grounds of the Patuxent River test center.

sounded. In seconds enemy fighter-bombers began sweeping over the field, torching a dozen well-camouflaged German machines. Lerche's Do 335 was completely exposed, however it escaped intact. That evening he departed on the last leg of his so far successful journey. With little faith in the troublesome undercarriage, Lerche took off for Oberpfaffenhofen and left the gear down. To any marauding enemy fighter this would be a sign of surrender. After a brief flight Oberpfaffenhofen came into view. The flight and landing were completed without incident.

Immediately after landing, Lerche's "Anteater" was towed to the relative safety of the airfield perimeter. Several days after Lerche's arrival American armored units reached Oberpfaffenhofen. The war was over. Lerche was made a prisoner of war, while his aircraft fell into American hands. Soon after their arrival all symbols of the Nazi past were eliminated. The swastikas on the aircraft's tail were completely overpainted, while only remnants of the wing and fuselage crosses and manufacturer's code VG+PH were left visible. Then the Americans painted their own insignia on the machine. The only external clue to the aircraft's original identity was the number 102, the last three digits of the aircraft's Werknummer, *which remained on both sides of the dorsal fin. Before the Dornier reached the homeland of its new owners, it would first have to cover thousands of nautical miles on the deck of an aircraft carrier. Before the start of this journey the aircraft was checked thoroughly and then flown to Cherbourg with another "Anteater".*

The aircraft's last flight in Europe began in Oberpfaffenhofen. En route stops were made at Neubiberg and Roth before the Do 335 landed at the French seaport. There the Americans had set up a large collection point for captured enemy aircraft. The aircraft were cocooned in a protective layer of sealant and tied down to the deck of the carrier Reaper.

Soon after their arrival in the USA, the two Dorniers were separated. The other Do 335, which has yet to be identified with certainty, was assigned to the USAAF, while "102" went to the Navy. Both services flight-tested their captured machines. Their interest satisfied, the Americans' interest in the high-tech German aircraft waned and they were left to languish. Over time the trails of most of these aircraft disappeared, including the second "Anteater" brought to the USA. Its trail can only be followed until 1947, while all information concerning its subsequent fate consists of rumor. One logical explanation was its transfer to one of the many American military "bone yards" and subsequent scrapping. Without proof, however, this is mere speculation. No one though of preserving these treasures for posterity. With few exceptions these aircraft fell victim to the smelting furnace, to be reborn as frying pans or other household implement. Some of the Luftwaffe aircraft have survived, however. At the Silver Hill Depot, for example, types such as the He 219, Ju 388, Go 229 and Ta 152 await restoration. In the case of "102" fate was somewhat kinder. For many long years the aircraft languished out of doors. When the US Navy was finished with "102" it was transferred to the Smithsonian Institute. In the late 1940s the Smithsonian had little interest in showing a German aircraft in its hallowed halls, and so this rare machine was stored in a depot for many long years. Lerche's "Anteater" had to wait a long time, until aviation enthusiasts from Germany tried to persuade the Smithsonian to restore the aircraft. The museum declined, however, as it had more pressing restoration projects to deal with. It responded with a proposal for the Do 335 to be restored in Germany.

The last "Anteater" decades later. This photo from Silver Hill shows the aircraft in poor condition. In the background is a Grumman Bearcat.

102 in the open at Silver Hill in the company of a Northrop Black Widow and a Chance-Vought Corsair. (Der Flieger, issue 5/1976)

The necessary agreement with the Smithsonian was concluded. The big day for all involved came on 10 October 1974. Packed into the belly of a Lufthansa cargo jet, the "Anteater" departed New York for its Bavarian homeland. On arrival at Rhein-Main airport the Dornier was transferred to two Transalls of the Bundesluftwaffe, and on 26 October the aircraft was flown to the airfield from where it had begun its odyssey. The circle was complete after thirty years! As the accompanying photos show, the aircraft was in desperate condition. Nevertheless, an initial inspection by Dornier revealed that the tail jettisoning system and the brake and fire-extinguisher systems were fully functional. During cleaning the Dornier technicians removed several bird's nests and a dozen American mice. Like most restoration jobs, the Do 335 required a great deal of work.

Years on inadequate storage had left their mark. Several thousand volunteers worked long hours on the project. The cost of re-

Left: *The precious cargo in the belly of a Lufthansa jumbo jet. (Der Flieger, issue 5/1976)*

storing the last Do 335 was considerable, being equivalent to the cost of a new Do 335 in the 1940s.

The Dornier was restored to original condition, with even the original cockpit instruments retained. The aircraft was painted in RLM 81/82 and 65. Regrettably, the propellers and spinners of the restored aircraft were painted black instead of the correct RLM 70, however this in no way detracts from the outstanding efforts of the restorers. As a final touch, "102" was fitted with an original set of Dunlop tires. The job was completed on 10 December 1975.

The "Anteater" made its debut the following year at the Hanover air show from 1-5 May 1976. That same month the aircraft went on display at the Deutsche Museum in Munich. Regrettably, the aircraft was only on loan until 1985. Subsequent negotiations delayed the return of the aircraft until December 1989.

The Dornier was returned to the United States and photographs which appeared on the internet in 1997 show that it is in disassembled condition in the Silver Hill Depot. Happily, a rumor that the Dornier was located on a children's playground with a smashed windscreen proved to be just that. The fact is that the aircraft is at Silver Hill.

The last stage from Frankfurt to Oberpfaffenhofen was made by Transall (50+52). (Der Flieger, issue 5/1976)

Completely stripped of paint, the aircraft during restoration work at Oberpfaffenhofen. (Der Flieger, issue 5/1976)

102 during its second roll-out. (Der Flieger, issue 5/1976)

This series of photographs depicts the restored aircraft from various angles.

Photograph of the cockpit, once the workplace of Hans-Werner Lerche.

The last surviving example of the Do 335 at Oberpfaffenhofen.

Hans Dieterle (left) completed the first flight in the V1 in October 1943. Next to him is Hans-Werner Lerche, Rechlin test pilot, who ferried 102 to Oberpfaffenhofen shortly before the end of the war.

Hans Dieterle and H.W. Lerche remember the past. (Der Flieger, issue 5/1976).

For many years the "Anteater" was one of the prize exhibits of the Deutsches Museum. (C. Vernaleken)

Help may be on its way, however. Extremely information suggests that a display hall is to be built for the aircraft stored at Silver Hill. According to information on the internet, the "Dulles Center" is to become a reality in 2003. This does mean, however, that is extremely unlikely that the Dornier will ever leave the USA again. Perhaps a political solution is the answer.

Hans Werner Lerche was not the only one to leave Rechlin in a Do 335, however. On 26 April 1945 engine specialist Dipl.-Ing. Heinz Fischer took off for Switzerland. As he possessed municipal citizenship in the city of Bern, he elected to fly to Dübendorf airfield near Zurich instead of to Bavaria. Probably assuming that he was over Swiss territory, Fischer activated the aircraft's ejection seat at a height of 300 meters. The seat failed to fire, however, and Fischer was forced to abandon the machine by the conventional method. To his dismay, however, he came down in the Vosges, 60 kilometers from the Swiss border. His "Anteater" crashed and burned in mountainous terrain.

If Fischer had landed safely at Dübendorf, as Mutke did with his Me 262 (now on display in the Deutsche Museum), another Do 335 would have been saved for posterity. The Swiss might have given the aircraft to the Deutsche Museum, as they did with the Me 262.

Time to say goodbye again: the "Anteater" during disassembly at the Deutsches Museum. (H. Schuller)

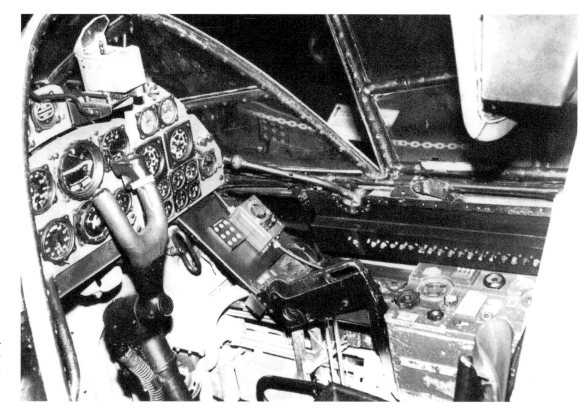

This photo, taken at Silver Hill in 1998, shows that the instrument panel is still complete. (C. Vernaleken)

Taken several years later, this photo shows that several instruments are already missing. In the foreground is the control column with pivoting fork grip. (C. Vernaleken)

102 at the Silver Hill Depot. Jens Kollehn took this sad photo in 1998.

14. Exotics

Development of the Do 335 "Twins"

Examination of Various *Zwilling* Designs

The twin-fuselage or Zwilling configuration was undoubtedly one of the most curious conceived in the hundred-year history of aviation. While not the exclusive domain of German aircraft designers, the twin-fuselage concept was more widely used by them than elsewhere. Heinkel employed the twin fuselage configuration for its He 111 Z glider tug, which was designed specially for the huge Me 321. There were also plans to develop the type for use as a strategic reconnaissance aircraft and long-range bomber. Messerschmitt also proposed twin-fuselage versions of the Bf 109 and its successors. The He 111 Z was the only German twin-fuselage design to come to fruition, however, and Heinkel had the most experience in the field. Plans for a twin-fuselage version of the Do 335 progressed no farther than the drawing board.

The Do/He 635 (P.1075)

The idea for such an aircraft based on the Do 335 had its origins in a specification issued by the RLM in late 1943. The resulting study proposed a long-range reconnaissance aircraft which was to be used in the maritime reconnaissance and U-boat cooperation roles. A corresponding design took shape on the drawing boards of the Heinkel company and was designated P.1075. As mentioned earlier, Heinkel-Vienna had been placed in charge of preparations for production of the night fighter versions of the Do 335 B. Heinkel also developed the extended-span wing of the high-altitude versions of the Do 335. During an RLM conference in November 1944 Junkers was instructed to construct thirty aircraft. The following extract from conference minutes of the Hauptausschuss fur Flugzeugbau *dated 1 November 1944 provides some details of the production plans:*

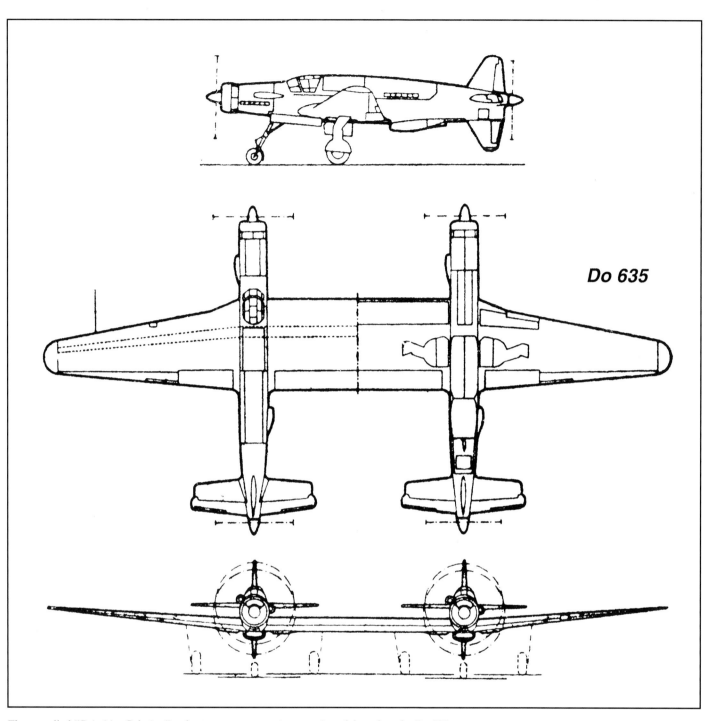

Do 635

The so-called "Primitive Solution", a long-range reconnaissance aircraft based on the Do 335.

"DWM will deliver sixty fuselages from the B-2/B-4 series to Junkers for thirty twins, provided the Chef TLR issues this requirement to the HAF. Metallbau Offingen will construct large wings for these twins. If necessary, the fuselages for the twins will be taken from the B-0 series by DWF instead of the B-2 series and the wings will be stockpiled."

The Dornier-Heinkel configuration was the simpler solution, but compared to the Junkers version it was much more of an improvisation. As described, the Dornier-Heinkel solution was an aircraft with standard production fuselages. The cruciform tails were not joined, and the only new component was a wing center-section joining the two fuselages. The outer wings were B-series components. Proposed power plants were four DB 603 E-1 engines. The undercarriage was taken from the Do 335 in order to avoid delays in the project. In terms of weight, ease of servicing and, not least, expenditure of materials, it was certainly not the last word. The aircraft was designed as a twin-seater. The pilot sat in the port fuselage, the radio operator in the starboard. The second cockpit was equipped with a duplicate set of controls in case of emergency. Both cockpits were to be pressurized and equipped with ejector seats. As the aircraft was designed for extremely long flights of up to twelve hours, the crews would face extreme mental and physical stresses. Given the limited space available, such missions would have been pure torture. These thoughts were expressed in a weekly report from Rechlin.

Technical Data for the Do/He 635

Wingspan	27.43 m
Length	13.85 m
Height	5.0 m
Gross weight	32 900 kg
Maximum speed	725 km/h at 6 400 m
Range	7 600 km
Power plants (4)	DB 603 E-1
Output	1,800 H.P. each
Crew	2

Junkers Ju 635

In the autumn of 1944 Junkers was instructed to continue development. Compared to the relatively primitive Dornier-Heinkel design, Junkers developed a much more versatile aircraft. While it was based on the Do 335, in several areas Junkers took a different path. The fuselage was stretched to 18.50 m. The port cockpit was designed to accommodate the pilot and radio operator, while the second cockpit housed a co-pilot. The second cockpit was smaller and equipped with a shallow canopy. The wing was a completely new design. This time-consuming measure was made necessary by the adoption of a revised undercarriage based on components taken from the Ju 352. The only components retained from the Do 335 were the two nosewheel members. The revised undercarriage in-

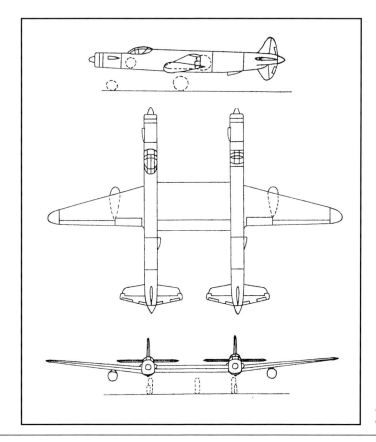

The more versatile design produced by Junkers was designated the Ju 635.

cluded two mainwheel units which retracted rearward into fuselage bays abeam the wing trailing edge. Plans also included provision for a third Ju 352 which could be attached to the wing center-section for takeoffs in overloaded condition. After takeoff the oleo would be jettisoned and returned to earth by parachute. The oleo was a single-wheel unit with oil-air damping. One relatively unique feature of this unit was the presence of two torque links mounted on the front and rear of the oleo. The strengthened version, intended for the Ju 352, was fitted with a 1440 x 520 tire. The original design called for a 1320 x 480 tire.

The intended power plants were four DB 603 E-1 engines, each producing 1,800 H.P. for takeoff. Given the aircraft's intended role, four engines required a considerable amount of fuel, and the design included wing, fuselage and external tanks. The redesigned wing housed two fuel tanks in each outer section, while the center-section contained four more tanks. As well, each fuselage housed three fuel tanks. Total fuel was bolstered by two jettisonable 300 to 1 000 liter tanks beneath the wings. The Ju 635 thus had a maximum fuel capacity of 15 846 liters. Fuel distribution was as follows:

- Two tanks in each outer wing with 312 and 541 liters.

- Four tanks in the wing center-section, 2 x 1915 liters and 2 x 1249 liters.

- Six fuselage tanks with 2 x 541 liters, 2 x 1665 liters, 1 x 916 liters (port) and 1 x 484 liters (starboard).

- Two external tanks up to 1 000 liters.

- Four 235-liter oil tanks in the fuselage.

- Two tanks in the outer wings for the MW 50 system, each holding 174 liters.

There was another Zwilling design with a total fuel capacity of 17 530 liters (including two 1 200-liter drop tanks). By way of comparison, the Fw 200 F, a long-range reconnaissance aircraft with

Table 22: Technical Data Ju 635

Wingspan	27.45 m
Length	18.50 m
Height	4.98 m
Wing area	80.50 m²
Depth of wing center-section	6.49 m
Distance between fuselages	7.98 m
Gross weight	33 000 kg
Maximum speed	720 km/h at 6 500 m
	539 km/h at sea level
Range	7 982 km
Service ceiling	11 000 m
Power plants (4)	DB 603 E-1
Output	1,800 H.P.
Equipment (in port or	one Rb 50/30 and one 250-l
starboard fuselage bay)	tank for GM-1
	five 50-kg marker bombs
Electronic equipment	FuG 10 or FuG 10 K3P,
	FuG 16 Z, FuG 101,
	FuG 25 A, FuG 217,
	FuG 200, FuG 224
De-Icing system	electrical system powered by
	two 3,000 Watt generators
Crew	3

extended range, had a maximum fuel capacity of 12 000 liters. The Ju 635 differed significantly from the Do/He 635, nevertheless both used components from the Do 335. Like its predecessor, the Ju 635 was unarmed, being equipped only with cameras. Though interesting projects, in the end neither Do 335 Zwilling was realized. In November 1944 orders were placed for a total of four prototypes and six pre-production aircraft, however the Emergency Fighter Program resulted their cancellation. Plans called for the initial production of three to four machines per month. Wind tunnel tests were carried out and a fuselage mock-up was built, however development work on the type continued until the end of February 1945.

15. Signs of the Future

Proposed Follow-One Projects to the Do 335

In spite of the Do 335's outstanding performance, designers continued to improve the type by adopting new technologies. A decision was reached in favor of so-called "mixed propulsion", a combination of piston and turbojet engines. Plans for such a design were on the drawing boards even before the maiden flight of the Do 335. This advanced project was dubbed the P.232/2. Development work on the project, which was based on the P.231/3, began in May 1943. The P.232/3 version followed in September of the same year. It was a high-speed bomber powered by DB 603 and Jumo 004 engines. This configuration appeared to offer promise, as piston-engined aircraft had proven to be limited to maximum speeds in the 700 km/h range.

The mixed propulsion system combined the reliability of the piston engine with the superior performance of the turbojet. It was anticipated that the piston engine would provide power for takeoff and landing and cruising flight, while the Jumo 004 would be employed for combat when superior performance was required. The Technische Amt *assigned the project a high priority as late as March 1945, however given the military situation this was extremely unrealistic. Becoming ever more out of touch with reality, late in the war the planners of the* Technische Amt *were still planning bomber projects which would not be realized until 1949! Technically speaking, the P.232 offered an ideal interim solution pending the perfection of turbojet technology, however like so many other advanced weapons systems it was stifled by the enemy's superiority and the time factor.*

Project P.232

As stated, this project existed in two versions, the P.232/2 and P.232/3. Both were designed around the DB 603 and Jumo 004 C power plants and were designed to carry a bomb load of 1 000 kg. Calculated maximum speeds were 808 km/h for the P.232/2 and 838 km/h for the P.232/3. Both designs were based on the Do 335, employing the latter's wing and forward fuselage. The aft fuselage was changed to accept the turbojet engine and a conventional tail. The undercarriage consisted of main and nosewheel members.

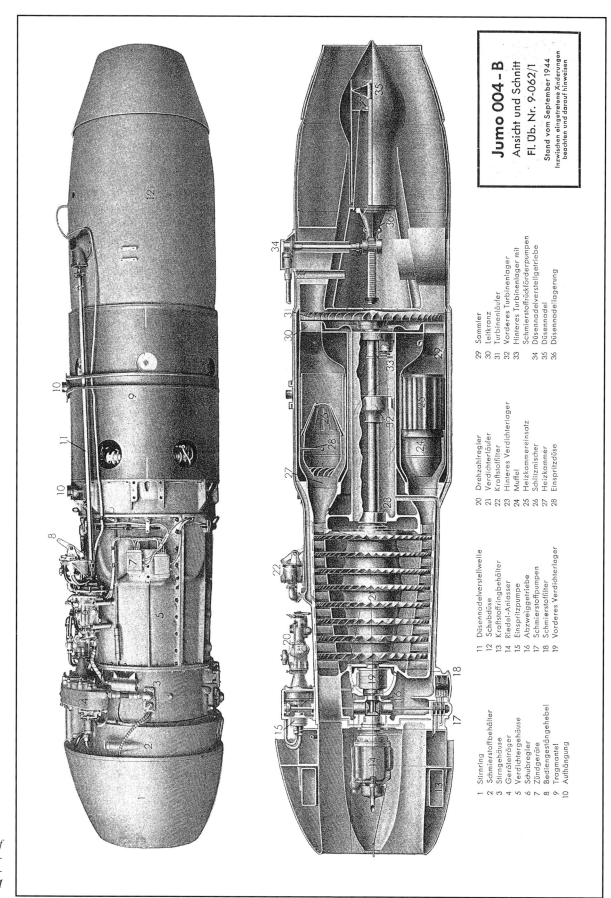

Jumo 004 - B
Ansicht und Schnitt
Fl. Üb. Nr. 9-062/1
Stand vom September 1944
Inzwischen eingetretene Änderungen
beachten und darauf hinweisen

1 Stirnring
2 Schmierstoffbehälter
3 Stirngehäuse
4 Geräteträger
5 Verdichtergehäuse
6 Schubregler
7 Zündgeräte
8 Bediengestängehebel
9 Tragmantel
10 Aufhängung

11 Düsennadelverstellwelle
12 Schubdüse
13 Kraftstoffringbehälter
14 Riedel-Anlasser
15 Einspritzpumpe
16 Abzweiggetriebe
17 Schmierstoffpumpen
18 Schmierstoffilter
19 Vorderes Verdichterlager

20 Drehzahlregler
21 Verdichterläufer
22 Kraftstoffilter
23 Hinteres Verdichterlager
24 Muffel
25 Heizkammereinsatz
26 Schlitzmischer
27 Heizkammer
28 Einspritzdüse

29 Sammler
30 Leitkranz
31 Turbinenläufer
32 Vorderes Turbinenlager
33 Hinteres Turbinenlager mit
   Schmierstoffrückförderpumpen
34 Düsennadelverstellgetriebe
35 Düsennadel
36 Düsennadellagerung

Air for the turbojet engine was provided by an air scoop positioned on the fuselage spine. The DB 603 G was supposed to power a Messerschmitt P8 propeller.

Fuel was contained in two fuselage tanks with capacities of 1 000 and 750 liters. There were also two wing tanks between the spars, each capable of holding 400 liters.

Daimler Benz DB 603 G

This version differed from the earlier A and E variants in having a higher compression ratio (8.3 to 1) and the use of 100 octane fuel. Propeller reduction was raised from 0.47 (DB 603 E) to 0.52. The G version had a single-stage supercharger. The two-stage supercharger was not introduced until the L version. The DB 603 G produced 1,900 H.P. for takeoff using C2 or C3 fuel. Detailed information on the DB 603 may be found in Chapter 9.

Junkers Jumo 004

The rear power plant was a Jumo 004 C turbojet engine. Its calculated output was 1 200 kg of thrust. This was achieved through the use of an afterburner. The engine proceeded no further than the test phase. During test runs with the afterburner it achieved 1 200 kg of thrust.

Plans called for the 004 E to go into production in 1945. The only production version of the engine was the less powerful 004 B, of which 6,010 examples (B-1 and B-2) were built from February 1944 to March 1945.

Project P.247

Another project based on the Do 335 was the P.247, which was projected in at least six versions. It was a single-seat fighter design

Cutaway model showing details of the Jumo 004's combustion chambers, shaft and compressor stage. (F. Klinger)

Table 23: Known Data for Projects P.232/2 and P.232/3

Technical Data	Project P.232/2	Project P.232/3
Wingspan	13.8 m	13.8 m
Length	14.0 m	14.0 m
Height	4.5 m	4.5 m
Wing area	38.5 m^2	38.5 m^2 or 33.5 m^2
Aspect ratio	5	-
Area (fin and rudder)	3 m^2	-
Area (tailplane)	7.75 m^2	-
Empty weight	5370 kg	5100 kg
Equipped weight	5830 kg	5560 kg
Useful load	2620 kg	2190 kg
Takeoff weight	8450 kg	7750 kg
Wing loading	219 kg/m^2	231 kg/m^2
Maximum speed (ground level)	660 km/h	675 km/h
Maximum speed (8700 m)	808 km/h	838 km/h
Service ceiling	13200 m	13300 m
Maximum boost altitude	8700 m	8700 m
Time to climb to 2000 m	2.9 min	2.5 min
Time to climb to 4000 m	6.0 min	5.0 min
Time to climb to 8000 m	14.5 min	11.8 min
Takeoff distance	740 m	580 m
Landing speed	148 km/h	148 km/h
Piston engine	DB 603 G	DB 603 G
Output	1900 HP	1900 HP
Turbojet engine	Junkers Jumo 004 C	Junkers Jumo 004 C
Thrust	1200 kp	1200 kp
Armament	2 x MG 151/20	2 x MG 151/20 / 1 x MK 103
	Bombs to 1000 kg	Bombs to 1000 kg
Crew	1	1

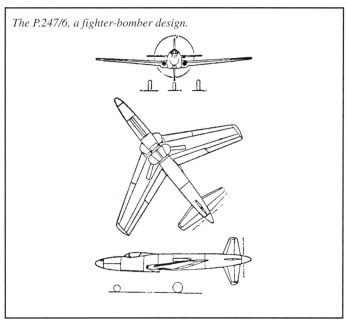

The P.247/6, a fighter-bomber design.

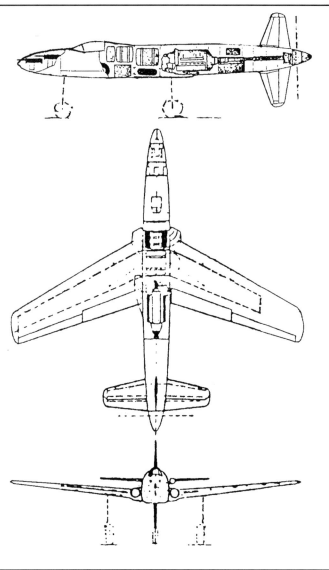

with a rear-mounted engine and pusher propeller. The aircraft was supposed to be powered by a Jumo 213 T with exhaust-driven turbo supercharger, producing 2,000 H.P., situated just aft of the center of gravity. Air inlets were located in both wing roots, while the supercharger air intake was positioned on the port side of the fuselage.

MW 50 boost was provided for increased performance, with a 75-liter tank for the methanol-water mixture. Like the Do 335, the P.247 employed the extension shaft system and a cruciform tail.

The advantages of this configuration were:

* improved visibility for the pilot
* central location of the armament
* better location for radar equipment
* improved effectiveness of the pusher propeller compared to a tractor propeller

Other features of this design were a blown canopy and tricycle undercarriage, made necessary by the rear-mounted propeller. The wing was swept. The fuselage housed a 110-liter oil tank, an unprotected fuel tank (260 l) and a protected fuel tank (400 l). Two integral fuel tanks were built into the wing leading edges (120 l).

The wing itself was a two-spar structure with a span of 12.5 meters and an area of 26 m2. Fuselage length was 12 meters.

The aircraft's armament of three MK 108 cannon was grouped in the nose.

The main undercarriage was equipped with 840x300 wheels, while the dimensions of the nosewheel tire were 630x220.

This design proceeded no farther than the drawing board, however it did spawn a number of other designs.

Project P.252

This project was also based on the P.247 design. Design work on the P.252, which was intended to fill the night, all-weather and heavy fighter roles, was carried out in February and March 1945. It was basically similar to the P.247 with the exception of the engines and a crew of three. The design was produced in three versions:

P.252/1

This was a two-seat variant with an unswept wing spanning 16.4 meters with an area of 43.20 m2. No other airframe dimensions are known.

Power was supplied by two Jumo 213 J engines driving counter-rotating pusher propellers by means of extension shafts. This resulted in a design with a tricycle undercarriage and cruciform tail. A total of 1 900 liters of fuel was provided for the two Jumo engines.

Other details of the design are sketchy. It is known that the armament was to have included two MK 108 cannon in a "Schräge Musik" installation. The nature of the forward-firing armament is not known.

P.252/2

This version incorporated numerous aerodynamic changes, although the basic configuration of tricycle undercarriage and cruciform tail was retained. Airframe dimensions are not known with certainty. The Zerstörer version was to have had a shorter fuselage than the night fighter, as no third crew member was required. A swept wing was a requirement given the high speeds at which the aircraft was designed to operate. The wing had a span of 18.40 meters and was swept 35 degrees. The P.252/II was also powered by two Jumo 213 engines driving pusher propellers. The fuel tanks were located between the engines. Intakes in the wing roots provided the engines with air. Armament was to include two obliquely-mounted MK 108 cannon, plus two MG 213/20 and two MK 108s mounted in the nose of the aircraft.

Table 24:

Wingspan	16.4 m
Length	5.2 m
Height	4.95 m
Wing area	43.2 m²
Empty weight	7310 kg
Equipped weight	8290 kg
Takeoff weight	maximum 10 700 kg
Maximum speed	900 km/h in 11300 m
Service ceiling	13400 m
Power plants (2)	Jumo 213 J
Output	2240 HP
Fuel capacity	2x1300 l, fuselage tanks
	2x600 l, wing tanks
Armament	3 x MK 108, 2 x MG 213 C
	1000 kg bombs
Crew	2

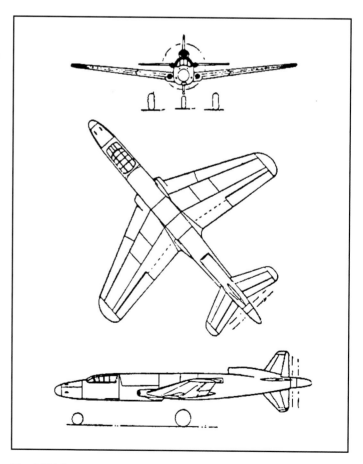

The P.252/3-01, a follow-on project with counter-rotating propellers.

P.252/3

This three-seat night fighter was to have been fitted with a redesigned laminar-flow wing. Compared to the earlier wing, it was reduced in span, sweep was reduced to 22.5 degrees and the root area was deepened. The rear fuselage was largely unchanged, apart from an air intake in front of the vertical stabilizer for the rear engine. Fuel capacity was increased significantly. Radar equipment was housed in the nose. Two MK 108 cannon were supposed to be located behind the cockpit in a "Schräge Musik" installation. It is also believed that the type was to have been equipped with heavy-caliber cannon, specifically two MK 214 A. The two 50-mm weapons were to have been mounted on either side of the cockpit. In their book Geheimprojekte der Luftwaffe, *Meyer and Schick claim that the planned weapons were in fact two MK 213 C 30-mm cannon. They also claim that two engines types were under consideration, the Jumo 213 J and the DB 603 LA. Fuel was housed in two* fuselage tanks with capacities of 700 and 1 100 liters. The fuselage also housed two 250-l oil tanks. A 200-l MW 50 tank was provided for increased performance.*

The calculated maximum speed of this version of the P.252 was 930 km/h at a height of 11 300 meters. This represented the absolute performance limit for piston-engined technology. Whether or not the aircraft would have proved capable of such speeds will regrettably never be known. The three versions of the P.252 never had a chance of becoming a reality, for by then jet-powered designs had absolute priority. By the time the plans for the P.252/1 and /2 projects were presented on 26 February 1945, Göring had already decided against Dornier. In spite of this, at least one further variant was developed. The feverish work carried out by numerous manufacturers on in some cases far-fetched projects allows only one conclusion to be drawn. They wanted to keep their remaining personnel busy and prevent them from being sent to the front.

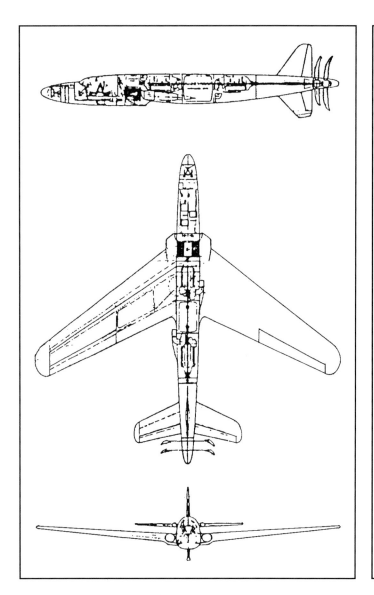

The project P.252/2-01.

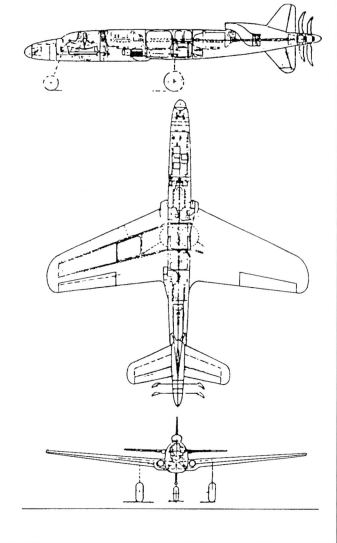

The P.252/3-01, a follow-on project with counter-rotating propellers.

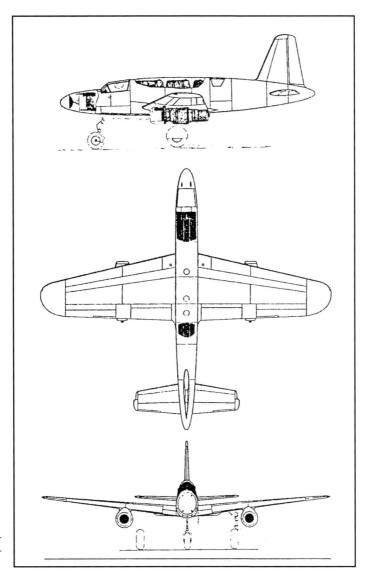

The P.256/1 was to have been powered by two Heinkel HeS 011 turbojets.

Project P.256

In an effort to remain in the race, within the space of barely half a month the Dornier team designed a heavy jet fighter with a very conventional airframe. The fuselage, which was not unlike that of the American B-26 Marauder, was 13.6 meters long. The crew consisted of pilot, radar operator and navigator. The latter's station was in the rear fuselage while the pilot and radar operator sat in a side-by-side cockpit.

Design features also included a tricycle undercarriage and conventional tail surfaces.

The design's laminar wing was derived from that of the Do 335 B series and had a span of 15.45 meters. Wing area was 41 m2. Propulsion was to have been provided by two Heinkel HeS 11 turbojet engines mounted beneath the wings. The engines were designed to produce 1 300 kg of thrust each. Takeoff-assist rockets would have been used to reduce takeoff distance.

The proposed armament of the P.256 was to have consisted of four MK 108 cannon in the fuselage nose and two similar weapons in a "Schräge Musik" arrangement. For fighter-bomber missions that aircraft was to be capable of carrying two 500-kg bombs.

Dornier's stopgap solution came to nothing, not least because its calculated performance, even with jet engines, was less than that of the P.252.

Table 25: Technical Data Project P.256

Wingspan	15.45 m
Length	13.6 m
Height	5.5 m
Wing area	41 m²
Wing loading	276 kg/m²
Equipped weight	6860 kg
Takeoff weight	11300 kg
	(with 3750 booster)
Maximum speed	882 km/h in 8000 m
Maximum range	?????
Service ceiling	13300 m
Power plant	Heinkel He S11 A
Thrust	1300 kp
Fuel capacity	???
Armament	6 x MK 108
Crew	3

Project P.254/Do 435

The P.254 project was based on the P.232 design and retained many components from the Do 335, including elements of the forward fuselage and the complete undercarriage. Most of the changes affected the rear fuselage and were associated with the design's mixed propulsion system. Two air intakes were added to the sides of the rear fuselage to feed air to the jet engines. As well, the ventral fin was deleted. A laminar-flow wing was designed to replace the wing of the Do 335. It spanned 15.45 meters and had an area of 41 or 43 square meters. The crew occupied separate positions and were provided with ejector seats. Versions were designed for the night fighter, high-altitude heavy fighter and long-range reconnaissance roles. The design was presented to the Technische Amt *in January 1945. The latter was convinced of the correctness of the concept and a development contract was issued to Dornier. The first prototype was to fly in May 1945 with initial deliveries of production aircraft to take place toward the end of the year.*

The RLM demanded the Jumo 213 J as an alternative to the DB 603 LA. Various combinations of power plants were proposed:

- Do 435 with DB 603 LA and Heinkel HeS 011 A
- Do 435 with Jumo 213 J and Heinkel HeS 011 A
- Do 435 with Jumo 222 and Heinkel HeS 011 A
- Do 435 with front- and rear-mounted Jumo 222 (most likely a proposal only)

The latter variant has been designated Do 435 A in some publications. It had a long slender fuselage with a length of approximately 17 meters. Drawings suggest that the Do 335's tail section would have been used. The cockpit was fitted with a bubble canopy. No confirmation of this design can be found.

Opposite Above: *The Do 435 design with a Jumo 213 DB piston engine and an HeS 011 turbojet.*
Opposite: *This version of the Do 435 haunts the literature. It is doubtful whether it in fact originated on a Dornier drawing board.*

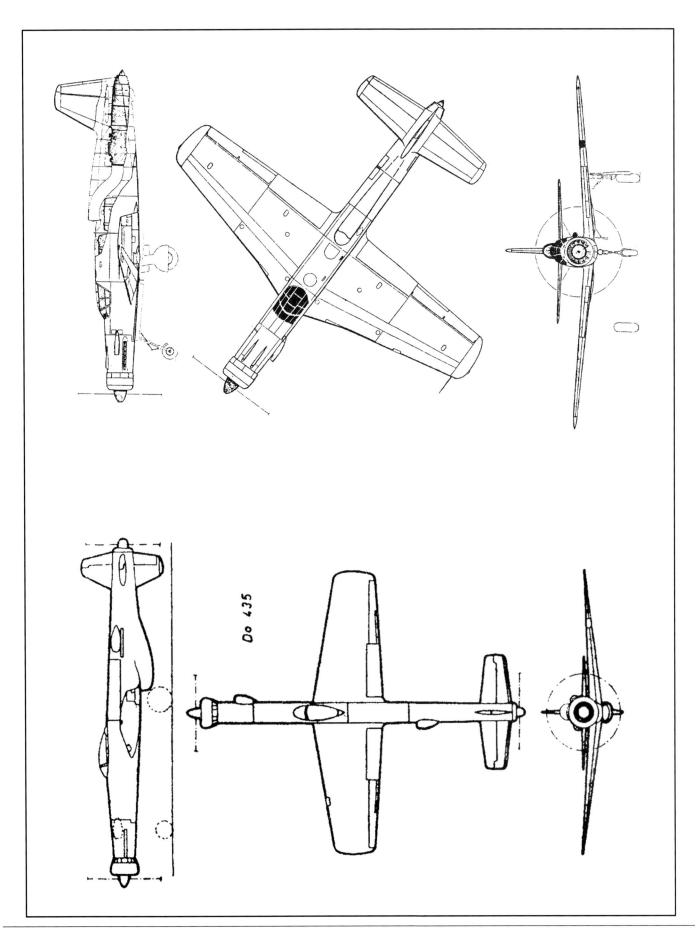

Do 435

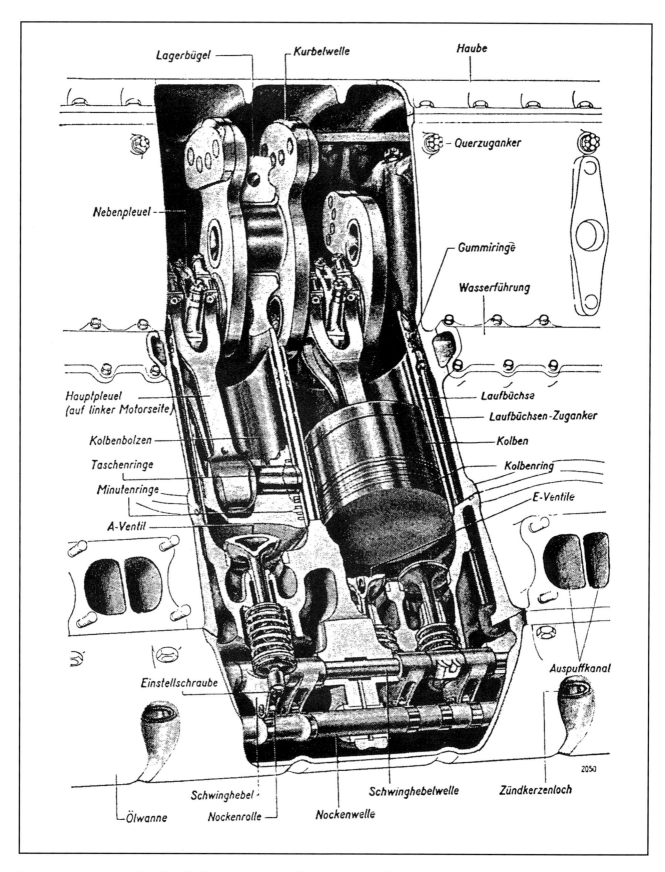

Drawing of the interior of the Jumo 213 engine (compare with photograph on following page).

Lagerbügel — Kurbelwelle — Haube

Querzuganker

Nebenpleuel

Gummiringe

Wasserführung

Hauptpleuel
(auf linker Motorseite)

Laufbüchsa

Laufbüchsen-Zuganker

Kolbenbolzen

Kolben

Taschenringe

Kolbenring

Minutenringe

E-Ventile

A-Ventil

Auspuffkanal

Einstellschraube

Schwinghebelwelle

Zündkerzenloch

Schwinghebel

Ölwanne

Nockenrolle

Nockenwelle

2050

Propulsion Technology

As described in the preceding text, the Do 435 was to have been powered by several combinations of power plants. The Jumo 213 was used only in an experimental role in conjunction with the Do 335, however its use was proposed for several projects. The Jumo 213 T was proposed for the P.247. The Jumo 213 J was among the power plants selected to power the Do 435. Like the aircraft it was to power, however, the Jumo 213 J was still in the project stage. The J version was designed to produce 2,240 H.P. for takeoff. This represented a significant increase over the A and E series, which produced 1,750 and 1,870 H.P. for takeoff respectively. This increase in power was achieved through various design changes. The following is a list of the most important changes compared to the Jumo 213 EB, based on original Junkers documents dated 19 January 1945:

- Cylinder liners – diameter increased from 150 to 154 mm.
- Cylinder head – each 2 inlet and 2 exhaust valves, 2 camshafts, increased casing rigidity.
- Reinforced attachment brackets.
- New main and secondary connecting rods plus pistons.
- Crankshaft – smaller gear diameter, increased gear reduction.
- More powerful supercharger.
- Four-blade VS-19 propeller.
- Propeller shaft lengthened by 40 mm.

The Jumo 213 was earmarked for follow-up designs to the Do 335. (F. Klinger)

The interior workings of the Jumo 213. (F. Klinger)

Interior of the Jumo 213. (F. Klinger)

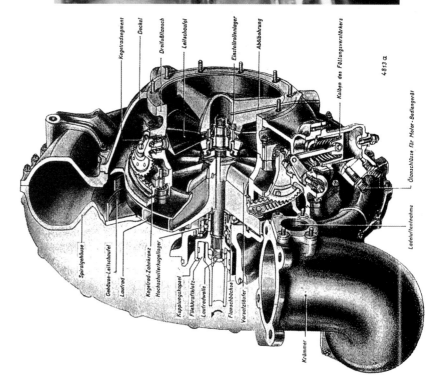

Details of the construction of the supercharger from a Jumo 213 A or C.

Jumo 222

The origins of this unlucky design go back to 1937, when Ferdinand Brandner was assigned the task of developing a 24-cylinder engine. After a development and construction period of two years, the first engine was started on the test bench on 24 April 1939. Numerous hurdles had to be overcome before the engine could enter production, however. Ultimately these obstacles caused the entire project to fail.

Ferdinand Brandner: "The tragedy of this engine design was the constant demand for increased power, resulting from airframe developments. This resulted in weight increases which prevented the engine from achieving the desired performance. As a result the Jumo 222 was developed to death."

The Jumo 222 was basically a 24-cylinder engine with its cylinders arranged in four rows of six cylinders each, a design which combined features of in-line and radial engines. In the course of

The Jumo 222 engine.

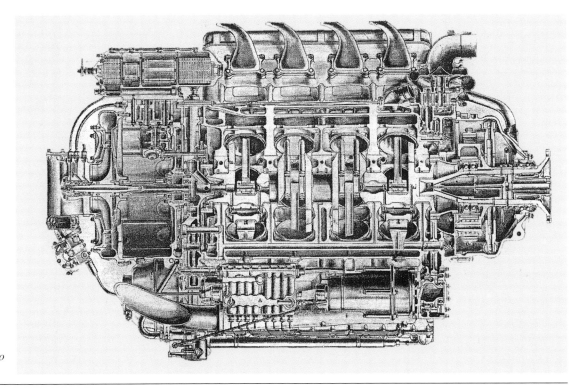

Cutaway drawing of a Jumo 222.

development the engine's volume was increased by enlarging cylinder hole diameter from 135 mm to 140 mm. The next step was to increase both the bore and stroke. The resulting differing piston displacements were 46.6, 49.8 and 55.5 liters. The output of the Jumo 222 rose from 2,000 H.P. to more than 2,500 H.P. then to 3,000 H.P. The Jumo 222 E/F was a high-altitude engine.

The last projected step foresaw a 36-cylinder version with a displacement of 70 liters and an output of 5,000 H.P.

Ferdinand Brandner outlined important events in the development of the Jumo 222:

- First run on 24 April 1939
- Certified for 2,000 H.P. in March 1940
- Jumo 222 dropped from production program on 24 December 1941
- Certified for 3,000 H.P. on 4 June 1942
- August 1942 – the RLM again considers the Jumo 222 in its production plans
- According to Production Plan 35 A of 11 February 1943 production is supposed to begin in Prague in October 1944
- According to Brandner, in 1943-44 twenty engines were available for the Fw 191 program. The latter did not enter production and the Jumo 222 A/B engines were assigned to Heinkel (He 219).
- In summer 1944 plans were sold to Japan. Brandner and the plans were supposed to go to Japan by U-boat in January 1945, however Brandner remained in Germany.
- In 1945 the Jumo 222 was assigned the highest priority, as it was the only available engine capable of 3,000 H.P.

Heinkel HeS 011

The rear component of the Do 435's propulsion system was an HeS 011 turbojet engine.

Design work was concluded in December 1942. Heinkel's power plant produced 1 200 to 1 300 kg of thrust, far more than Junkers' 004. Test runs began in 1944. These initially resulted in an output of 1 100 kg of thrust. One of the engine's most notable features was the design of its compressor. In the forward (axial) stage the intake flow moved into a so-called diagonal stage, which in turned opened into a three-stage axial compressor. The compressed air was guided into an annular combustion chamber, followed by a two-stage turbine.

In contrast to the Jumo 004, only a few examples of Heinkel's turbojet were built. Surviving records suggest the total was nineteen engines.

Production of the HeS 011A continued after the war for the Americans. The S 011 provided the basis for the S 021 turboprop engine.

Dornier's Do 435 was an attempt to provide a quick solution to the problem of the RAF's Mosquito bombers, which were largely immune to interception. Plans called for the first prototype Do 435 to fly in May 1945 with deliveries to the front-line units commencing by the end of the year. Like so many other plans, however, these were cancelled by Germany's defeat.

As the accompanying table shows, the use of mixed propulsion was not a purely German domain. As it turned out, however, the concept played only an insignificant role in the development of aviation, as manufacturers turned to pure-jet designs.

Size comparison of the Heinkel HeS 08 and Junkers Jumo 004 turbojet engines.

Table 26

Technical Data	P.254/Do 435	P.254/Do 435	Ryan FR-1	Curtiss XF-15 C-1
Wingspan	13.8 m	15.45 m	12.19 m	14.63 m
Length	13.2 m	13.4 m	9.86 m	13.41 m
Height	5.2 m	5.6 m	4.24 m	4.61 m
Wing area	38.5 m^2	41 m^2	22.25 m^2	37.16 m^2
Equipped weight	7585 kg	7725 kg	3488 kg	5737 kg
Takeoff weight	10500 kg	10640 kg	5285 kg	8481 kg (max)
Maximum speed	822 km/h	865 km/h	650 km/h	755 km/h
	in 7500 m	in 11200 m	in 5300 m	in 7700 m
Flying time/range	-	???	2607 km	2229 km
Power plant	DB 603 LA	Jumo 213 J*	Wright R-1830-72 W	Pratt & Whitney R-2800
Output (takeoff)	2300 HP	2240 HP	1350 HP	Version 34W 2100 HP
Turbojet engine	Heinkel He S 011 A	He S 011 A	GE J31	Allison-Chalmers (de Havilland H-1 "Goblin")

Table 26

Technical Data	P.254/Do 435	P.254/Do 435	Ryan FR-1	Curtiss XF-15 C-1
Thrust (for takeoff)	1300 kp	1300 kp	726 kp	1225 kp
Armament	2 x MG 151/20	2 x MG 151	4 x 12.7 mm MG	4 x 20 mm MK
		3 x MK 108		
	1 x MK 108, 2 x MK 108	1 500 kg bomb		
	as Nightfighter, 1 500 kg			
	bomb			
Crew	2 (nightfighter)	1	1	1
Start of development	1944	1944	1944	1944
First flight	-	-	6/25/1944	2/27/1945
Testing	-	-	qualification on	tested by US Navy from
			USS *Ranger*	November 45
			on 1 May 1945	
Extent of production	-	-	66 built	3 prototypes
Out of service	-	-	1947	-

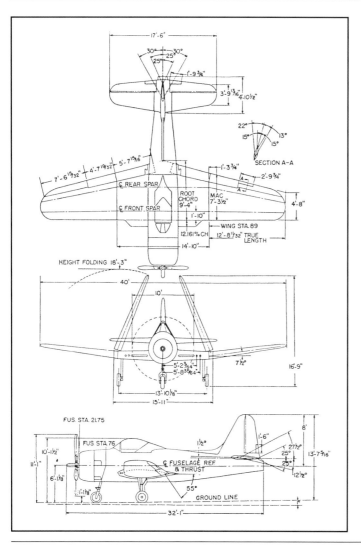

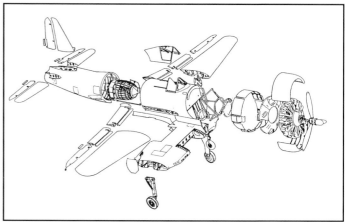

Exploded drawing of the Ryan Fireball.

Three-view drawing of the FR-1 with measurements in feet and inches.

Project P.273/3

In April 1943 the Do 335 took on its final form and received the blessing of the RLM. Dornier immediately began work on a high-altitude single-seat fighter based on the Do 335. The new design was assigned the project number P.273. The most significant change was a new wing with a span of 18 meters and area of 45.5 m2.

In keeping with its high-altitude role, the new design incorporated a pressurized cockpit and an ejection seat.

Power was to be provided by two DB 603 G engines.

Armament was to be in the form of two MG 151/20 and one MK 103 cannon, grouped in the same way as the Do 335's armament. The final design configuration was dated May 1943. Changing priorities doomed the design. In 1944 work began on a high-altitude heavy fighter, however it was dropped in favor of the Ta 512.

This last of the unrealized projects ended the evolution of the Do 335. In spite of its excellent performance, the Do 335 was ultimately representative of a dying breed, as the piston engine was superseded by the turbojet. The German surrender in May 1945 brought to abrupt end the development of the Do 335 and its advanced counterparts. The victors were interested only in Germany's jet research, which contributed significantly to postwar aviation development. Many German scientists worked on both sides of the Iron Curtain. In Germany, however, more than a decade was to pass before aviation awoke from a ten-year sleep.

Much more time would pass before the last "Anteater" returned to the land of its birth. Its initial sorry state soon gave way to restored beauty at the hands of Dornier workers. A unique piece of aviation was thus saved from certain decay.

Rumors concerning the Do 335 still persist. Divers claimed to have discovered an unusual aircraft in a Bavarian lake. This story has tantalized admirers of the Do 335, however it has yet to be confirmed. Only the future will reveal if an "Anteater" still sleeps in a watery grave.

The following table compares the P.273.3 and the BV 155:

Table 27:

Technical Data	P.273/3	BV 155 B
Wingspan	18 m	20.5 m
Length	13.7 m	12 m
Height	ca. 5 m	4.17 m
Wing area	45.5 m²	41.5 m²
Takeoff weight	9100 kg	5521 kg
Maximum speed	835 km/h in 8700 m	523 km/h in 6000 m
		650 km/h in 12000 m
		690 km/h in 16000 m
Maximum altitude	max 16000 m	16950 m
Power plants	DB 603 G	DB 603u + TKL-15
Output	1900 HP	1810 HP
Armament	1 x MK 103	1 x MK 108
	2 x MG 151/20	2 x MG 151/20

Bibliography

This book is based largely on original documents, which make possible a much more accurate picture than secondary literature. Most important are various parts of the Do 335 Handbook and a technical description dated 1944. The descriptions of engines are based mainly on the handbooks for the DB 603, HM 60 R and Jumo 213. Space limitations prevented a more detailed description of some engines, specifically the Jumo 222 and the HeS 011 turbojet.

Selected publications were used in certain places and are listed below:

Beauvais, Kössler, Maier, Regel: Flugerprobungsstellen bis 1945
Butler: War Prizes
Ebert/Kaiser/Peters: Willi Messerschmitt – Pionier der Luftfahrt
Eichholtz: Geschichte der deutschen Kriegswirtschaft, Band 3
Giger: Kolben-Flugmotoren
Green: Warplanes of the Third Reich
Köhler: Ernst Heinkel – Pionier der Schnellflugzeuge
Lange: Typenhandbuch der deutschen Luftfahrttechnik
Ruff, Ruck, Sedlmayer: Sicherheit und Rettung in der Luftfahrt
Schliephake: Flugzeugbewaffnung
Sengfelder: Flugzeugfahrwerke
Smith: Aircraft Piston Engines
Wachtel: Claude Dornier – Ein Leben für die Luftfahrt
Wagner: Hugo Junkers – Pionier der Luftfahrt
OKH list of production designations for weapons, ammunition and equipment, Berlin 1944

Most of the photos used in this book came from the Dornier archives and were kindly made available by Frau Burgmaier. Recopying of original documents was unavoidable, as most were unsuitable for reproduction. Ralf Swoboda produced the color drawings. The author wishes to thank all those persons and institutions without whose support this project would not have been possible. Special appreciation goes to Jürgen Bela, Jens Kollehn, Fritz Klinger, Arnd Siemon, Harald Schuller, Christoph Vernaleken and Herr Zuerl of the publisher of the same name. Photos were also taken from the already legendary publication Der Flieger, *publication of which began in 1921 and which became an institution until it ceased printing. Finally the author would like to thank Alfred Schliebner for photographs and valuable information which were made available at the last minute, so to speak.*

Appendix: drawing of the forward engine (DB 603) with mount and accessories.

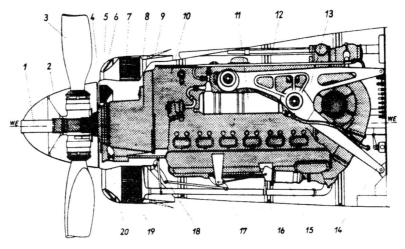

1	Schußkanal (MK 103) in der Luftschraubenhaube
2	Luftschraubenhaube
3	Luftschraube
4	Panzerung am Luftschraubengetriebegehäuse
5	Stirnhaube
6	Kühlerpanzerung
7	Schmierstoffkühler
8	Klappenträgerring
9	Kühlerklappe
10	Motor
11	Kühlstoffbehälter
12	MG 151
13	Triebwerksgerüst
14	Brandwand Spant 1
15	Hydraul. Temperatur-Regler
16	Triebwerksverkleidung
17	Umlenkwelle zur Kühlerklappenverstellung
18	Antriebshebel der Kühlerklappenverstellung
19	Kühlstoffkühler
20	Innere Strömungsverkleidung